Politic...

Po...

De...

Charles F. Andrain

San Diego State University

Politics and Economic Policy in Western Democracies

Duxbury Press
North Scituate, Massachusetts

Politics and Economic Policies in Western Democracies was edited and prepared for composition by Amy L. Ulrich. Interior design was provided by Joanna Prudden Snyder. The cover was designed by Elizabeth Rotchford.

Duxbury Press
A Division of Wadsworth, Inc.

Library of Congress Cataloging in Publication Data

Andrain, Charles F
Politics and economic policy in Western democracies.

Includes index.
1. Economic policy. 2. Inflation (Finance) and unemployment. 3. Income distribution. I. Title.
HD82.A634   338.9   79-10163
ISBN 0-87872-228-9

Printed in the United States of America
1 2 3 4 5 6 7 8 9 — 83 82 81 80 79

Contents

Foreword

Public policy is the lifeline of society. It is the network of complex decisions that provide for the satisfaction of societal needs and the creation of demands by groups and individuals alike. If there can be such a phenomenon as a hybrid between what is the structure of an institution and the nature of individual behavior, then that is the *form* in which public policy appears. In turn, the *content* of public policy is the elaborate maze of perceptions, decisions, implementations, and evaluations that shape and determine how all that is valued and scarce in society is allocated. Of course the entire allocation process is largely the function of the nature of social stratification, which determines the societal worth, as well as the life chances and access, individuals and individual members of groups and classes might enjoy.

The postindustrial societies of the end of the twentieth century are peculiar variants of the classical models depicting the specifics of a market economy, planning, and property. During the 1970s we had to accept increasingly the notion that the realm of the *public* and the *private* have become blurred and enmeshed in a complex of twilight spheres, thereby causing much societal conflict and debate over just what is and where is the boundary line between the two. Much of what has been the sacrosanct property of the private sense of activity and identity now has become a matter of public challenge and controversy through the means of regulation, controls, and above all taxation policies. At the same time public actions and decisions, just as public institutions and political processes, have become often the handy vehicles for special interests of such a narrow and well-defined nature that they approximate the vision and reality of the private realm. Single-issue politics shakes and frightens the traditional mold of American politics just as the endless expansion of governmental activity, intervention, and control elicits the anger of the frustrated and alienated citizen. But above all these debates looms the mighty issue of an uncertain future of scarcities and the dilemmas of growth, expansion, and constraints. We debate, argue, and puzzle over the nature and character of a sustainable society for our age and the next century. The parameters are fairly well set— what we tend to argue about is how to "get there." And this "how to get there" ambiguity is really the conflict of public policy in terms of tradeoffs, priorities, and options.

Charles Andrain's book is a monumental, yet precisely constructed work leading through the harrowing maze of policy contradictions and conflicts in our societies. The dilemma of our very specifically urgent present, the push-and-pull effects of inflation and unemployment, clearly occupy the center stage in the dramatic convulsions of a world economic order that is neither satisfied with "business as usual" in performance nor adequately equipped to conjure up visions of acceptable alternate solutions and success scenarios. Sadly enough, the governments of the postindustrial world keep stumbling through without the slightest perception of the consequences, middle and long range, of their current policy choices and actions.

The question of linkages between the ideological, cultural, and structural fibre of economic policies as yet eludes the policymaker and implementor alike. This excellent work, while representing a serious breakthrough in a comparative public policy analysis, reminds us that the hallmarks of a viable and sustainable society are based on the courage of the imagination, the compassion of the heart, and the clarity of the intellect. Charles Andrain's book painfully reminds us how woefully inadequate we are in facing the challenges of the future while it offers us a positive example, clear thinking, and common sense.

Arpad von Lazar
Professor
Programs in International
    Development and Energy
The Fletcher School of Law
    and Diplomacy
Tufts University

Medford, Massachusetts
April 1979

Preface

During the 1970s, the problems of rising unemployment and inflation confronted leaders in nearly all Western societies. Whereas in the early 1960s both unemployment and inflation remained at relatively low rates, the situation changed drastically during the early 1970s. In most countries the sum of price increases and unemployment levels increased successively over each of three time periods: 1961–1965, 1966–1970, and 1971–1975. Western economies no longer appeared so responsive to the "fine tuning" of economists who postulated the appropriate mix of fiscal and monetary policies to secure the best tradeoff between inflation and unemployment. Policymakers faced a dilemma. Should they spend less public funds to restrain inflation, or should they spend more to lower the jobless rate? The concurrent growth of inflation and unemployment also made citizens more sensitive to the issue of income equality. Politicians and social scientists disagreed both about the desirability of greater equality and about the precise empirical effects of taxation and government transfer programs to income distribution.

Examining these issues, this book aims to explore the content and impact of public economic policies, especially those dealing with taxes, expenditures, the money supply, interest rates, foreign exchange rates, the regulation of private economic activities, and public ownership of industries. In particular, the book stresses the consequences of these policies on the degree of inflation, unemployment, and income equality. What policies affect the rates of unemployment and inflation? Which social groups bear the greatest burdens and secure the most favorable benefits? How do these public policies influence the distribution of income? By analyzing economic policies in seven Western countries—the United States, Canada, Britain, West Germany, Sweden, France, and Italy—this book provides some tentative answers to these questions.

Despite the importance of these economic problems, few social science studies have adopted an explicit crossnational focus. Most investigations explore the effects of economic policies within the United States; comparisons are made among states, not nations. Some analyses also examine the causes of unemployment, inflation, and income inequality within a particular foreign country, such as Britain, Canada, or

Sweden. Few studies have tested the validity of generalizations derived from one nation. In this work I hope to rectify some of these deficiencies. By studying seven Western societies with similar economic and political structures, I reduce the complexities influencing policy outcomes. Since they are all industrialized, modified market economies with competitive electoral systems, I can draw more valid conclusions about the relationships between policy contents and impacts than if I were to analyze just one country or many dissimilar nations.

This book combines empirical data with theoretical perspectives to explain the findings. It synthesizes economic analyses of the causes of unemployment, inflation, and inequality. It also explores the credibility of explicit hypotheses derived from various theories—for example, the demand-pull and cost-push explanations of inflation. Three theoretical dimensions—cultural values, political structures, and economic structures—help explain the different policy contents in the United States and Western Europe.

As a method for understanding the content and impact of economic policies, the institutional approach used by John Kenneth Galbraith, John Blair, and Gunnar Myrdal generates the most useful explanations. Imperfect competition, rather than a fully competitive market, is the dominant characteristic of contemporary Western economies. In the emerging corporate state, three institutions—government, concentrated industries, and labor unions—possess the power to shape the market's operation. Concentrated industries (oligopolies) administer prices. If demand declines, they may lower production rather than prices. Curtailed supplies mean higher unemployment. Dominant in the governmental sector and concentrated industries, labor unions win higher wages than do personnel in more competitive firms, especially retail trade and the personal services. Particularly in Sweden and Britain, the wages gained by unionized employees set the standards for earnings made by workers in nonunionized firms. On the whole, most government policymakers respond more readily to the demands of corporate executives and union leaders than to the preferences of the less well-organized small-scale entrepreneurs or consumers.

These three institutions exert a reciprocal influence on each other. They bargain with one another over their shares of the economic pie. No Western government operates solely as the executive committee of the capitalist or working class. Although the political power of labor and business varies from country to country and changes over different historical periods, government officials, corporate heads, and labor union leaders jointly shape the content of economic policies and also affect policy outcomes.

The institutional approach adopts an interdisciplinary focus. To gain the best understanding of economic problems, we can no longer concentrate on just purely "economic" phenomena like changes in the money supply and increases in the gross national product. Instead, we need to rely on the insights of the economists, sociologists, and political scientists. Economists stress the production, distribution, and consumption of scarce resources such as income and wealth. In this book, I use theories assessing the interaction between supply and demand to probe the causes of unemployment, inflation, and income distribution. From a sociological perspective, cultural values and the social stratification system (the ranking of groups according to their political power, wealth, and status) represent two concepts for explaining the content of public policies. The political scientist's attention to the distribution and exercise of political power, especially to the roles played by government institutions, political parties, labor unions, and concentrated industries, helps us understand the limits as well as the possibilities of public policies for attaining particular objectives.

Consistent with the institutional orientation, this book takes a historical overview of the policy process. Economic conditions are rarely in equilibrium. Rather, disturbances in both the national and the international environments often produce significant changes. For this reason, we need to examine the dynamic process by which economic changes occur over time. Lacking a historical perspective, political scientists and economists underestimate the tendency for policy impacts to change over different periods. For example, from 1960 through 1965 fiscal and monetary policies secured a negative tradeoff between inflation and unemployment—that is, within each of the seven Western nations, as prices increased, jobless rates declined. During the 1970s, however, this inverse association no longer held true. Inflation and unemployment rose concurrently. More than any other condition, the quadrupling of oil prices by the Organization of Petroleum Exporting Countries in late 1973 led to higher general inflation. Increased costs for petroleum products also lowered aggregate demand. Unemployment consequently increased. In sum, rather than concentrating on just one time period, this book analyzes the impact of public policies over a number of years, primarily between 1960 and 1975. By so doing, it emphasizes the tendency for general conclusions about inflation, unemployment, and income equality to rest on a specific historical base.

Several different people have assisted in the preparation of this book. I especially appreciate the contributions made by the following individuals. I began the manuscript in spring 1975 and completed it during fall 1978 while I was a research associate at the Institute of

International Studies, the University of California at Berkeley. Dr. Carl G. Rosberg, Jr., director of the IIS, facilitated my research at the University. Two of my colleagues at San Diego State University—political scientist Brian Loveman and economist Ibrahim Poroy—made several helpful suggestions. Professors Stanley Rothman of Smith College and Alexander Groth of the University of California at Davis reviewed the manuscript for Duxbury Press. At Duxbury several individuals assisted me in the preparation of this work: Robert J. Gormley, publisher; Patrick Fitzgerald, political science editor; James C. Blair and Sylvia Dovner, production editors; and Amy Ulrich, copy editor. While Gary Zimmerman was a graduate student at Essex University, he gathered valuable information in England. Grace Gonick and Peggy McCroskey efficiently typed the manuscript.

Introduction

Throughout the Western world economic problems have recently become more severe than at any time during the last thirty years. In North America and Western Europe, the 1970s saw a simultaneous rise in both inflation and unemployment rates. Unlike the pre–World War II period, during the last quarter of the twentieth century growing unemployment accompanied escalating price increases. Even young college graduates experienced difficulties finding professional jobs. Older citizens felt the severe impact of inflation on their housing and health care costs. Hospital bills, doctors' fees, and residential expenses shot up faster than the general cost of living. By the 1970s, when the tradeoff between inflation and unemployment seemed to bring the worst of all possible worlds, concern with economic inequalities began to mount. As taxes and government expenditures rose to provide a wide variety of social services, some groups feared that income distribution was growing too equal. Faced by high inflation and unemployment, other individuals felt that the gap between rich and poor was not narrowing but widening.

Under deteriorating economic conditions, few citizens can ignore the decisive impact of government policies on their welfare. Within the Western nations today, governments at all levels spend between 30 percent and 45 percent of the gross national product (GNP). Total tax revenues as a proportion of the GNP range from about 25 percent in Portugal to nearly 50 percent in Denmark. Changes in interest rates and in the money supply affect business expansion, individual borrowing, consumer purchasing power, and ultimately the rates of inflation. Modifications of foreign exchange currency rates, such as the devalua-

Chapter One

tion of the British pound and the appreciation of the German mark, also influence national levels of inflation and unemployment. In turn, these fiscal and monetary policies shape the distribution of income among a nation's citizens.

Politics and Economic Policy

As government has expanded its role in the economy, citizens in Western democracies have come to perceive a close linkage between politics and public economic policies. Although in the United States the majority of Americans still retain a self-reliant ideology, they now expect the government to assume some responsibility for dealing with inflation, unemployment, and poverty. Even more than Americans, Canadian and European citizens expect their political leaders to tackle these issues through implementing appropriate public policies.

Although these problems have long plagued societies, not until the twentieth century did Western governments give priority to public policies that provide direct services to individuals. When the nation-state system first came into existence during the sixteenth century in England, Holland, France, and Spain, governments concentrated on maintaining the territorial integrity of the fragile nation. Most public policies involved defense, foreign affairs, internal order, and the raising of financial revenues through levying taxes and printing currency. Beginning with the middle of the nineteenth century, the mobilization of physical resources assumed greater importance as a distinctive state activity. Government policies stimulated the construction of public works, such as roads, railways, and canals. Public subsidies promoted industry, commerce, and agriculture. During the twentieth century the growing popularity of democratic values, the rising strength of socialist movements, the industrializing process, and the severe effects of two world wars led political figures to design public policies that allocated social benefits to individuals. Since World War II, governments have spent an increasing proportion of public revenues on such programs as unemployment compensation, family allowances, social security, health, and education.[1] Even in the United States, where private agencies retain a greater authority over these issues than they do in Canada or Western Europe, the federal government has expanded its role as provider of social services.

Despite the growing importance of public policies designed to cope with unemployment, inflation, and economic inequalities, until recently

American political scientists focused less attention on policy research than did professors teaching before the First World War. According to Dwight Waldo, who analyzed several political science journals published between 1909 and 1971, political scientists prior to World War I placed their greatest emphasis on comparative politics and on substantive public policy analysis, especially economic policies involving industry, commerce, labor-management relations, agriculture, and fiscal issues. In contrast, during the early 1970s political scientists concentrated on such topics as political parties, interest groups, voting behavior, and public opinion.[2] Only in the last few years have political scientists begun to reestablish the former close linkage between politics and policy. Major universities have instituted schools and centers for policy research. Private organizations, such as the American Enterprise Institute, the Brookings Institution, and the Institute for the Study of Labor and Economic Crisis, assess the outcomes of current economic policies and recommend proposals for policy changes. Magazines like *Policy Analysis, Policy Studies Journal, Policy Review, Politics and Policy, Policy Sciences,* and *Social Policy* report the latest research findings about the causes and effects of economic policies.

Political theorists have long recognized the close connection between politics and policy. From the time of Plato and Aristotle, political activity has involved the making and carrying out of decisions with public consequences. Both "politics" and "policy" have their roots in the Greek work *politeia* (citizenship, government, constitution). In French *politique* means both politics and policy. Similarly, in German the term *politik* refers to both politics and policy.

Political institutions, including government agencies, exercise the authority to make decisions binding on the whole community. Because public policies involve a wide range of issues and affect a large number of individuals, these policies have the capacity to influence the whole society. From this perspective, politics cannot exist apart from public policy. Contemporary political scientists thus interpret politics as the formulation and implementation of public policies; they explore the impact of these policies on the society, especially on different social groups. By the same reasoning, public policies comprise those sets of decisions affecting a large number of citizens within a society.[3]

Especially in the industrial West, so-called "private" organizations like multinational corporations, concentrated industries, and labor unions also exert a significant impact on the public. They try to shape the content of public economic policies and help administer government programs, such as incomes policies, that are designed to restrain price and wage increases. The wage demands made by trade union leaders and the pricing decisions taken by large corporations obviously exert profound public consequences. Consequently, the policies of all three institutions—government, unions, and corporations—should be regarded as "public" decisions. As Robert Vaison argues:

> *A policy is public, then, not because of the legal status of the particular organization (or individual) formulating it but rather because of the nature and the effect of the policy itself. It is public if it directly or indirectly affects members of the society outside the organization initiating the policy.*[4]

This book focuses primarily on three types of public decisions that significantly affect the public welfare: (1) fiscal policies concerning taxes and expenditures, (2) monetary policies influencing the money supply, interest rates, and international currency exchanges, (3) programs involving government ownership of economic firms. This volume also assesses the effects of these government policies, as well as the impact of business corporations and labor unions, on unemployment, inflation, and income equality.

Public policy analysis involves not only the exploration of actually enacted policies but also an investigation of the power of government and social groups to block new programs. Often the power to prevent the enactment of a new policy becomes just as important as the power to initiate a policy. For example, until the twentieth century, national governments in the Western world took few active steps to solve unemployment problems. Before then, the individual, family, private charity association, church, or local government assumed major responsibility for alleviating the distress suffered by the unemployed. Even during this century, most policymakers in North America and Western Europe have not placed the pursuit of economic equality at the top of their political agendas. Instead, economic growth, increased productivity, and price stability have assumed higher priority.[5] We should view as public policies both the actions to realize full employment and income equality as well as the decisions to refrain from implementing programs that would lower jobless rates and reduce economic inequalities.

The Comparative Analysis of Economic Policies

During the last decade, crossnational policy research has come to occupy a more central place on the political science agenda. Until recently, most American policy researchers studied the United States. Social scientists compared American cities or states, rather than different nations. Today, however, crossnational policy investigations have become increasingly popular.

Yet those who compare several nations face a dilemma. An investigation of diverse countries expands the complexity of conditions affecting unemployment, inflation, and economic equality. Public policies constitute only one variable shaping an outcome like unemployment. Other factors, including the heterogeneity of a population, age patterns within a nation, distinctive cultural values, and unique patterns of peer group interaction also affect unemployment levels. Unfortunately, even if several nations share similar economic policies, other nonpolicy variables may vary. Since in all Western countries youth between fifteen and twenty-four face the greatest difficulties finding a job, one nation may have a higher unemployment rate than another because it contains a larger proportion of young people under twenty-five years old. Faced with such divergent conditions, the comparative analyst cannot easily trace the precise interaction among distinctive policy and nonpolicy variables. We can find few national cases for comparison that share all traits in common except a different policy content or method of implementation. Without knowing the distinctive interrelations among the parts of a social system, we cannot evaluate policy performance. For these reasons, efforts to assess the causal impact of public policies across several nations become risky.

Although crossnational comparisons do make analysis more complex, they are needed to test the validity of generalizations derived from one society. Some American economists have hypothesized that a large annual increase in the money supply causes rapid price increases. They also assume that high unemployment compensation as a percentage of people's regular wages leads to higher jobless rates. Other analysts believe that greater government expenditures for education, health, and social services have increased income equality. Yet these hypotheses have been investigated mainly in the American context; crossnational comparisons enable us to test their validity in other societies.

Crossnational comparisons also provide opportunities to evaluate governmental performance throughout different countries. For example, by examining policies that deal with unemployment, inflation, and economic inequality in various nations, we can discover how these programs operate and how they affect different groups. Then we can link this information about systemic performance to such criteria as efficiency, equality, and freedom for businessmen, workers, and consumers.

This book uses a comparative approach to examine public policies in seven Western countries: the United States, Canada, Britain, West Germany, Sweden, France, and Italy. These nations have similar sociopolitical backgrounds. They are all industrialized, fairly wealthy market economies with competitive electoral systems. Analysis of a few comparable cases makes it possible to consider the effects of the social context.[6] Since this comparative strategy reduces the number of complex conditions influencing a policy outcome, we can draw more valid conclusions about the linkages between policy contents and their consequences.

The Institutional Approach

This analysis of economic policies in Western democracies uses the institutional approach to the study of political economy.[7] Institutionalists examine the interactions among three key institutions of contemporary industrial societies: governments, labor unions, and concentrated industries. Particularly in the highly industrialized, modified market economies of the Western world, these three institutions, rather than some impersonal forces of a fully competitive market, influence the degree of unemployment, inflation, and income equality. By emphasizing capital-intensive economic activities, rather than production involving a large labor force, concentrated industries may increase the unemployment rate of unskilled workers. Governments and concentrated industries administer prices that do not fully respond to changes in supply and demand; therefore, inflation results. If labor unions obtain wage hikes exceeding their increases in labor productivity, they may aggravate the inflationary situation. The struggle among government officials, corporate executives, and union leaders over scarce economic resources largely shapes the distribution of wealth among individuals and groups.

The institutional approach is obviously interdisciplinary, rather than purely "economic" or "political," for it explores the relationships among political power, wealth, and cultural values. Political scientists concentrate on understanding the distribution and exercise of political power—that is, the use of resources to attain public consequences. Economists give priority to the production and distribution of wealth. They examine efficient methods to maximize production and ways to allocate scarce resources among impersonal factors of production (land, labor, capital). Institutional economists pay particular attention to the distribution of income among concrete groups and individuals. "Value" and "social stratification" are variables studied by sociologists. They assume that cultural values shape the purposes and priorities of political action, influence the selection of specific policies, and justify the policies chosen by political leaders. Sociologists also assume that the patterns of social stratification—the ranking of individuals and groups according to their political power, wealth, and prestige—influence both the content and the outcomes of public policies.

Guided by the interdisciplinary focus, institutional economists believe in reciprocal causation. Factors within the whole social system, not just political or economic determinants, shape public policies. For this reason, the policy analyst must explore the causal interdependence among values, political power, wealth, and general patterns of social stratification.

Taking an evolutionary, historical view of political economy, institutionalists examine how the economy changes over time. As different personnel come to hold government offices, policies may change. Depending on the political, military, and economic conditions in a country, the relative power of the national government, unions, and corporations over specific policy issues may also change. For this reason, institutionalists regard generalizations as relative to historical time and space, rather than universally valid. Generalizations true in one country may not be equally valid elsewhere; explanations for inflation in one time period may lack validity at a different historical period. Thus the conclusions reached by policy analysts are not timeless, but are bound to a specific historical context. By examining economic policies mainly between 1960 and 1975, this book assesses the changing impact of these public policies on unemployment, inflation, and economic equality.

In conclusion, this book investigates the content and the impact of public economic policies. Part I explores the substance of these policies and then assesses the cultural, political, and economic factors that explain the diverse policy content across the seven nations. Part II evaluates the consequences of these policies on inflation, unemployment, and income equality. Part III provides a concluding overview of the public policy process.

Notes

1. See Richard Rose, "On the Priorities of Government: A Developmental Analysis of Public Policies," *European Journal of Political Research* 4 (September 1976):247–89.

2. Dwight D. Waldo, "Political Science: Tradition, Discipline, Profession, Science, Enterprise," in Fred I. Greenstein and Nelson Polsby, eds., *Handbook of Political Science* (Reading, Mass.: Addison-Wesley, 1975), vol. 1, pp. 84, 99.

3. For these interpretations of "politics" and "policy," see Sheldon S. Wolin, *Politics and Vision: Continuity and Innovation in Western Political Thought* (Boston: Little, Brown, 1960), pp. 2–7; Heinz Eulau, "The Place of Policy Analysis in Political Science: The Interventionist Synthesis," *American Journal of Political Science* 21 (May 1977):420.

4. Robert Vaison, "A Note on 'Public Policy'," *Canadian Journal of Political Science* 6 (December 1973):662.

5. See Elliot J. Feldman, "Comparative Public Policy, Field or Method?" *Comparative Politics* 10 (January 1978):287–305, especially 289, 300–01; John A. Garraty, *Unemployment in History: Economic Thought and Public Policy* (New York: Harper & Row, 1978); Charles W. Anderson, "The Logic of Public Problems: Evaluation in Comparative Policy Research," in Douglas E. Ashford, ed., *Comparing Public Policies: New Concepts and Methods* (Beverly Hills, Calif.: Sage Publications, 1978), pp. 27–33.

6. In this book, I use what Arend Lijphart calls "The Comparable-Cases Strategy in Comparative Research," *Comparative Political Studies* 8 (July 1975):158–77.

7. For analyses of the institutionalist methodology, see Philip A. Klein, "American Institutionalism: Premature Death, Permanent Resurrection," *Journal of Economic Issues* 12 (June 1978):251–76; Wallace C. Peterson, "Institutionalism, Keynes, and the Real World," *Challenge* 20 (May-June 1977):22–32; Alfred S. Eichner, "Post-Keynesian Theory: An Introduction," *Challenge* 21 (May-June 1978):4–10; Allan G. Gruchy, "Institutional Economics: Its Influence and Prospects," *American Journal of Economics and Sociology* 37 (July 1978):271–81; Gunnar Myrdal, "Institutional Economics," *Journal of Economic Issues* 12 (December 1978):771–83.

PART

I *Policy Contents*

Part I analyzes the content of economic policies within seven Western nations; it considers the areas of life affected by the policies. Chapter 2 focuses on economic policies dealing with taxes, expenditures, the money supply, interest rates, and government ownership of economic firms. Chapter 3 then offers some explanations for the less activist policies pursued by the United States government compared to most other Western governments. Here, cultural values, the power of political structures like governments and political parties, and the power of economic structures, such as concentrated industries and labor unions, become crucial explanatory variables.

The Content of Economic Policies

Throughout the Western world, citizens tend to associate governments with economic policies, especially those policies involving taxes, expenditures, interest rates, and the regulation of business. Since 1960 total government expenditures as a percentage of the gross national product have showed dramatic increases. Taxes, especially social security contributions, have also sharply risen. Not surprisingly, then, when survey interviewers question samples of a population about the main ways that government affects them, people most often refer to tax policy. For example, during 1973 Louis Harris and his associates in the United States asked a random sample of Americans to assess the most important effect of government on their personal lives. Nearly 50 percent cited taxes as the most important effect of the federal and the state governments. About one-third perceived taxes as the main consequence of local government operations.[1] No other government activity evoked such a high percentage of responses. Despite the different tax policies carried out by various political systems, similar popular identifications between government and taxes occur in other Western countries as well.

Using a crossnational perspective, this chapter explores three types of economic policies: (1) fiscal decisions involving taxes and expenditures, (2) monetary policies that deal with the money supply and interest rates, and (3) programs for implementing government ownership of industries.

Chapter Two

Fiscal Policies

Fiscal policies, which refer to a government's tax and spending programs, probably represent the most important political decisions affecting citizens' welfare. In this regard, both the absolute *levels* as well as the *types* of taxes and expenditures exert a crucial impact. Tables 2–1, 2–2, and 2–3 present information about these two fiscal policies in seven Western industrialized nations. For comparative purposes, the tables present taxes and expenditures as a proportion of a country's gross national product.

As indicated by table 2–1, the fiscal policies pursued by the United States and Sweden showed the sharpest contrasts. From 1965 through 1974, the Swedish government enacted the highest levels of taxes and expenditures as a precentage of the gross·national product. In contrast, U.S. governments at all levels—national, state, and local—raised the lowest proportion of tax revenues and spent the smallest percentage of

Table 2–1 Levels of Taxes and Expenditures as a Percentage of Gross National Product, 1965–1974

Country	Expenditures		Taxes	
	1965–1969	*1970–1974*	*1965–1969*	*1970–1974*
United States	27.4	30.5	26.4	28.3
Canada	28.0	34.0	30.1	33.9
United Kingdom	32.3	34.9	33.3	34.9
West Germany	32.0	34.3	33.4	35.8
Sweden	33.1	40.3	38.0	42.6
France	34.2	34.7	37.0	37.0
Italy	31.3	35.6	29.8	30.6

NOTE: Data pertain to all levels of government: central, state-provincial in the three federal systems (United States, Canada, West Germany), and local. Taxes include revenues actually gathered by all governmental levels.

SOURCE: For data, see *National Accounts of OECD Countries, 1975* (Paris: OECD, 1977), vol. 2; *1962–1973* (Paris: OECD, 1975), *1961–1972* (Paris: OECD, 1974); *Revenue Statistics of OECD Member Countries, 1965–1974* (Paris: OECD, 1976), p. 74. Data on the gross national product at market prices appeared in *Revenue Statistics of OECD Member Countries, 1965–1974* (Paris: OECD, 1976), p. 98.

the GNP. The economic policies carried out by the Canadian government resembled those of the United States; Canada ranked second lowest in expenditures and third lowest in taxes. The Federal Republic of Germany and the United Kingdom ranked between the two North American nations and Sweden.

During two different time periods, 1965–1969 and 1970–1974, most nations maintained the same rankings in terms of taxes as a proportion of the GNP. Although in all nations except France the levels of taxes increased from one period to the next, the rank orderings of the countries remained the same. For example, while the U.S. governments collected the lowest taxes, Swedish citizens paid the highest taxes as a share of the national income.

The expenditures data reveal greater changes, however. True, government expenditures as a proportion of the GNP rose in every nation. Yet the rankings of Italy and France dramatically changed. Between 1965 and 1969 the French government ranked highest in expenditures, but during the early 1970s its spending dropped to fourth place. Over the same period, Italy's government showed just the opposite trend. Expenditures rose from third lowest to second highest behind Sweden.[2]

Although fiscal surpluses tended to decline between 1965 and 1974, most nations still managed to avoid a deficit during these years. As table 2–1 shows, taxes generally exceeded expenditures, especially during the last five years of the 1960s. The French, German, and Swedish governments accumulated the largest surpluses. Only Italy and the United States showed a fiscal deficit for all governmental levels. In particular, between 1970 and 1974 the Italian government ranked second lowest in taxes but second highest in expenditures. Even though in all seven countries current receipts included revenues other than taxes— for example, property income, compulsory fees, fines, penalties, and current transfers received from the rest of the world—nontax revenues did not suffice to balance the Italian governments' budgets. A similar, but less severe, fiscal problem plagued the U.S. governments.

The types of taxes and éxpenditures as well as the levels represent divergent policy priorities across nations. Let us look first at the pattern of government expenditures during the early 1970s. As indicated in table 2–2, French and especially Italian policies expressed a comparatively strong commitment to spending money on social service programs, including health care, old age pensions, child allowances, and unemployment benefits. However, their fiscal preference for education and health programs appeared relatively weak. The U.S. and German policies demonstrated divergent value priorities. The United States ranked high on educational expenditures, but low on health and general social service programs. West German expenditures showed an exactly reversed pattern: government spending on health and social services exceeded allocations for education. The Canadian and especially the Swedish governments spent a relatively high percentage of their national incomes on all three domestic policies.

Among the seven countries, the British and U.S. governments achieved the highest levels of military expenditures as a percentage of the GNP. Perhaps because Canadians live under the U.S. nuclear umbrella, Canada ranked the lowest on defense spending as a proportion of the total national income.

Comparisons over time indicate that in all seven nations expenditures for health, education, and income maintenance (transfer payments for old-age pensions, child allowances, unemployment insurance, pub-

Table 2–2 *Types of Government Expenditures as a Percentage of Gross National Product, 1973*

Country	Total Government Expenditures[a]	Education[b]	Health[c]	Social Services[d]	Military[e]
United States	29.9	6.7	2.8	12	6.1
Canada	33.7	8.0	6.0	19	2.0
United Kingdom	34.6	6.3	4.3	17	4.9
West Germany	35.2	4.1	4.6	22	3.4
Sweden	40.6	7.7	6.5	24	3.7
France	35.0	5.3	4.2	19	3.5
Italy	37.0	5.4	1.2	22	3.0

[a]Expenditures by all levels of government. See *National Accounts of OECD Countries, 1975* (Paris: OECD, 1977), vol. 2.

[b]Public education and subsidized private education at all government levels. See *UNESCO Statistical Yearbook* (Paris: UNESCO Press, 1976), pp. 378–88.

[c]Medical care and other health services, including national health insurance, public health, and expenditures under workmen's compensation. See Ruth Leger Sivard, *World Military and Social Expenditures 1976* (Leesburg, Va.: WMSE Publications, 1976), pp. 21–22.

[d]Health care, old-age pensions, unemployment benefits, and family allowances. See *Vision: The European Business Magazine,* no. 66 (May 1976):33.

[e]Government spending on defense. See *The Military Balance: 1976–1977* (London: The International Institute for Strategic Studies, 1976), p. 78.

lic assistance) rose between the early 1960s and the early 1970s. In particular, health expenditures as a proportion of the total national income dramatically escalated; in Canada, the United States, and West Germany, they more than doubled during this ten-year period. Spending for education and income maintenance, however, showed more modest increases. In contrast, defense expenditures as a percentage of the GNP either declined or remained roughly constant.[3]

Besides varying in their patterns of government spending, societies also place reliance on different types of taxes. Among the seven nations, most tax revenues for all levels of government derive from three types: personal income taxes, social security contributions, and taxes on goods and services (notably retail sales, value-added, and excise taxes). Although both the value-added tax in Europe and the sales tax in the United States and Canada are levied on goods and services, methods of collection differ. Consumers pay the retail sales tax when they purchase a good. However, government officials collect the value-added tax at several stages of the production process. The value-added tax represents the difference between the selling price of a good, like shoes, and the costs arising from a firm's outlays for manufacturing and distributing those shoes. Only the value added by each firm—for example, the rancher, tanner, shoe manufacturer, wholesaler, and the retailer—incurs a tax.[4]

Table 2–3 presents information about tax revenues gathered by all levels of government. According to this table, whereas Swedish citizens bear the heaviest tax burdens, Americans pay relatively low taxes as a percentage of the gross national product. The French and Italians pay low personal income taxes but high social security contributions and high taxes on goods and services. In Canada and the United Kingdom, personal income taxes are higher than social security contributions and taxes on goods and services. The West German governments tax their citizens at comparatively moderate rates.

Between 1965 and 1974 total taxes as a percentage of the GNP increased in every nation, with Sweden and Canada experiencing the sharpest rises. Everywhere, social security and personal income taxes grew. Except in Sweden, taxes on goods and services showed a slight decline. In all countries except the United States and the United Kingdom, taxes on net wealth and immovable property (land and buildings, for example) decreased a bit over the ten-year period.

The economic policies of the United States and Sweden show a marked divergence in their patterns and levels of taxation. Swedish policymakers finance programs for education, health, and income maintenance with high personal income and value-added taxes. At both the national and local government levels, Sweden levies the highest personal income taxes, double the U.S. rate. The taxes on goods and services—mainly value-added taxes—amounted in 1974 to 11 percent of the gross national product, over twice the U.S. percentage. The U.S. government exacts a much lower tax tribute from its citizens. As in Sweden, the personal income tax raises more money than the sales tax. Yet these tax burdens as a percentage of the GNP are less than one-half as large in the United States.

The two Latin nations, France and Italy, rely on social security and value-added taxes; personal income taxes represent a relatively unimportant source of revenue. Tax evasion has always been widespread in these countries, and government officials have found it more efficient to collect taxes indirectly through taxes on the production and distribution of goods, rather than directly on personal incomes. Compared with the United States and Britain, expenditures for social security are higher in France and Italy; social security taxes are also higher.

Although diverging somewhat in their expenditures policies, the Canadian and British governments have employed similar tax policies. The citizens in both countries pay fairly high personal income taxes, at least compared with France and Italy. However, social security contributions amount to comparatively low percentages of the gross national products. In both Canada and Britain, taxes on goods and services produce more revenue than social security payroll taxes.

Neither property taxes nor corporation income taxes constitute an important source of government revenue in most of these countries. The three English-speaking nations—the United Kingdom, the United States, and Canada—raise the comparatively greatest revenues through taxes on property and net wealth. In the other countries these taxes exert little fiscal impact, since they comprise less than 1 percent of the GNP. Only in the United States and Canada do taxes on corporate income represent more than 10 percent of the total tax revenues. Yet over the last ten years, these taxes have declined in importance. For instance, in 1965 the U.S. and Canadian governments raised about 15 percent of their revenues through corporate income taxes; by 1974 this figure had decreased to between 11 and 12 percent. During this ten-year period, social security contributions and personal income taxes as a proportion of total taxes increased.[5] Despite the heavier burden of corporate income taxes in Canada and the United States, these taxes have become less important over the years; they have been offset by rising personal income and social security taxes.

Monetary Policies

Monetary policies also affect a nation's economic welfare, particularly its inflationary tendencies. Monetary policies include decisions about the money supply and interest rates. Under the term *money supply* fall several different types of money: currency in circulation outside banks and checking accounts in the banks (M1), savings deposits at commercial banks, and deposits held by savings banks and credit institutions. The monetary information analyzed in this chapter is based on currency and checking accounts; this narrower measure of money has a similar meaning across different nations and therefore can be used to make crossnational comparisons of increases in the money supply. The price of money refers to interest rates, which determine the cost of borrowing money. Central banking systems in each country establish a dis-

Table 2–3   Types of Taxes as a Percentage of Gross National Product

Country	Date	Total Taxes[a]	Taxes on Goods and Services[b]
United States	1965	24.9	4.8
	1974	28.9	4.7
Canada	1965	27.3	9.7
	1974	34.8	9.6
United Kingdom	1965	30.5	9.4
	1974	35.6	9.0
West Germany	1965	32.6	9.8
	1974	37.6	9.0
Sweden	1965	35.6	10.8
	1974	44.2	11.0
France	1965	36.5	13.2
	1974	37.5	12.4
Italy	1965	29.1	10.8
	1974	31.9	10.3

[a]Revenues gathered by all levels of government.

[b]General sales taxes, value-added taxes, excise taxes, and taxes levied on the import and export of goods.

count rate—that is, the interest charges paid by member commercial banks to secure funds from the central bank.

When formulating monetary policy, government officials face the following dilemma: How can they best achieve a rapid economic growth rate while avoiding escalating price increases? Generally, if the central banks want to pursue an expansionary monetary policy, they will institute low interest rates and high annual increases in the money supply. Such a policy encourages businesses to borrow money for investment and leads consumers to seek loans to purchase goods on credit. A restrictive monetary policy involves low increases in the quantity of money and high interest rates.

Perhaps because of the desire to avoid an unfavorable tradeoff between inflation and the economic growth rate, few nations pursue a consistently expansionary or restrictive monetary policy toward both

Social Security Taxes	Income Taxes		Taxes on Net Wealth and Property[c]
	Personal Income	*Corporate Income*	
4.1	7.6	3.9	3.4
6.7	9.8	3.2	3.5
1.6	6.3	4.2	3.2
3.2	12.2	4.4	3.0
4.7	9.5	1.8	3.4
6.1	12.5	2.9	3.7
9.6	8.2	2.5	1.2
13.2	11.5	1.8	0.8
5.6	16.0	2.2	0.3
8.5	19.9	1.5	0.2
13.6	3.7	1.9	0.6
15.7	4.1	3.1	0.1
9.9	3.2	2.0	0.5
13.3	4.9	1.6	0.0

[c]Taxes on land and buildings paid by both corporate enterprises and households.
SOURCE: *Revenue Statistics of OECD Member Countries, 1965–1974* (Paris: OECD, 1976), pp. 74–89.

interest rates and the money supply. According to table 2–4, between 1960 and 1974 only two countries followed consistent policies, although in opposite directions. The United Kingdom had the highest interest rates during the three time periods (1960–1964, 1965–1969, 1970–1974) and comparatively low increases in the quantity of money, especially during the 1960s. Italy adopted the most expansionary policy, with relatively low interest rates and large yearly rises in the money supply. The other five governments adopted slightly divergent policies toward the supply and price of money. For example, Germany combined low interest rates with moderate increases in the money supply. In contrast, the Federal Reserve Board, the central banking system in the United States, made comparatively low increases in the quantity of money but established moderate interest rates. The French government chose high increases in the money supply along with moderate to high interest rates. Compared with the United States, Canada and Sweden experienced generally higher yearly rises in the money supply and higher interest rates too.

Table 2–4 *Interest Rates and Increases in Money Supply*

Country	% Increases in Money Supply[a] (annual averages)			Interest Rates[b] (%/year)		
	1960–1964	1965–1969	1970–1974	1960–1964	1965–1969	1970–1974
United States	2.5	5.0	6.3	3.3	5.0	6.0
Canada	5.1	6.6	10.8	3.8	6.1	6.3
United Kingdom	2.9	3.2	10.9	5.3	7.2	9.1
West Germany	9.1	6.7	9.9	3.2	4.2	5.5
Sweden	6.0	5.7	9.5	4.6	5.9	5.8
France	13.9	6.0	12.3	3.7	4.9	9.0
Italy	13.6	14.5	19.6	3.5	3.6	5.7

[a]Money refers to M1—currency outside banks and checking accounts in banks. See *Main Economic Indicators, Historical Statistics: 1960–1975* (Paris: OECD, 1976); *Main Economic Indicators, Historical Statistics; 1955–1971* (Paris: OECD, 1973); *Rates of Change in Economic Data for Ten Industrial Countries: 1956–1975* (Federal Reserve Bank of St. Louis, October 1976).

[b]Official discount rate. See *Main Economic Indicators, Historical Statistics: 1960–1975* (Paris: OECD, 1976).

When we look at the changes in monetary policy over time, we see a general tendency for both interest rates and the quantity of money to rise. Particularly in the United States, Canada, the United Kingdom, and Italy, during each five-year period between 1960 and 1974, the average yearly increase in the money supply grew larger. Interest rates showed an even more dramatic rise; in all seven nations except Sweden, the banking discount rates successively increased over each five-year period. Apparently, central banking officials wanted to check the severe inflation that accelerated during the early 1970s, an inflation caused partly by increases in the money supply.

All seven nations employ similar techniques for increasing and decreasing the money supply. These methods include the following: (1) ordering the printing presses to print more or less money, (2) buying and selling government bonds, (3) raising or lowering the discount rate, (4) altering the minimum reserve requirements, and (5) changing the ceiling on the amount of money banks can lend. All seven countries use the first four methods. Since they are the most important types of monetary policies, let us briefly examine their modes of operation.

First, although the central banks in these seven economies have the authority to print more money, they seldom rely on this technique to expand the money supply. Deposits in the banks generally exceed in value the currency in circulation outside the banks. When central banking officials want to expand the money supply, they are more likely to release additional funds for loans than to order the printing press operators to manufacture more francs, dollars, or pounds.

Second, especially in the United States, Canada, the United Kingdom, and Italy, the central banks rely on the purchase and sale of government securities as the prime method to change the supply of money. To increase the money supply, the central bank buys government securities and deposits the payments in commercial banks; thereby it increases the funds available to banks for making loans to businesses and individual consumers. To reduce the money supply, the central bank sells government bonds to commercial banks. Because banks use their funds to purchase these securities, they have less money for lending to their customers; therefore, expansionary tendencies in the economy subside.

Third, the central bank may lower the discount rate (the interest rate determining the price of loans made to other banks). By this strategy, the cost of loans declines and more money becomes available for use in the economy. Decreasing the money supply involves the opposite strategy—that is, a raise in the discount rate. The Bank of England's control of the money supply partly rests on its authority to change the discount rate when loaning money to the discount houses.

Fourth, through altering the reserve requirements, the central banking system affects the quantity of money. In these seven countries, banks must hold in cash (or reserve) a certain percentage of the deposits in the bank. Changes in reserve requirements are most frequently made in Germany, France, Sweden, and the United Kingdom, where the central banks raise or lower the minimum reserve ratios. Whereas a lower ratio increases the money supply, a higher ratio reduces the quantity of money. U.S. and Canadian central banks pursue this monetary strategy less often. In the United States the reserve requirement rarely changes. Although the Bank of Canada is legally forbidden to change the reserve ratio for checking and savings accounts, it can alter the reserve ratio for Canadian treasury bills and short-term loans to securities dealers. This limited authority over minimum reserve requirements affects the credit available for investment purposes.[6]

Two variables mainly explain variations in the money supply across these seven nations: (1) the power relationships between public and private banks and (2) the independence of the central banks from elected political leaders—that is, the president and legislators in the United States and France; the prime minister and cabinet ministers in the rest of Europe and Canada. Michael Parkin hypothesizes that in a Western market economy with a political democracy, the greater the power of the private banks and the greater the autonomy of the central banks from elected political leaders, the lower will be the annual increases in the money supply.[7] Although this explanation may hold true for the United States, France, and Italy, it does not explain monetary policies in the other countries.

Why does the central banking system in the United States follow restrictive policies toward the money supply? As Parkin suggests, private banks exercise extensive political power in the United States. Unlike the situation in other Western societies, no single central public bank even operates. Congress has delegated to a quasi-private corporation—the Federal Reserve System—the authority to regulate the money supply. Although the president appoints and the Senate approves members of the Board of Governors of the Federal Reserve System for fourteen-year terms, these members retain a high degree of independence from elected political leaders. Both in public sessions and in private meetings where crucial economic decisions are made, they often challenge the policies formulated by the president and Congress. Since the twelve regional banks own the Federal Reserve Bank and since Board members enjoy a fairly long tenure, the Bank appears more accountable to private bankers than to either the president or Congress. Specifically, decisions about banking regulations, credit, and money supply are made each month in secret by the chairman of the Board of Governors, the head of the Federal Reserve Board of New York, and the Federal Open Market Committee (FOMC), an agency staffed by professional economists sensitive to the interests of the private banking community. As the key decision-making agency, the FOMC consists of twelve members; of these twelve, seven are members of the Federal Reserve Board and the remaining five are presidents of the Federal Reserve banks. Even though the president appoints members of the Federal Reserve Board, neither he nor Congress chooses the Bank presidents, who are elected by boards of directors of the twelve banks. As expected from this arrangement, the decisions of the FOMC represent the monetary preferences of bankers and corporate businessmen. Between 1960 and 1974 they upheld relative low annual increases in the quantity of money.[8]

The banking situation in France and particularly in Italy contrasts dramatically with the U.S. Federal Reserve System. In these two countries the central banks—the Bank of France and the Bank of Italy—as well as most commercial banks are publicly owned, either directly by the government, as in France, or by state holding companies, such as the Istituto per la Ricostruzione Industriale (IRI) in Italy. Elected government officials exercise much greater control over the central banks than do U.S. political leaders. As a result of the desire to maintain an expansionary economy, since 1960 the French and especially the Italian banks have decreed relatively high annual increases in the money supply.

In short, the United States, France, and Italy all reveal a close relationship between the power of private banks and the political independence of the central bank, on the one hand, and the annual rate of increase in the money supply, on the other. The United States' restrictive monetary policies partly stem from the influential power of private banks. The more expansionary French and Italian policies result from the weaker power of private banks and the more limited autonomy of the central bank from elected political leaders.

Yet the power of private banks and the independence of central banks from elected officials do not so clearly explain policies toward the money supply in Canada, Britain, Sweden, and Germany. The banking systems in these four nations share similar features. All four have a public central bank: the Bank of Sweden has been publicly owned since 1668, the Bank of Canada was established in 1934, the Bank of England was nationalized in 1946, and the German Bundesbank was created in 1957. In all these countries, decentralized financial institutions, especially privately owned ones, play a key role in banking transactions. Most commercial banks and credit institutions are privately owned.

Despite these similarities in banking structure, the monetary policies of Britain and Sweden diverge from those of Canada and West Germany. According to most observers, the central banks in Germany and Canada have somewhat greater autonomy from elective parliamentary leaders than do those in Britain and Sweden. Although the heads of parliament voice general economic policies, the Bundesbank and the Bank of Canada retain considerable discretion in making decisions about money supply increases and availability of credit.[9] In contrast, the Bank of England and the Bank of Sweden come under slightly greater control by the prime minister and the cabinet. These structural arrangements between elected officials and the central bank might lead us to assume that Sweden and Britain would pursue more expansionary policies than Canada or West Germany. However, just the opposite tendency appeared during the 1960s and 1970s. Over this fifteen-year period (1960–1974), the Bundesbank and the Bank of Canada instituted larger annual increases in the money supply than did the Bank of England or the Bank of Sweden. Thus neither the autonomy of the publicly owned central bank nor the economic power of private banks so clearly explains recent monetary policies in these four countries as in the United States, France, and Italy.

Government Ownership Policies

The power of government in the economic sector involves not only fiscal and monetary policies but also policies toward government ownership of economic firms. When a large number and variety of industries fall under public ownership, then government officials have the potential power to affect directly both the employment situation and prices of goods. However, where privately owned firms are pervasive, government wields less direct control over inflation and unemployment. Under this condition, it must rely primarily on fiscal and monetary policies.

According to table 2–5, the United States and Canada feature the highest degree of private ownership. Sweden, Germany, and Britain occupy an intermediate position on the nationalization scale. The greatest extent of public ownership exists in France and Italy.

Throughout Western Europe and North America, government ownership has extended the furthest over the transportation and communication industries. Except in the United States, governments have achieved total ownership or both governments and private firms own these industries. With the capital goods industries—that is, those pro-

Table 2–5 Ownership of Economic Firms

Economic Firm	Italy	France	Sweden	West Germany	Britain	Canada	United States
Transportation							
highways	G	G	G	G	G	G	G
railroads	G	G	M/G	G	G	M/G	M/P
airlines	G	M/G	M/G	M/P	M/G	M/G	P
auto manufacturing	M/P	M/P	P	M/P	M/P	P	P
Communications							
radio/television	G	G	P	G	M/G	M/P	P
telephones	G	G	G	G	G	M/P	P
postal service	G	G	G	G	G	G	M/G
Power Industries							
gas	M/G	G	M/G=P	G	G	P	P
electricity	M/G	G	M/G=P	M/G	G	M/G	M/P
coal	M/G	M/G	M/P	P	G	P	P
oil	M/G	M/G=P	M/G=P	M/P	M/P	P	P
steel	M/G	M/P	M/G	M/P	G	P	P
Banks	G	M/G	M/P	M/P	M/P	M/P	P

NOTE: The table estimates the degree of government ownership during the early 1970s. G refers to ownership by the government, either central or local. P indicates private ownership. Mixed ownership includes three types: *M/G* means that government ownership predominates; *M/P* means that private ownership predominates; *M/G=P* refers to a balance between government and private ownership.

SOURCE: (1) Anthony King, "Ideas, Institutions and the Policies of Governments: A Comparative Analysis," *British Journal of Political Science* 3 (July 1973):292–96; (2) Martin C. Schnitzer and James W. Nordyke, *Comparative Economic Systems,* 2nd ed. (Cincinnati: South-Western Publishing Co., 1977), pp. 189–93; (3) Stuart Holland, "Europe's New Public Enterprises," in Raymond Vernon, ed., *Big Business and the State: Changing Relations in Western Europe* (Cambridge, Mass.: Harvard University Press, 1974), pp. 25–44; (4) *Encyclopaedia Britannica: Macropaedia* (Chicago: Encyclopedia Britannica, 1975), vol. 3 (Canada), pp. 725–33; vol. 7 (France), pp. 599–601, 610; vol. 8 (Germany), pp. 58–59; vol. 9 (Italy), pp. 1101–02; vol. 15 (Public Enterprises), pp. 198–202; vol. 17 (Sweden), pp. 847–50; vol. 18 (United Kingdom), pp. 880–85; (5) Kevin Allen and Andrew Stevenson, *An Introduction to the Italian Economy* (New York: Barnes and Noble, 1974), pp. 217–63; G. Corti, "Perspectives on Public Corporations and Public Enterprises in Five Nations," *Annals of Public and Co-operative Economy* 47 (January-March 1976):47–48.

ducing the power resources needed to manufacture a variety of products—the ownership pattern becomes more mixed. Generally, both government as well as private companies assume responsibility for producing steel, coal, oil, and electricity, although private firms often predominate over the first three of these resources. Similarly, in most countries except the United States, a nationalized central bank, along with several private commercial banks, handle basic financial activities.

Although all seven countries operate under mixed economies, where government and private industries share economic tasks, the United States features by far the highest degree of private ownership. As in the other nations, for example, a public organization dominates the handling of the mail. Yet the U.S. Postal Service, a semigovernmental corporation, must compete with a private agency, the United Parcel Service, which delivers more parcels than does the Postal Service. Some large publishing firms have even undertaken to deliver their own magazines. Besides the postal service, only railroads and electricity fall under partial government ownership; here, however, the private sector dominates. Some city governments own their electricity plants. Several public hydroelectric power projects exist; of these the Tennessee Valley Authority, controlled by the Tennessee state government, is perhaps the most famous. Although the railroads come under private ownership, quasi-public corporations, the National Railroad Passenger Corporation (AMTRACK) and the Consolidated Rail Corporation (CONRAIL), operate the railways.

Does private ownership imply lack of government control? Not necessarily. Compared with the other six countries, the United States has the greatest regulation of privately owned firms by central and state governments, which also provide extensive subsidies to private industries. Economic units that are nationalized in Europe fall under government regulation in the United States. For example, a federal or state regulatory agency exists for nearly every industry listed in table 2–5. The Interstate Commerce Commission regulates the rates and routes of railroads and most trucking firms. The Civil Aeronautics Board and the Federal Aviation Administration regulate the airlines. The Environmental Protection Agency assumes responsibility for protecting citizens from auto pollution; the National Highway Traffic Safety Administration encourages automobile manufacturers to produce safe cars. The Federal Communications Commission regulates radio, television, and interstate telephone and telegraph services. State public utility commissions oversee gas, electricity, and telephones. At the federal level, the Federal Power Commission regulates interstate rates, routes, and transmission of electric power and natural gas. The Department of Energy controls the price of domestic crude oil and gasoline. Finally, several agencies supervise the banking industry; these include the Federal Deposit Insurance Corporation, the Comptroller of the Currency, and the Federal Reserve Board. Besides controlling the money supply, the Federal Reserve Board enforces the Consumer Credit Protection Act, the Equal Credit Opportunity Act, and the Bank Holding Company Act.[10]

Despite all these government regulations and extensive subsidies, most observers agree that private firms have gained control over the regulatory agencies, rather than vice versa. After appointing members of the regulatory agencies, government officials can no longer exert very much control over them. Instead, heads of the regulated companies come to exercise the dominant influence. In most instances, the regulatory agency strives to guarantee certain profits and to avoid service failures; other aspects of management remain beyond the scope of the regulators' control. For example, private railroad managers, labor union leaders, and private banking officials dominate CONRAIL and AMTRACK. Under the provisions of the Railroad Revitalization and Regulatory Reform Act of 1975, the Interstate Commerce Commission relinquished some authority to regulate the railroads. Since the president now appoints only two of the eleven members of CONRAIL's board of directors, that board has come under even greater domination by managers of privately owned railroads. The structures of CONRAIL and AMTRACK enable these "quasi-public" agencies to secure subsidies, grants, and loans from the government while escaping any detailed regulation by governmental organizations.

Similarly, the Federal Communications Commission issues few regulations over radio and television stations; private businesses run these stations primarily to provide advertising media accessible to virtually the whole population. Compared with European radio-television stations, where no more than 5 percent of broadcast time is devoted to advertising, on U.S. stations advertisements take up between 20 and 25 percent of the total broadcast hours.[11]

Other regulated industries show a similar pattern of private business control. As William G. Shepherd has observed:

> [*The federal and state*] *commission has formal powers to direct or control; but in practice it usually negotiates and often merely acquiesces. In some cases, regulators are irrelevant or passive to company behavior, or even serve to legitimize it.*[12]

The history of weak central government power in the United States, combined with political beliefs hostile to an activist state, explains the subordination of the regulatory agencies to privately owned businesses.

Although Canadians, like Americans, live in a private enterprise economy and in a federal political system, Canadian federal and provincial governments have undertaken more extensive public ownership. In most sectors of the economy, either government and private firms compete in the same industry or else privately owned companies hold exclusive control. For instance, the Canadian Broadcasting Corporation, a federal government agency, owns some radio and television stations throughout Canada; yet private stations are more numerous. Influenced by diverse ideologies, such as classical conservatism, liberalism, and socialism, Canadian leaders seem more committed than American politicians to operating a truly mixed economy where government firms and private industries carry out similar economic activities. Compared with practices in the United States, Canadian economic policies, like European ones, follow a more corporate model. Government leaders try to secure harmonious, cooperative relations among the three large-scale corporate institutions: government, business, and labor unions. Bureaucracies dominate all three sectors. The community and group take precedence over the individual parts. Although private ownership prevails, state control and regulation over "private" businesses has become widespread.[13]

The three northern European countries, Sweden, Germany, and Britain, experience an intermediate degree of public ownership that is greater than in Canada and the United States but less than in France and Italy. Despite the moderate size of the government sector, the scope of central government control appears limited. Over 90 percent of Swedish industries are privately owned. Government participation in industrial activities, such as oil production, takes the form of joint-stock companies; under this arrangement, both the central government and private firms hold joint shares, often half each, in the corporation. Like the German government, the British government has relied on public corporations to manage the economy. Although financed by public funds, these corporations, such as the British Broadcasting Corporation, retain a high degree of independence from the cabinet ministers. Their employees are not viewed as civil servants.

Among the seven Western countries, the French and Italian governments manage the most comprehensive publicly owned economic sector. Compared with German, Swedish, and British public corporations, French public enterprises experience more direct regulation by cabinet ministers in the central government. Yet in contemporary French corporate society, the heads of the national civil service, the large private corporations, and the public enterprises enjoy close working relationships. Fulfilling a managerial, technocratic role, the same individuals often move freely from one sector to the other; they become dependent on each other for resources, expertise, and information. Since managerial and professional types dominate all large-scale organizations, public and private enterprises operate similarly. Under this corporate structure, public corporations may enjoy more independence from cabinet ministers than do privately owned firms. For example, the French central government wields greater power over private credit banks than over the state-owned financial institutions.[14]

In Italy as well, the emergence of the corporate state blurs the old distinction between the public and private economic sectors. The central government itself owns outright only the railroads and the postal service. Nearly all the other publicly owned economic firms function as state holding companies of which the IRI (Instituto per la Ricostruzione Industriale) and the ENI (Ente Nazionale Idrocarburi) operate the greatest number of firms. Established in 1933 by Mussolini's corporate state, the IRI today manages a vast array of different economic activities, including highways, airlines, auto manufacturing, radio, television, telephones, steel, and banking. The ENI concentrates on oil and gas production, oil refining, nuclear energy, engineering, and chemicals. A complicated structure pervades this state holding sector. The central government's Ministry of State Participation supposedly supervises the IRI and the ENI. Below them come the financial holding companies, to which private shareholders make contributions. At the bottom level the operating companies—over 350 throughout Italy—carry out economic activities somewhat as do privately owned firms. Under this complex arrangement, the governmental Ministry of State Participation finds it difficult to exert significant power over the economic decisions made by the operating companies, partly because the IRI top managers control banking officials as well as a large number of representatives in the Chamber of Deputies, the lower house of the Italian parliament.[15] In short, extensive public ownership, as found in Italy, does not necessarily imply widespread control exercised by elected political leaders. Despite the variations in degree of public ownership, all these nations operate modified market economies; private economic firms retain considerable independence to shape the decisions made by the central government.

Notes

1. See Louis Harris, *Confidence and Concern: Citizens View American Government,* a survey of public attitudes by the Subcommittee on Intergovernmental Relations of the Committee on Government Operations, U.S. Senate, part 2 (Washington, D. C.: Government Printing Office, 1973), pp. 63–71.

2. Changes in government spending over time must be interpreted cautiously. Increases in government expenditures as a percentage of the GNP may stem from general price increases, from rapid spending increases, or from a declining economic growth rate. See Morris Beck, "The Expanding Public Sector: Some Contrary Evidence," *National Tax Journal* 29 (March 1976):15–21; Rudolf Klein, "The National Health Service," in Rudolf Klein, ed., *Social Policy and Public Expenditure 1975: Inflation and Priorities* (London: Centre for Studies in Social Policy, 1975), p. 83.

3. For data on changes in expenditures for education, income maintenance, and health as a percentage of the gross domestic product between the early 1960s and the early 1970s, see *The OECD Observer*, no. 92 (May 1978):10. Information about defense expenditures as a percentage of the gross national product appear in the yearly reports of *The Military Balance*, issued by The International Institute for Strategic Studies in London.

4. For a discussion of the value-added tax, see Martin C. Schnitzer and James W. Nordyke, *Comparative Economic Systems,* 2nd ed. (Cincinnati: South-Western Publishing Company, 1977), p. 205; George F. Break and Joseph A. Pechman, *Federal Tax Reform: The Impossible Dream?* (Washington, D. C.: The Brookings Institution, 1975), p. 119; Richard A. Musgrave and Peggy B. Musgrave, *Public Finance in Theory and Practice,* 2nd ed. (New York: McGraw-Hill, 1976), p. 337.

5. *Revenue Statistics of OECD Member Countries, 1965–1974* (Paris: OECD, 1976), pp. 83–88.

6. For analyses of banking systems and monetary policies in several countries, see Schnitzer and Nordyke, *Comparative Economic Systems,* pp. 142–43, 186–88, 213–16, 242–44, 299–302, 324–27; *The Role of Monetary Policy in Demand Management: The Experience of Six Major Countries,* OECD Monetary Studies Series (Paris: OECD, 1975), pp. 25–50; Ian M. Drummond, *The Canadian Economy: Structure and Development,* rev. ed. (Georgetown, Ont.: Irwin-Dorsey, 1972), pp. 67–79; Kevin Allen and Andrew Stevenson, *An Introduction to the Italian Economy* (New York: Barnes and Noble, 1974), pp. 157–73.

7. Michael Parkin, "The Politics of Inflation," *Government and Opposition* 10 (Spring 1975):201.

8. See Sandford F. Borins, "The Political Economy of 'The Fed'," *Public Policy* 20 (Spring 1972):175–98; E. Ray Canterbery, "The Awkward Independence of the Federal Reserve," *Challenge* 18 (September/October 1975):44–48; Henry S. Reuss, "Federal Reserve: A Private Club for Public Policy," *The Nation* 223 (October 16, 1976):370–72.

9. Schnitzer and Nordyke, *Comparative Economic Systems,* pp. 188, 235; Drummond, *The Canadian Economy,* pp. 72–73; John T. Woolley, "Monetary Policy Instrumentation and the Relationship of Central Banks and Governments," *The Annals of the American Academy of Political and Social Science* 434 (November 1977):151–73, esp. p. 172.

10. See the extensive discussion of federal governmental regulations in *Business Week,* April 4, 1977, esp. pp. 52–56.

11. See James A. Dunn, Jr., "Railroad Policies in Europe and the United States: The Impact of Ideology, Institutions, and Social Conditions," *Public*

Policy 25 (Spring 1977):205–40, esp. pp. 228–36; *UNESCO Statistical Yearbook, 1974* (Paris: UNESCO Press, 1975), pp. 849–50, 870–71.

12. William G. Shepherd, *The Treatment of Market Power: Antitrust, Regulation, and Public Enterprise* (New York: Columbia University Press, 1965), p. 149. See also James Q. Wilson, "The Rise of the Bureaucratic State," in Nathan Glazer and Irving Kristol, eds., *The American Commonwealth 1976* (New York: Basic Books, 1976), pp. 95–100.

13. G. Horowitz, "Conservatism, Liberalism, and Socialism in Canada: An Interpretation," *The Canadian Journal of Economics and Political Science* 32 (May 1966):143–71; J. T. McLeod, "The Free Enterprise Dodo Is No Phoenix," *Canadian Forum* 56 (August 1976):6–13.

14. Schnitzer and Nordyke, *Comparative Economic Systems,* p. 186.

15. Allen and Stevenson, *An Introduction to the Italian Economy,* pp. 217–50; G. Corti, "Perspectives on Public Corporations and Public Enterprises in Five Nations," *Annals of Public and Co-operative Economy* 47 (January-March 1976):74.

The Cultural and Structural Context of Economic Policies

As chapter 2 has shown, the U.S. government pursues the least activist economic policy in the Western world. Compared with Canadian and European governments, it authorizes the lowest total public expenditures as a percentage of the GNP, collects the lowest tax revenues as a proportion of the GNP, practices the most restrictive policies for increasing the money supply, and has brought under public ownership the fewest economic firms.

What variables best explain the divergent content of economic policies in the United States, Canada, and Europe? Policy analysts have focused on two general aspects of the social system: culture and structure. Political culture denotes those beliefs, values, and symbols that give meaning to political life. Individuals use cultural values to perceive, understand, and evaluate the political universe. Political structure refers to the patterns of interaction among individuals, particularly as found in the society's groups and institutions. When members of these groups and institutions use their resources to shape public policies, they exercise political power. As crucial structural variables, power relationships partially explain a specific policy content, like the level of government expenditures or the selection of private agencies to implement a public policy.

Although we can make analytical distinctions between culture and

Chapter Three

structure, obviously these two variables interact empirically in the actual policy process.[1] Neither beliefs nor structural arrangements operate in a vacuum independent of the other. Beliefs about freedom and equality, individualism and collectivism, and equity and efficiency help to shape the content of public policies. As the famous English economist John Maynard Keynes observed:

> *The ideas of economists and political philosophers, both when they are right and when they are wrong, are more powerful than is commonly understood. Indeed the world is ruled by little else.*[2]

True, ideas do have consequences on policy, but they become realized only through particular structural arrangements. Thus beliefs about the need for individual hard work as a means to overcome poverty cannot easily take effect where the economic structures provide few employment opportunities. Political leaders have difficulty realizing ideas of freedom and equality under hierarchical, authoritarian structures. Yet even within similar economic and political structures, such as those existing in the market societies of North America and Western Europe, public economic policies reveal divergent contents. Part of this divergence stems from the diverse beliefs held by leaders and citizens of each society.

Cultural Beliefs

The cultural sector of society revolves around the production and distribution of symbols and beliefs; these cultural beliefs influence the content of public policies in the following ways.[3] First, values shape the purposes and priorities of political action; they specify those issues that political leaders regard as most important. In this respect, elite perceptions of appropriate political action become crucial. How do public officials define the scope of political activity; that is, what particular problems do they perceive should be resolved through political means? If elite preferences veer toward the political solution of problems, for what specific projects should the government allocate resources? Should national defense take priority over health and social security? What role, if any, ought the government to play in coping with unemployment, inflation, and income inequality?

Second, once political leaders have decided that they should try to resolve certain social problems through the public policy route, beliefs influence the selection of the most desirable and feasible policies. For example, public officials may decide to tackle the inflation problem through governmental methods. Should they emphasize fiscal or monetary restraints? If they favor the fiscal alternative, should they raise taxes or cut government expenditures? Leaders who want to maximize the economic freedom of the private sector will probably favor a policy of lower expenditures. Similarly, leaders supporting a strengthened private sector will prefer that private business firms, rather than a government bureaucracy, administer public programs to lower unemployment. Most likely, they will regard government subsidies to private firms for training in job skills as not only more desirable but also more efficient than jobs directly created by the government.

Third, government officials use cultural beliefs to justify selected policies and to gain acceptance for these policies. Legitimacy means that groups accept the justified right of political leaders to make morally binding public policies. By securing acceptance of important government decisions, political leaders attempt to legitimate their rule and the political system. For example, Bismarck (1815–1898), chancellor of Germany, used cultural beliefs about hierarchical responsibility to justify social security and health insurance programs introduced during the 1880s. By justifying these two policies in terms of the need for the paternalistic German state to care for the needs of the workers, Bismarck hoped to win the allegiance of the working class toward the monarchical state.[4]

Among all countries, even the democratic societies of the Western world, the beliefs held by policymakers carry special weight in shaping the content of public economic policies.[5] To a greater extent than European policymakers, U.S. leaders articulate beliefs about freedom and equality, individualism and collectivism, and populism and elitism that discourage activist economic policies.

Freedom and Equality

The American concept of freedom and equality derives primarily from classical liberalism, the most influential belief system shaping the American policy process. According to basic liberal principles, people should enjoy equal rights before the law and equal opportunities to achieve. Rather than guaranteeing greater equality of opportunity, a strong government threatens to produce political elitism vested in a centralized bureaucracy. Thus classical liberals have historically supported limited, decentralized government.

Political leaders in American society interpret freedom to mean the right of private business firms to achieve independence from government control. American liberals have opposed government "interference" in the private sector, except to grant subsidies for private businesses and to provide some benefits for the very poor and aged. Under this conception of the state's role, the government acts as a referee to regulate the playing of the political game. The players are mainly heads of private corporations and powerful lobbyists. Political leaders try to maintain a general adherence to the rules, so that these powerful groups gain their "fair shares." In this rule-oriented game, different government agencies play specialized roles.[6] The legislature ratifies the victories secured by the strongest group coalitions. The judges make the rules consistent and systematic; they may even invalidate state and federal legislative actions that act contrary to private group interests. For example, between 1870 and 1935 the U.S. Supreme Court declared unconstitutional state and national legislative decisions that set a minimum wage, abolished child labor, established workmen's compensation, enacted an income tax, and outlawed agreements under which employees pledged not to join a union if they wanted to keep their jobs. The administrative agencies regulate the group contest after the basic laws have been passed and adjudicated.

By contrast, European leaders articulate ideologies that grant the state more positive power to deal with social problems. In Canada and England, conservatism and socialism, as well as liberalism, attract significant followings. The two dominant parties in Italy voice the beliefs of Catholic conservatism and secular communism. Germany has experienced political struggles among Catholic conservatives, social democrats, and economic liberals dedicated to the "social market." In France conservatism, socialism, and communism exert the major influence on the shaping of contemporary public policy. Except for liberalism, all these ideologies envision a positive role for the central government; government must act as an economic manager, not just as a referee. Instead of merely responding to crises, government should initiate actions to ward off problems. It needs to assume greater responsibility for instituting comprehensive public policies. In sum, Americans perceive freedom as independence from government control, but Europeans interpret freedom to mean the right of the government to plan for the public welfare.

Individualism and Collectivism

Different attitudes toward collectivism and individualism also distinguish American cultural beliefs from European conceptions of politics. As the dominant belief system in the United States, liberalism accords a high priority to individualism. At the time of the writing of the U.S. Constitution in the early 1780s, the ideas of John Locke and Adam Smith, two advocates of classical liberalism, enjoyed popularity among the political leaders. Both stressed a strong individualist strain, assuming that each individual is motivated primarily by the desire to advance his or her self-interest (wealth and status). Government should therefore function as the agency to protect private property and maintain individuals' security against those who threaten their material possessions.[7] Government should also promote the conditions necessary for individuals to achieve success. Social mobility occurs mainly through free competition among individuals, rather than through government assistance to collective groups. This value placed on individualism has led to fairly high expenditures on education, for policymakers historically have viewed the American public school system as the most appropriate mechanism for attaining equality of individual opportunity. In line with their laissez faire liberal traditions, most Americans regard the public good as the aggregate sum of private individual interests.

During the twentieth century, these individualistic beliefs of classical liberalism have received less support on the European continent and even within England itself, the original home of liberalism. Although they disagree on the specific nature of the public interest, conservatives, socialists, and communists all believe that government should promote the collective welfare, a good that transcends the sum of aggregated individual interests. European leaders place less faith than Americans do in the ability of private enterprises to realize the common welfare. Europeans want the government to represent the interests of the comprehensive whole, not just the individual parts. For this cultural reason, European leaders have displayed greater support than have U.S. officials for comprehensive economic policies that include the whole population. For example, public housing projects are constructed for low- and middle-income persons, not only for the poor. Health care policies enroll nearly all citizens, not just the poor, disabled, elderly, and veterans. Child allowances provide cash benefits for all families with children, regardless of their income.[8]

Populism and Elitism

Although in democratic countries the "demos" or people supposedly decide public policies, the beliefs of political elites (those leaders who have the power to make authoritative decisions for a society) exercise greater impact on shaping the content of most public policies than do beliefs of the mass public. Especially when a conflict occurs between elite and mass beliefs, the preferences of the policymakers carry greater weight.

Elite attitudes, rather than mass preferences, better explain different tax policies in the United States, England, and Sweden. Tax revenues as a percentage of the gross national product are higher in Sweden and Britain than in the United States. From this policy difference, we should not conclude that the American public is more resistant to increased taxation than are the British or Swedish. Indeed, public opinion polls taken in the two European nations indicate widespread public opposition to higher taxes. In 1969, 63 percent of Swedish citizens believed that the tax burden must be reduced at any cost; 70 percent felt that tax rates were far too high. Similarly, in 1967, 81 percent of English voters wanted income taxes reduced. U.S. surveys have found similar attitudes toward increased taxation. According to Gallup national surveys, in 1966, 76 percent of the American people opposed increased income taxes; three years later 69 percent held that federal income taxes were too high, 25 percent regarded them as "about right," and less than one-half of 1 percent believed them too low.[9] Despite the similar stands taken by the public in the three countries, Swedish and British government leaders have raised taxes more drastically than have U.S. officials; thus, the total tax revenues as a percentage of the gross national product between 1965 and 1974 grew by 8 percent in Sweden, 5 percent in Britain, and 4 percent in the United States.[10]

Among all Western democratic countries, the majority of the population—over 60 percent—supports comprehensive government expenditures on old-age pensions, health care, and employment opportunities.[11] Of course, if faced with the prospect of higher taxes, citizens show less enthusiasm for increased spending for these social services. Yet even during 1975, a year of escalating prices, rising unemployment, and increasing taxes, national sample surveys in France, the United Kingdom, and West Germany revealed a widespread reluctance to reduce both taxes and social services. One question asked: "Which of these two statements comes closest to your own opinion? Taxes and wage deductions for social security and health programs should be reduced, even if this means a cut in services. Social security and health programs should be improved, even if this means higher taxes and wage contributions." Of those who offered an opinion, 66 percent in France, 59 percent in Germany, and 53 percent in Great Britain preferred improving health and social security programs, even at the cost of higher taxes.[12]

Even in the United States, where opposition to the welfare state is supposedly the strongest, national sample surveys taken since the 1930s have consistently found widespread popular support for public policies providing health care, social security, and employment opportunities. Approximately 70 percent of the American public favors government antipoverty programs, including public jobs and unemployment programs. For example, in 1973, 68 percent agreed with this statement: "The federal government has a deep responsibility for seeing that the poor are taken care of, that no one goes hungry, and that every person achieves a minimum standard of living." The public even prefers federal government action to private business action as the best way to eliminate poverty. In 1969, 41 percent believed that the federal government should assume the main responsibility for antipoverty programs, only 12 percent advocated that private industry take the primary responsibility, and 34 percent wanted both to play an equal role. In 1977, 80 percent of the American people supported public service jobs for the unemployed who could not find employment in private industry.[13] As implied by these findings, Americans lean toward government provision of jobs and unemployment compensation, rather than toward a guaranteed annual income, as the best way for public officials to secure economic welfare. Employment opportunities secured by governmental efforts seem more in agreement with the individualistic Lockean heritage.[14]

Popular attitudes also strongly support greater government assistance for the ill and the elderly. For instance, in 1976 two-thirds of the American public favored increased government expenditures for old-age pensions. That year over 50 percent wanted the government to spend more on health care programs.[15] A majority of the American people have also supported a comprehensive health insurance program for all citizens, not just the very poor and the elderly. In late 1976 only a quarter of the American population favored retaining the voluntary system of health care. Nearly 40 percent wanted the government to establish a compulsory health insurance program for everyone; under this program, employers and employees would share the costs, while the federal government would pay the health bills of the unemployed and those not in the work force. About 30 percent preferred a universal insurance system administered by the federal government and financed wholly by federal tax revenues. Only 14 percent wanted the state governments to manage national health insurance, and only 15 percent wanted insurance companies to assume the major responsibility for implementing public health programs.[16]

Despite public support for social service programs, U.S. national government leaders have moved more slowly than have European officials to meet these popular demands for health care, old-age pensions, and employment assistance. As chapter 4 shows, the U.S. government has taken less active steps to find jobs for the unemployed. Among the seven countries in 1975, unemployment benefits as a proportion of average earnings for manufacturing workers were lowest in the United States. U.S. public health programs include only about a quarter of the population; Canada and Western European nations have comprehensive public health programs enrolling over 90 percent of the people. Table 2–2 showed that during the early 1970s only Italy ranked lower than the United States in government spending for health care programs as a percentage of the gross national product. In contrast, rankings on government expenditures for old-age pensions place the United States in an intermediate position behind Sweden, France, and Italy, tied with Canada, and ahead of the United Kingdom and West Germany. An aged couple in the United States received in 1975 a pension amounting to 57 percent of earnings made during the year before retirement. An elderly couple in Sweden received a cash payment of 76 percent of preretirement earnings, but in the United Kingdom a pension amounted to only 39 percent.[17]

The attitudes of U.S. policymakers, rather than public opinions, better explain these policy differences between the United States and other Western societies. Although national sample surveys demonstrate similar widespread popular support for government expenditures on medical care, social security, and employment opportunities in all countries including the United States, elite preferences differ across nations. European government officials favor comprehensive social service programs. In the United States, however, national leaders show greater concern for the elderly than for the poor and the unemployed. Therefore, national government expenditures for social security and Medicare programs, which directly benefit the aged, assume higher priority than spending on employment opportunities, unemployment compensation, and a universal public health insurance program.

At the local level of government as well, U.S. political leaders display greater opposition to government expenditures for social services than does the general population. Sidney Verba and Norman Nie supervised interviews with local leaders and citizens in sixty-four communities throughout the United States. According to their survey findings, community leaders experienced fewer severe personal problems with bad housing, unemployment, and ill health than did lower status, less well educated, and politically inactive citizens. As a result, the local elites were less likely to believe that government agencies should play an active part supplying housing, employment, and medical care to disadvantaged citizens. These community leaders felt that the individual, not the government, should resolve welfare problems. They viewed high taxes, poor education, and air pollution as the social problems most worthy of government attention.[18] Thus, at both the national and local levels, the reluctance of governments to allocate funds for social welfare and health stems more from leader preferences than from popular opposition.

Political Structures

Political structures interact with cultural beliefs to influence the content of public economic policies. In the contemporary Western industrialized context, the most powerful political structures include those organizations, like government agencies, political parties, and interest groups, which gain the resources needed to initiate or to veto public policies.

In the seven democratic societies examined here, government agencies and political parties play an especially key role in the policy process. Everywhere government officials have the primary responsibility for selecting policy alternatives and choosing the best ways to implement a public policy. Although political parties within democratic systems have less control than do government bureaucrats over policy implementation, parties do provide a means for mass participation in political life. They organize elections to representative institutions, offer citizens a choice of legislative candidates, influence voters' attitudes toward political issues, and shape the policy positions taken by legislators. For these reasons, the composition of political parties within a nation offers some explanations for crossnational variations in policy contents.

Governmental Institutions

The centralization of government refers to the geographical concentration of powers as well as to the division of powers at the national level. The United States, Canada, and West Germany are federal systems; the central, state (provincial), and local governments all share in the decision-making process. In contrast, France, Italy, Britain, and Sweden are unitary states; the central government exercises the dominant authority over local government. Of the seven nations, the United States features the greatest division or balance of powers at the central level; the president, Congress, Supreme Court, and numerous semi-autonomous organizations like regulatory agencies and the Federal Reserve Board participate in making public policies. Canada and the European nations, however, grant the national parliament the leading decision-making role. Only France has a system where the president exercises more decisive power than the prime minister, whom he appoints. In the other societies, the party or parties securing the most votes in parliamentary elections select the prime minister, who appoints his cabinet. The legislative and executive powers are thus fused, rather than separated, as in the United States.

Analysts have assumed that in a more decentralized political system, government expenditures as a proportion of a gross national product will be lower than under centralized arrangements. Within the decentralized structures, business executives who oppose high government expenditures will presumably wield effective veto power at the local and regional levels. To what extent does this assumption hold true? Generally, a modest statistical association does exist. Between 1970 and 1974 the most decentralized system, the American, spent the lowest percentage of national wealth on government expenditures at the national, state, and local levels. The other two federal systems, Canada and West Germany, expended a smaller percentage than did the four unitary states of France, Italy, Sweden, and the United Kingdom. However, the main divergence lay between the United States, which spent the least (30 percent), and Sweden, which spent the most (40 percent). The other governments expended about the same proportion of the GNP (34–35 percent) during this period.

The historical strength of the central state helps explain the greater degree of public ownership in Europe than in North America. The French in particular have traditionally lived under a strong state; French monarchs secured unitary rule over their territory as early as the sixteenth century. Although Italy was unified at a much later date (1870) and the monarchy never attained the wide scope of power reached in France, the Italians also adopted a unitary state. Mussolini ruled between 1922 and 1943; he strengthened the central political institutions. At the end of the war, many Fascist institutions, like the IRI, remained in operation. Most of the senior civil servants holding office in the early 1970s joined the administration during the 1930s.

The other three European states, however, retained stronger local institutions. Although the Swedish monarch gained dominance during the early sixteenth century, an independent peasantry and nobility restrained his powers.[19] Similarly, local notables in England, such as justices of the peace, along with an independent parliament checked the rise of a centralized bureaucratic state. Certainly, the various regions in Germany, such as Prussia, Bavaria, and Saxony, long exerted significant political autonomy. Although Bismarck and, later, Hitler attempted to centralize government power, after World War II the West Germans, under American pressures, established a federal political system. Today the länder (the ten German "states") play a key role in federal decision making. Civil servants from the länder bargain with bureaucrats in the federal government to secure concrete benefits, such as educational and economic development funds, for the länder. The need for widespread consensus gives both cabinet ministers and civil servants in the länder veto power to block redistributionist policies.[20]

Political Parties

The European pattern suggests that the political power of left-wing parties, both socialist and communist, provides a less convincing explanation for the extent of public ownership than does the degree of government centralization. Americans associate socialism with a commitment to expand the public economic sector. As we have seen, France and Italy have the largest number and variety of nationalized industries; socialists, however, are weaker there than in England, Sweden, and Germany. Although the communist party is stronger in the two Latin countries, it participated in an Italian central coalition government only between 1943 and 1947. The French Communist party joined a popular front government in 1936 and again from 1945 through 1947. Except during these brief periods, the two communist parties between 1930 and 1977 wielded only limited influence over the central government's economic policy. In Germany, Sweden, and Britain, extensive nationalization actually occurred during the late nineteenth and early twentieth centuries before the socialist parties came to government power.

Looking at patterns of government spending, we see that the power of socialist and communist parties more strongly influences the level than the type of expenditures. Socialist parties exert the greatest government power in Sweden, Britain, and Germany but are weaker in Canada and weakest in the United States. As table 3–1 shows, the greater the socialist strength in parliamentary elections between 1972 and 1974, the higher the total government expenditures as a percentage of the GNP in 1974. The combined parliamentary strength of communist and socialist parties exerts a slightly weaker effect on levels of government spending. However, socialist power does not so clearly explain the types of activities to which European governments allocate a high proportion of funds. Of the three countries where the socialist parties are strongest, the British government spends the highest percentage of the GNP for the military; Germany gives priority to income maintenance programs; and Sweden emphasizes education and health.

Despite the weakness of the socialist party in Canada and especially in the United States, the spending policies of the two governments diverge on important issues. The U.S. government spends the most for defense purposes; Canadian officials, who live under the American nuclear umbrella, spend the least. Compared with the U.S. government, the Canadian government places higher priority on public health expenditures. The two governments share a similar commitment only toward education.

What features in Canada and the United States explain their policy variations? One explanation lies in the strength of the socialist party in three out of the ten provinces—British Columbia, Manitoba, and Saskatchewan—where the New Democratic Party (NDP) has formed the government.[21] The health and social welfare policies enacted by these provincial governments have influenced federal governmental action

Table 3–1 Government Expenditures and Electoral Strength of Left-Wing Parties

| | Percentage of Total Popular Vote, 1972–1974 | | | |
Country	Socialists	Communists	Socialists and Communists	Government Expenditures (% of GNP) 1974
United States	0	0	0	31.5
Canada	15	0	15	35.7
United Kingdom	39	0	39	39.1
West Germany	46	0	46	37.8
Sweden	44	5	49	44.5
France	20	21	41	35.4
Italy	17	27	44	36.8

NOTE: The Pearson correlation coefficient (r) between government expenditures and electoral strength of socialists is .84; the r between government expenditures and electoral strength of socialists and communists is .75.

SOURCE: For data on parliamentary election results, see Thomas Mackie and Richard Rose, *The International Almanac of Electoral History* (London: Macmillan, 1974): *European Journal of Political Research* 2 (September 1974):293–98; *European Journal of Political Research* 3 (September 1975):319–28. For data on total government expenditures as a percentage of the GNP for 1974, see *National Accounts of OECD Countries, 1975* (Paris: OECD, 1977), vol. 2.

too. At the federal level in Ottawa, the dominant Liberal party ruled for a brief time (1972–1974) in a coalition government with the New Democratic Party. Furthermore, although both Canada and the United States are federal systems, Canada has a parliamentary government where legislative and executive powers are fused. In Canada the election of a Liberal parliamentary majority in Ottawa or an NDP plurality in a western province ensures that the Cabinet will enact the program of its party leaders. The United States, however, divides decision-making power between a separately elected president and Congress. This sharing of power makes enacting government policies for social welfare more difficult. Since World War II either a Democratic Congress has faced Republican presidents hostile to expanded welfare programs, or else activist Democratic presidents have had to negotiate compromises with Democratic committee chairmen who oppose redistributionist policies, such as progressive taxes.

Although more egalitarian than Republican leaders, most Democratic officials in the United States do not strongly support government expenditure policies that will transform the life conditions of the poorer segments of the population. Compared with Republicans, Democratic leaders favor more positive government initiatives in the areas of jobs, health care, and general social welfare. Yet at the national and especially the local levels, Democratic leaders show at best restrained enthusiasm for these programs. Certainly their policy positions do not resemble those taken by the socialist parties in Canada, England, or Sweden. During 1971 and 1972 Allen Barton supervised interviews with over five hundred leaders of important organized groups throughout the United States. His questions dealt with several issues of tax and expenditure policy, including the needs for a higher tax on capital gains, a more effective inheritance tax, a reduction of income differences, a top limit on incomes, and a job-creating program administered by the federal government. On all these issues, the Democratic politicians took a "centrist" position between heads of "conservative" organizations (American Conservative Union), business leaders, and Republican politicians, on the one hand, and ethnic minority leaders, heads of "liberal" organizations (Americans for Democratic Action), and labor union leaders, on the other. The Democratic politicians expressed attitudes like those held by career civil servants and mass media executives.[22]

At local levels, the government system interacts with the party system to produce a political situation where leaders pay less attention to the needs of poorer citizens than to those of the more affluent. European countries tend to have partisan elections at local levels of government; the presence of socialist parties and socialist political ideologies, with their commitment to redistributive programs, encourages greater participation by blue-collar workers and stronger elite attention to their policy concerns.[23] In the United States, however, two-thirds of cities over 5,000 persons, mainly in the West, hold nonpartisan elections. Studies of city councils in the San Francisco Bay Area indicate that Republicans, compared with Democrats, have more economic resources, stronger motivation to become politically active, and higher rates of participation in local elections. The absence of party cues to guide the voters' choices means that particularly in the poorer and larger cities with over 50,000 population, Republican leaders gain the electoral advantage in local nonpartisan offices. Partisan ballots would enable more Democrats to win local elections. But even those Democrats elected to nonpartisan offices do not always take egalitarian attitudes toward government expenditures. If "egalitarian policies" refer to the use of government actions to provide more houses, jobs, and social services to the poor, the Republican leaders are the least egalitarian and the Democratic partisan officials are the most egalitarian. Democratic nonpartisan leaders take issue positions closer to the Republican positions than to the Democratic partisan representatives. In part, their opposition to redistribution policies stems from similar occupational backgrounds; many Republican and nonpartisan Democratic leaders are small-scale business owners, realtors, local developers, and doctors. All these groups possess the wealth and education, as well as the motivation, to participate actively in local politics. Given their business-oriented backgrounds, they tend to oppose comprehensive state or federal government programs that will help solve the problems associated with high unemployment, ill health, substandard housing, and racial segregation. For them, lower taxes take priority over higher government expenditures to deal with these problems.[24]

Economic Structures

At the most general level, economic structures concentrate on the production and distribution of wealth. Economic resources (forms of wealth) include the classical trilogy: *land* (natural assets such as land, water, air, fuel, oil, minerals), *labor* (human skills, knowledge, expertise, entrepreneurial abilities), and *capital* (physical machines, equipment, tools, buildings, and so forth). Various types of monetary income—wages, salaries, rent, interest, and dividends—stem from the use of these economic resources. Technological developments involve attempts to maximize the productive capacity of land, labor, and capital. In turn, the distribution of wealth reflects certain patterns of structural interaction: ownership and control of scarce resources, property relationships, and the division of labor.

Both the production and the distribution of economic resources shape the content of public policies. Comprehensive social service programs are found most often in a wealthy, industrialized economy that can supply the resources needed to finance these policies. The distribution of wealth partly determines access to the political system. Generally, those groups possessing the greatest economic assets have the best opportunity to translate their preferences into public policies. This section focuses on two aspects of the economic structure that affect the content of policies: (1) the level of economic development, (2) the strength of labor unions and the private business sector in the policy process.

Level of Economic Development

A crossnational survey of *sixty* countries indicated that the higher the level of economic development (measured by gross national product per capita), the greater the government expenditures for nondefense programs.[25] Governments in wealthy countries spent more money for civilian projects. Yet when we look at the *seven* wealthy, industrialized countries examined here, no relationship whatsoever holds between the GNP per capita in 1974 and civilian government expenditures as a percentage of the GNP in 1974 (see table 3–2). Although Sweden and the United States are the wealthiest nations, the Swedish governments spent by far the highest percentage (41 percent) of the GNP on nonmilitary programs; the U.S. governments allocated the lowest percentage (25 percent) of the GNP for civilian public expenditures. Regardless of their level of economic development, the other five countries expended about the same proportion (34 percent) of the GNP for nondefense policies.

The Political Power of Labor Unions and Private Business Firms

The political power of labor unions and private business firms offers a clearer explanation for the content of public economic policies than does aggregate wealth. We assume that in countries where government expenditures, especially for social services, are comparatively high and where monetary policies are expansionary, unions play the more crucial role in the political process. However, where private business firms dominate policy making, taxes and expenditures are lower and fewer nationalized industries exist. As the following section shows, in nearly all Western democratic nations industrialists exert greater power over the policy process than do union leaders. From a comparative perspective, the private business sector exercises the most decisive political power in the United States. These structural patterns partly explain the divergent economic policies found in the United States and other Western societies.

The success of trade unions in shaping economic policies depends on the goals of the union and the power needed to attain these goals. What public policies do unions want to see realized? In general, they seek concrete economic benefits, such as full employment, the maintenance of their jobs against the threat of automation, wage increases that exceed price rises, expanded fringe benefits (health insurance, pensions), healthier working conditions, and the preservation of union autonomy in the collective bargaining process. Particularly during the 1970s, when inflation rose to double-digit figures, union leaders demanded that any

Table 3–2 Wealth and Government Spending on Civilian Programs, 1974

Country	GNP per capita (in constant U.S. dollars)	Nonmilitary Government Expenditures[a] (% of GNP)
Sweden	8450	41.1
United States	7099	25.4
Canada	6935	33.6
West Germany	6842	34.2
France	6386	31.8
United Kingdom	4089	34.0
Italy	3074	33.9

[a]Figures obtained by subtracting defense expenditures from total government expenditures at all levels. See *The Military Balance 1976–1977* (London: The International Institute for Strategic Studies, 1976), p. 78; *National Accounts of OECD Countries, 1975* (Paris: OECD, 1977), vol. 2.

NOTE: The Pearson correlation coefficient between GNP per capita and government expenditures is .13.

SOURCE: Data on GNP per capita from *Statistical Abstract of the United States,* 97th ed. (Washington, D. C.: Government Printing Office, 1976), p. 877.

incomes policies formulated by the government guarantee workers the continued right to strike for higher pay and the right to press for wage gains that exceeded the rise in the cost of living.

In short, union leaders have historically campaigned for reformist policies, like free collective bargaining, tax reductions for workers, and restraints on price increases. Since the mid-nineteenth century, when unions began to organize the workers in Western societies, few unions have made "radical" demands for a fundamental change in the political and economic systems. Instead, they have sought more advantageous positions within the existing capitalist framework. During the 1970s, for example, retaining the jobs held by employed workers took priority over finding jobs for the unemployed. Policies to narrow the wage gap between high and low paid employees found little enthusiasm among unions representing the higher-income workers. Fearful that government managers would operate like private corporate executives, unions in Britain, Sweden, and West Germany have not pressed for extensive public ownership of industries. Instead, they have supported programs to establish greater working class or trade union representation on company boards of directors.[26]

Although union members throughout the Western world have shared similar policy objectives, they have exercised differing degrees of power in realizing their goals. Swedish, British, and German unions have probably enjoyed the greatest success. The union movements in the United States, Canada, France, and Italy have played a less decisive role in influencing the content of economic policies. What structural factors explain these crossnational differences? One indicator of a union's potential power is the inclusiveness of its membership. Swedish, German, and British unions have enrolled a high percentage of the civilian labor force; over 40 percent of workers in Britain and Germany belong to a union, and in Sweden that figure exceeds 70 percent. Most government employees are trade union members; for example, over three-quarters of German civil servants are unionized. Unlike the American situation, where the Supreme Court has forbidden unions in the armed forces, in Sweden and Germany the union movement has even spread to the military. Nearly all career personnel within the Swedish Armed Forces belong to a military union. In France, Italy, and North America, however, unions have achieved less success in organizing the work force. No more than one-third of civilian workers are union members. Especially in the United States the union movement has become weaker since the end of World War II. In 1953 union members constituted 25.5 percent of the total labor force, but by 1974 that proportion had declined to 22 percent. As more people have taken jobs in the service sector and as the number of manufacturing jobs has decreased, U.S. unions have lost members. Although during recent years government employees have joined such unions as the American Federation of State, County, and Municipal Employees, the National Education Association, and the American Federation of Teachers, in 1974 only one-fifth of all public employees belonged to a union, a far lower percentage than in Sweden or Germany.[27] Thus, the lower share of the work force unionized in the United States, compared with Sweden, Germany, and Britain, means that union leaders possess less potential power to shape economic policy making.

More importantly, Swedish, German, and British unions have demonstrated greater political unity. Their alliance with the Social Democratic and Labour parties has given union leaders more power to translate their preferences into public policies. During the late nineteenth century socialist political parties and unions established close cooperation; both struggled for the expansion of the suffrage and for an improvement in the workers' conditions. Except in England, where the unions created the Labour party in 1900, the socialist party usually organized the union movement, as happened in Germany during the 1880s and in Sweden in 1898. Today the largest, most powerful unions—the Swedish Trade Union Federation (LO), the German Confederation of Trade Unions (DGB), and the British Trades Union Congress (TUC)—give extensive financial, electoral, and political support to the socialist parties. In exchange, when the social democratic parties hold government office, union officials gain direct access to the Cabinet ministers who formulate economic policies.[28]

Compared with Swedish, British, and German union movements, the unions in France and Italy are more politically fragmented. Particularly after World War II, when the Soviet Union posed a military threat to Western Europe, communist and noncommunist parties organized separate unions. In Italy the Christian Democrats and Republicans formed two unions independent from the General Confederation of Italian Labor, long dominated by an alliance of communists and socialists. In France the Socialists and left-wing Catholics refused to participate in the Confédération Générale du Travail, which after the war came under Communist party influence. Only recently have the Italian and French unions begun to adopt a nonpartisan stance. Divisions within the union movement thus parallel the split among the political parties.[29]

In the United States and Canada, neither the unions nor the socialist/communist parties exercise dominant political power. Although giving greater electoral support to the Democrats, U.S. unions attempt to maintain good terms with both parties. One of the largest unions, the Teamsters, enjoys closer relations with the Republicans than with the Democrats. Canadian unions exert even less political influence than do U.S. labor organizations. The U.S. and Canadian economies are closely interlocked; U.S. corporations make extensive investments in Canada. Partly for this reason, over one-half of Canadian trade unionists belong to the Canadian Labour Congress, which is affiliated with the AFL-CIO; rather than attaching themselves to a major Canadian party, they have aligned with a U.S. union. Some Canadian unions, however, have established links with the socialist New Democratic Party; yet in recent elections it has failed to gain more than 20 percent of the total national vote.[30]

Not only political fragmentation but also geographical and economic sources of disunity plague the North American union movements and hinder them from exercising important political power over the policy process. Canada has a federal system, in which the provincial governments wield the authority to pass industrial relations laws. Regional linguistic and economic differences accompany political decentralization. The bilingual heritage has meant the establishment of a separate union, the Confederation of National Trade Unions (CNTU), in French-speaking Quebec. Moreover, different types of economic activity characterize the diverse regions. For instance, Ontario and Quebec concentrate on manufacturing, the Maritime provinces specialize in fishing, and economic life on the prairies revolves around farming. All these geographical, linguistic, and economic cleavages promote a decentralized union movement in which the local affiliates are generally more powerful than the central federation.[31]

Similarly, in the United States geographic and economic differences hinder the formation of a centralized union structure. For example, state governments and employers in the South have opposed union efforts to organize the workers in the new manufacturing industries. Historically, craft and industrial unions articulated divergent economic policies and organized separate organizations. Not until 1955 did the craft-based American Federation of Labor merge with the industrial Congress of Industrial Organizations to establish the AFL-CIO. Even today such power unions as the Teamsters and the United Auto Workers remain outside the AFL-CIO. As in Canada, central union leaders can exert only limited power over local branches; often the national union leadership cannot prevent local members from calling a strike. Because of the decentralized structure, national union officials wield less effective influence over economic policy making than do leaders of the more centralized unions in Sweden.

Compared with most European nations, the United States also experiences stronger opposition to trade union activities within firms. Unlike their European counterparts, U.S. managers show greater reluctance to recognize unions or to allow them to organize the workers. European employers demonstrate less support than do American managers for price competition. Unions often raise production costs. If all the plants have similar working conditions and labor costs, then one firm can gain no "unfair" advantages over other enterprises by charging lower prices for goods. The strong state tradition in European nations also leads European business managers to support state planning and provision of social services by the government. Business leaders accept the need for business and government to make joint economic decisions. In the United States, however, the laissez faire classical liberal heritage has made employers more reluctant to rely on the state for planning economic welfare. Influenced by the adversary principles of common law, individual American entrepreneurs seek autonomy from state interference, just as they want to retain their freedom from union "meddling" in plant operations.[32]

In sum, among the seven countries, the union movements in Germany and especially Sweden, play the most effective role in shaping economic policies. They have enrolled a high proportion of the work force. Employers have accepted the need to work closely with union officials. Their close ties with socialist parties have given national union leaders direct access to Cabinet ministers when the social democrats hold governmental office. As a partial result of their political power, German and Swedish union leaders have rarely felt the need to call strikes. During the 1970s Swedish and German workers lost the fewest days per one thousand employees because of strike activity.

Despite the similar labor situations in Sweden and Germany, German unions exert somewhat less political influence than does the Swedish labor movement. Less than half the German work force belongs to a union. The central union officials allow local affiliates in the DGB to negotiate collective bargaining agreements. Although supporting the rights of unions to represent the workers' interests in codetermination agreements, especially in the iron, steel, and coal industries, German management retains considerable autonomy on the shop floor. Because of some religious differences separating Protestant and Catholic workers, the alliance between the DGB and the Social Democratic party is weaker than the linkages of the LO to the Swedish Socialist party.[33]

Although the British Labour party and the unions retain a close alliance, the unions in Britain have exercised less effective power over economic policy making than have Swedish unions. Although the British trade unions largely finance Labour party activities and form the largest voting bloc in meetings of the party's annual conference, their influence over members of Commons, even the Labour MPs, has been limited. Several autonomous occupational unions remain independent from the national Trades Union Congress leaders. Local union officials, shop stewards, and committees of stewards exert decisive power over collective bargaining. The national TUC wields only limited influence over the Parliamentary Labour Party and the prime minister. If the unions and the Labour government articulate divergent policies toward, for example, wage restraints and strike legislation, then even the Labour MPs sponsored by the unions will usually vote according to their party's policy positions.[34]

In France and Italy the alliance between the dominant unions and the communist parties has deterred union leaders from attaining their policy goals, especially a progressive income tax benefiting the working class. Since noncommunist parties, the French Gaullists and the Italian Christian Democrats, have dominated the national governments during the last twenty years, the unions have exerted only limited power over economic policy making. Historically, French and Italian industrialists have tried to deny unions the right to organize the work force. For this reason, unions in the two Latin countries have wielded less effective influence than those in northern Europe.

Finally, the North American situation also reveals a weak role for unions in the policy process. Particularly in the United States, employers have attempted to keep unions out of their plants, as evidenced by General Motors' resistance to UAW organizing efforts in the South. Historically, unions gained their greatest influence during the New Deal days of Franklin Roosevelt and the Great Society period of Lyndon Johnson, when union leaders successfully persuaded Congress to pass legislation establishing the Social Security program, public health care for the aged, and the right of trade unions to bargain collectively. Today as in the past, however, unions make up only one group of the Democratic coalition. If union leaders fail to win support from Democratic legislators, a Democratic president, or some other groups—Northern Catholics, Southern whites, ethnic minorities, urban residents, business leaders, and intellectuals—then even a Democratic majority in Congress may not support union policies for full employment, progressive taxes, universal health insurance, and laws facilitating union organization. Certainly, this situation existed during the 1970s, when the Democratic Congress supported the policy preferences of business groups more frequently than those of AFL–CIO officials.

In the other Western nations except perhaps Sweden, unions appear to exert less effective political power than do employers. Of course, unions retain an important veto power. Threats or actual steps to strike may paralyze an entire nation, as happened when the British coal miners and the Canadian mail carriers called strikes. However important this veto power, unions' ability to initiate new policies seems less pervasive. Despite some movements toward joint management of firms by employers and union leaders, the entrepreneur still retains the dominant authority over the business process in the modified market economies of the Western world. This authority gives private businessmen the potential power to shape the content of economic policies.

The influential part played by business firms stems from their responsibility for making crucial economic decisions in a private enterprise, market economy. Business managers handle the allocation of capital, a process involving decisions about the purchase of new equipment, the location of new plants, the investment of resources at home or overseas, and the determination of the ratio of labor to capital that will most efficiently increase productivity. Private business enterprises also produce consumer as well as capital goods. They decide the price of these goods and services; they set the wages paid to workers who produce the goods.[35] All these decisions obviously affect the economic welfare of large segments of the public. As Charles Lindblom points out, this decision-making power gives private business entrepreneurs considerable influence over the policy process.

> *Businessmen generally and corporate executives in particular take on a privileged role in government that is, it seems reasonable to say, unmatched by any leadership group other than government officials themselves. . . . A market system requires that on many points the enterprise be legally protected in a right to say no to the state. More important, its privileged position permits it to obstruct policies such as those on environmental pollution and decay, energy shortage, inflation and unemployment, and distribution of income and wealth.*[36]

Because private enterprises possess this authority over economic decision making, Western central governments can exert only limited control over them. For instance, if government imposes too high business taxes, then corporations may decrease investment at home or else increase their investments overseas. Whichever the decision, higher unemployment among the manufacturing labor force will result. If expenditures for social services reduce the profits of the business sector, corporate leaders will mount opposition to these expenditures. Attacks on the "welfare state mess" will perhaps persuade legislators to decrease government spending for social services and raise expenditures for business investment.

The exercise of political power involves the struggle to attain certain public consequences. What general policy goals have entrepreneurs sought in Western societies? Not all business firms occupy the same economic position. While some produce for the domestic market, others concentrate on exporting their goods overseas. Small-scale competitive firms may articulate different economic interests than do large-scale, oligopolistic multinational corporations. The political party affiliations of entrepreneurs also differ. For these reasons, businessmen may not hold identical viewpoints toward specific economic policies involving energy, health, social security, and taxes. Even if they do not share the same stand on all issues, they generally all agree on the need to maintain the private enterprise market system. Before government agencies make a particular economic decision, business leaders seek close consultation with the government officials charged with formulating and implementing the policy. Corporate managers often pressure government officials to restrain union leaders from demanding high wages and rights to participate more extensively in economic decision making. Throughout the Western world, most businessmen also oppose egalitarian economic policies, especially progressive income taxes. In their view, low taxes on corporations will give business an economic incentive to invest, increase productivity, and thereby maximize long-term profits.[37]

Studies conducted in the United States and Britain indicate that the positions taken by business leaders on specific economic policies reflect their general corporate objectives. For example, in 1971 American corporate executives, compared with national presidents of labor unions, expressed greater opposition to placing a higher tax on capital gains, raising the inheritance tax, ending the oil depletion allowance, spending more on welfare services, reducing income differences, increasing the political power of the poor, enlarging the workers' role in management, and establishing some public ownership of corporations now under private control. Similarly, in Britain business groups want to see government play a reduced role in economic affairs. Since the end of World War II they, unlike union officials, have opposed nationalization of the steel industry, government operation of the national insurance program, rent controls, and public planning of towns and counties.[38]

How effective are business leaders in winning government support for their policy positions? To what extent do U.S. corporate executives, compared with their European counterparts, attain their objectives? Although the evidence for all seven countries remains scanty and inconclusive, private economic elites—bankers, lawyers, managers, doctors, corporate executives—appear to exert more power over government policy in the United States than in most other Western countries. Supportive of the business position, the U.S. federal government during the 1970s failed to raise inheritance or capital gains taxes, to spend more money on welfare reform, to reduce income differentials, to enlarge the political power of the poor, to increase workers' role in management, to nationalize private industries, or to establish a comprehensive public health insurance program. (However, in 1975 Congress did vote to end the oil depletion allowance for large companies, a position favored by union leaders but opposed by business.) As Lindblom points out, in U.S. society business groups possess an important veto power over public policies. For example, the political power wielded by private insurance companies, private hospitals, and private medical associations has effectively blocked the establishment of a comprehensive public health program for all citizens. In Canada and Europe, however, private organizations lacked this veto power; during the post–World War II period, governments there possessed the power to implement policies extending health care benefits to all people, not just the aged and the poor.

In the United States, business leaders also have the power to initiate new programs. Historically, they have played a key role in deciding which issues should be resolved through government; that is, their decisions influence which specific issues are placed on the political agenda. Particularly between 1840 and 1932, few other private or public organizations challenged business dominance. Since feudalism never existed, no landed aristocracy could control the government leaders. Not until 1935, with the passage of the Wagner Act that gave unions the right to collective bargaining, did union membership begin to grow beyond 7 percent of the work force. Before that time, union officials exerted only limited influence over public policies. Moreover, the lack of American involvement in foreign wars and the absence of a rigid class structure deterred the establishment of a strong state administered by a powerful civil service. No professional government bureaucracy emerged until the Depression days of the 1930s. Even today, with the growth of a stronger federal bureaucracy, unions, and consumer public interest groups, the American private business sector retains its ability to shape the broad outlines of public economic policies. Through such organizations as the Council on Foreign Relations, the Committee on Economic Development, the Business Council, and the Brookings Institution, corporate executives, bankers, and lawyers recommend specific policies intended to resolve certain problems. In turn, congressmen, professional civil servants, and the president and his staff select the detailed procedures for implementing these policies; their role revolves around deciding the amount of government spending, the type of expenditures, and the particular agencies that will best realize the policy goals.[39]

Paradoxically, European societies combine a more centralized government structure with more pluralistic relations between private business elites and the government. Historically, countervailing organizations have checked the political power exercised by entrepreneurs and lawyers with strong business ties. During the nineteenth century, corporate leaders had to compete for influence with the landed aristocracy, the high clergy within state churches, and a professional bureaucracy. At the end of the century, trade unions and socialist parties began to play an active part in political life. Throughout most contemporary European societies, the working class is more widely organized into unions and socialist/communist parties than in the United States. All these other groups thus check the political power of the business sector. As a result of this reduced business influence, European governments, compared with the U.S. government, have nationalized more industries, established greater public planning for the economy, and instituted longer lasting incomes policies designed to restrain price and wage hikes. In European nations overall taxes, expenditures, and increases in the money supply are higher than in the United States. European government expenditures for social services like health care, family allowances, and unemployment compensation are also a higher proportion of the gross national product. All these policy contents partly reflect the tendency for European leaders to achieve a greater sharing of political power among professional civil servants, socialists, union officials, and business executives.

Notes

1. Erik Allardt, "Revolutionary Ideologies as Agents of Cultural and Structural Change," in Nancy Hammond, ed., *Social Science and the New Societies: Problems in Cross-Cultural Research and Theory* (East Lansing: Social Science Research Bureau, Michigan State University, 1973), pp. 152–58.

2. Quoted in Joseph A. Pechman, "Making Economic Policy: The Role of the Economist," in Fred I. Greenstein and Nelson Polsby, eds., *Handbook of Political Science* (Reading, Mass.: Addison-Wesley, 1975), vol. 6, p. 23.

3. For analyses of the functions of cultural beliefs in the policy process, see Martin Rein, *Social Science and Public Policy* (New York: Penguin Books, 1976),

p. 142; Thomas J. Bossert, *Political Argument and Policy Issues in Allende's Chile,* unpublished Ph.D. dissertation, Department of Political Science, University of Wisconsin, Madison, 1976, pp. 2–10.

4. See Gaston V. Rimlinger, *Welfare Policy and Industrialization in Europe, America, and Russia* (New York: Wiley, 1971), pp. 338–39.

5. For an emphasis on the importance of political beliefs, see Anthony King, "Ideas, Institutions and the Policies of Governments: A Comparative Analysis: Part III," *British Journal of Political Science* 3 (October 1973):409–23; David Vogel, "Why Businessmen Distrust Their State: The Political Consciousness of American Corporate Executives," *British Journal of Political Science* 8 (January 1978):45–78.

6. Earl Latham, "The Group Basis of Politics: Notes for a Theory," *The American Political Science Review* 46 (June 1952):376–97.

7. See Sheldon S. Wolin, *Politics and Vision: Continuity and Innovation in Western Political Thought* (Boston: Little, Brown, 1960), chapter 9; Louis Hartz, *The Liberal Tradition in America* (New York: Harcourt, Brace and World, 1955); G. Horowitz, "Conservatism, Liberalism, and Socialism in Canada: An Interpretation," *The Canadian Journal of Economics and Political Science* 32 (May 1966):143–71; Gad Horowitz, "Notes on 'Conservatism, Liberalism, and Socialism in Canada,' " *Canadian Journal of Political Science* 11 (June 1978):393.

8. Arnold J. Heidenheimer, Hugh Heclo, and Carolyn Teich Adams, *Comparative Public Policy: The Politics of Social Choice in Europe and America* (New York: St. Martin's Press, 1975), p. 279.

9. Joachim Vogel, "Taxation and Public Opinion in Sweden: An Interpretation of Recent Survey Data," *National Tax Journal* 27 (December 1974):502; Arthur Seldon, *Taxation and Welfare* (London: The Institute of Economic Affairs, 1967), p. 18; *The Gallup Poll: Public Opinion 1955–1971* (New York: Random House, 1972), vol. 3, pp. 2005, 2191.

10. *Revenue Statistics of OECD Member Countries, 1965–1974* (Paris: OECD, 1976), p. 74.

11. For an analysis of public opinion poll data from the United States, Canada, the United Kingdom, Australia, West Germany, France, Sweden, and Denmark, see Richard M. Coughlin, *Ideology and Social Policy: A Comparative Study of the Structure of Public Opinion in Eight Rich Nations,* unpublished Ph.D. dissertation, Department of Sociology, University of California at Berkeley, 1977, chapters 3 and 4, esp. pp. 156, 211, 228, 239, 242, 274, and 281.

12. See Coughlin, *Ideology and Social Policy,* pp. 370, 451. If we include the non-responses ("don't knows" and refusals to answer), which constituted 28 percent in France, 18 percent in Great Britain, and 30 percent in West Germany, the support for expanded programs for health and social security is 47 percent in France, 44 percent in Britain, and 41 percent in Germany.

13. Seymour Martin Lipset and Earl Raab, "The Message of Proposition 13," *Commentary* 66 (September 1978):45; Hazel Erskine, "The Polls: Government Role in Welfare," *Public Opinion Quarterly* 39 (Summer 1975):251–74.

14. See Joe R. Feagin, *Subordinating the Poor: Welfare and American Beliefs* (Englewood Cliffs, N.J.:Prentice-Hall, 1975), pp. 132–41. In 1972, 72 percent of a

sample of American adults preferred a guaranteed job plan, but only 28 percent favored a guaranteed income plan.

15. William Schneider, "Public Opinion," *Politics Today* 5 (September–October 1978):10; Lipset and Raab, "The Message of Proposition 13," pp. 44–45. According to the National Opinion Research Center survey data collected during the spring of 1976, 60 percent of Americans surveyed believed that the government was spending too little on health care, 31 percent felt that government expenditures were about right, and only 5 percent wanted a cutback in government spending for medical care. See NORC codebook National Data Program for the Social Sciences Spring 1976 General Social Survey, variable 137. These data were made available through the Interuniversity Consortium for Political and Social Research.

16. Hazel Erskine, "The Polls: Health Insurance," *Public Opinion Quarterly* 39 (Spring 1975):128–43; *The Gallup Opinion Index*, no. 139, February 1977, pp. 26–27. In 1972, 20 percent of the American sample wanted local organizations run by citizens and doctors to administer a national health insurance program. Between 1972 and 1976 public support for administration of a national health care plan by the federal government dropped from 40 percent to 28 percent.

17. See Constance Sorrentino, "Unemployment Compensation in Eight Industrial Nations," *Monthly Labor Review* 99 (July 1976):21; "Main Features of Selected National Health Care Systems," *Research and Statistics Note*, no. 9–1973, U.S. Department of Health, Education, and Welfare, Social Security Administration, May 18, 1973, pp. 2–5; U.S. House of Representatives, Committee on Ways and Means, *National Health Insurance Resource Book*, rev. ed. (Washington, D. C.: Government Printing Office, 1976), pp. 294, 407; Leif Haanes-Olsen, "Earnings-Replacement Rate of Old-Age Benefits, 1965–1975, Selected Countries," *Social Security Bulletin* 41 (January 1978):4.

18. Sidney Verba and Norman H. Nie, *Participation in America: Political Democracy and Social Equality* (New York: Harper & Row, 1972), pp. 267–343.

19. Francis Castles, "Barrington Moore's Thesis and Swedish Political Development," *Government and Opposition* 8 (Summer 1973):317–18.

20. Gerhard Lehmbruch, "Party and Federation in Germany: A Developmental Dilemma," *Government and Opposition* 13 (Spring 1978):151–77.

21. See William M. Chandler, "Canadian Socialism and Policy Impact: Contagion from the Left?" *Canadian Journal of Political Science* 10 (December 1977):755–80. Canadian civil servants and legislators more strongly support government expenditures for social services than do American civil servants and legislators. This pattern holds true at both the federal and provincial (state) levels. See Robert Presthus, "Aspects of Political Culture and Legislative Behavior: United States and Canada," *International Journal of Comparative Sociology* 18 (March-June 1977):13; Robert Presthus and William Monopoli, "Bureaucracy in the United States and Canada: Social, Attitudinal, and Behavioral Variables," *International Journal of Comparative Sociology* 18 (March-June 1977):181.

22. Allen H. Barton, "Consensus and Conflict among American Leaders," *Public Opinion Quarterly* 38 (Winter 1974/75):507–30.

23. See Verba and Nie, *Participation in America*, pp. 297–98, 336–41; Norman H. Nie and Sidney Verba, "Political Participation," in Fred I. Greenstein and

Nelson Polsby, eds., *Handbook of Political Science* (Reading, Mass.: Addison-Wesley, 1975), vol. 4, pp. 40–70.

24. See Willis D. Hawley, *Nonpartisan Elections and the Case for Party Politics* (New York: John Wiley, 1973); Arnold J. Heidenheimer, Hugh Heclo, and Carolyn Teich Adams, *Comparative Public Policy: The Politics of Social Choice in Europe and America* (New York: St. Martin's Press, 1975), p. 112; Hugh A. Bone and Austin Ranney, *Politics and Voters,* 4th ed. (New York: McGraw-Hill, 1976), pp. 70–71.

25. Robert W. Jackman, *Politics and Social Equality* (New York: John Wiley, 1975), pp. 181–87.

26. See William H. Form, "Job vs. Political Unionism: A Cross-National Comparison," *Industrial Relations* 12 (May 1973):224–38; Ronald Inglehart, *The Silent Revolution: Changing Values and Political Styles among Western Publics* (Princeton, N.J.: Princeton University Press, 1977), p. 213, 280; Lewis Minkin, "The Labour Party Has Not Been Hi-Jacked," *New Society* 42 (October 6, 1977):6–8; Neil Elder, "The Swedish General Election of 1976," *Parliamentary Affairs* 30 (Spring 1977):199–201.
      The British TUC leaders showed less enthusiasm for securing public ownership of industries than for obtaining full employment, better working conditions, improved living standards, and free collective bargaining. The Swedish LO supported a Meidner fund plan to gradually transfer control of industries to elected union representatives.

27. Union membership as a percentage of the work force includes the following estimates: Sweden, over .70%; Britain, 43%; West Germany, 41%; Italy, 33%; Canada, 30% to 35%; United States, 22%; France, 20% to 25%. See the following sources: (1) *Encyclopedia Americana* (New York: Americana Corporation, 1975), vol. 5, p. 380 (Canada); vol. 11, p. 724 (France); vol. 12, p. 614 (West Germany); vol. 13, p. 259 (Britain); vol. 15, p. 570 (Italy); vol. 26, p. 109 (Sweden); (2) *The Gallup Opinion Index,* June 1975, no. 120, p. 23; (3) U. S. Department of Labor, Bureau of Labor Statistics *Handbook of Labor Statistics 1975—Reference Edition* (Washington D.C.: Government Printing Office, 1975) p. 389; *Handbook of Labor Statistics 1977,* pp. 291–93; (4) *Facts and Figures on Government Finance,* 19th ed. (New York: Tax Foundation, 1977), p. 25; (5) A. H. Raskin, "The Big Squeeze on Labor Unions," *The Atlantic* 242 (October 1978):41–48; (6) George V. Haythorne, "Prices and Incomes Policy: The Canadian Experience, 1969–1972," *International Labour Review* 108 (December 1973):487; (7) Lewis J. Edinger, *Politics in West Germany,* 2nd ed. (Boston: Little, Brown, 1977), p. 228; (8) William Gomberg, "Unions in the Military: Three European Cases," *Monthly Labor Review* 101 (April 1978):39–40.

28. See Richard J. Willey, "Trade Unions and Political Parties in the Federal Republic of Germany," *Industrial and Labor Relations Review* 28 (October 1974):38–59; Nils Elvander, "In Search of New Relationships: Parties, Unions, and Salaried Employees' Associations in Sweden," *Industrial and Labor Relations Review* 28 (October 1974):60–74; Lewis Minkin, "The British Labour Party and the Trade Unions: Crisis and Compact," *Industrial and Labor Relations Review* 28 (October 1974):7–37.

29. Peter R. Weitz, "Labor and Politics in a Divided Movement: The Italian Case," *Industrial and Labor Relations Review* 28 (January 1975):226–42; Peter

Weitz, "The CGIL and the PCI: From Subordination to Independent Political Force," in Donald M. Blackmer and Sidney Tarrow, eds., *Communism in Italy and France* (Princeton, N. J.: Princeton University Press, 1975), pp. 541–71; Jean-Daniel Reynaud, "Trade Unions and Political Parties in France: Some Recent Trends," *Industrial and Labor Relations Review* 28 (January 1975):208–25; George Rose, "Party and Mass Organization: The Changing Relationship of PCF and CGT," in *Communism in Italy and France,* pp. 504–40.

30. Robert Presthus, *Elites in the Policy Process* (London: Cambridge University Press, 1974), pp. 173–76, 205; Robert Presthus, "Interest Group Lobbying: Canada and the United States," *The Annals of the American Academy of Political and Social Science* 413 (May 1974):56; David Kwavnick, "Pressure Group Demands and the Struggle for Organizational Status: The Case of Organized Labour in Canada," *Canadian Journal of Political Science* 3 (March 1970):72; Desmond Morton, "Labour's New Political Direction: Is the CLC Serious?" *Canadian Forum* 57 (October 1977):11–13.

31. Robert N. Stern and John C. Anderson, "Canadian Strike Activity—Is Centralization the Solution?" *Monthly Labor Review* 101 (April 1978):40–42; Kwavnick, "Pressure Group Demands and the Struggle for Organizational Status," p. 72.

32. See Everett M. Kassalow, "How Some European Nations Avoided U. S. Levels of Industrial Conflict," *Monthly Labor Review* 101 (April 1978):37–39; Robert J. Goldstein, "Political Repression and Political Development: The United States and Europe, 1789–1917," paper presented at the Western Political Science Association convention, Los Angeles, March 17, 1978, pp. 9–11. For a detailed analysis of the governmental and private business techniques used to repress American labor unions between 1873 and 1936, see Robert Justin Goldstein, *Political Repression in Modern America* (Cambridge, Mass.: Schenkman, 1978).

33. See U. S. *Handbook of Labor Statistics 1977,* pp. 378–379; Douglas A. Hibbs, Jr., "On the Political Economy of Long-Run Trends in Strike Activity," *British Journal of Political Science* 8 (April 1978):153–75; Douglas A. Hibbs, Jr., "Industrial Conflict in Advanced Industrial Societies," *American Political Science Review* 70 (December 1976):1033–58; Michael Shalev, "Strikers and the State: A Comment," *British Journal of Political Science* 8 (October 1978):479–92; M. Donald Hancock, "Productivity, Welfare, and Participation in Sweden and West Germany: A Comparison of Social Democratic Reform Prospects," *Comparative Politics* 11 (October 1978): 11; Jack Barbash and Kate Barbash, *Trade Unions and National Economic Policy* (Baltimore: Johns Hopkins University Press, 1972), pp. 169–74.

34. See Minkin, "The British Labour Party and the Trade Unions," pp. 7–37; Minkin, "The Labour Party Has Not Been Hi-Jacked," pp. 6–8; William D. Muller, "Union–M. P. Conflict: An Overview," *Parliamentary Affairs* 26 (Summer 1973):336–55; Timothy May and Michael Moran, "Trade Unions as Pressure Groups," *New Society* 25 (September 6, 1973):570–73; Andrew Martin, "Labor Movement Parties and Inflation: Contrasting Responses in Britain and Sweden," *Polity* 7 (Summer 1975):427–51. Union-sponsored Labour MPs constitute about 30 to 40 percent of the total number of Labourites in Commons; they show the greatest readiness to submit to party discipline as enforced by the party whip.

35. David M. Kotz, *Bank Control of Large Corporations in the United States* (Berkeley: University of California Press, 1978), p. 146.

36. Charles Lindblom, *Politics and Markets: The World's Political-Economic Systems* (New York: Basic Books, 1977), pp. 172, 347.

37. Lindblom, *Politics and Markets,* pp. 205, 233.

38. Barton, "Consensus and Conflict among American Leaders," pp. 513–514; Christopher Hewitt, "Policy-Making in Postwar Britain: A Nation-Level Test of Elitist and Pluralist Hypotheses," *British Journal of Political Science* 4 (April 1974):210.

39. Vogel, "Why Businessmen Distrust Their State," pp. 45–78; Thomas R. Dye, "Oligarchic Tendencies in National Policy-Making: The Role of the Private Policy-Planning Organizations," *The Journal of Politics* 40 (May 1978):309–31; Peter J. Freitag, "The Cabinet and Big Business: A Study of Interlocks," *Social Problems* 23 (December 1975):137–52.

PART
II *Policy Outcomes*

Besides investigating the cultural and structural variables that affect the content of public policies, political scientists trace the effect of policies on economic conditions. Part II of this book explores the impacts of fiscal and monetary policies on unemployment, inflation, and income equality. Each chapter has the following format: First, I discuss ways to define and measure unemployment, price rises, and income equality across different nations. The Organisation for Economic Cooperation and Development, the U.S. Bureau of Labor Statistics, and the International Monetary Fund provide data for measuring the three outcomes. These measurements are then used to indicate the degree of unemployment, inflation, and inequality found in the seven Western countries studied in this book.

Second, each chapter presents different theoretical explanations to account for the effects of public policies. An "explanatory" generalization states the relationship among variables.[1] For example, if the central banking system rapidly increases the supply of money, then price rises will occur. If government, private businesses, and consumers decrease their aggregate demand (total spending for goods and services), then the unemployment rate will increase. As these two examples imply, theoretical explanations in economics focus on the interaction between demand and supply variables. High unemployment may stem from a low supply of highly demanded skilled labor or from insufficient total demand by government, private business firms, and consumers. The demand-pull explanation for inflation assumes that the total demand stimulated by government, businesses, and households exceeds the supply of goods. In contrast, the cost-push explanation suggests that three oligopolistic organizations—concentrated industries, labor unions, and government agencies—raise the costs of supplies, thereby causing prices to rise above existing demand. The sources of income inequality reflect power relationships in contemporary Western economies. Political leaders often fail to listen sympathetically to the policy demands of poorer citizens. Because low-income groups lack political power, they usually do not receive as high a supply of public benefits, like government services, income transfers, and tax concessions, as do wealthier citizens.

Third, after discussing each theoretical explanation, I investigate the credibility of specific hypotheses derived from the theories by analyzing data, mainly from 1960 through 1975, and by synthesizing the research findings of economists and political scientists. I have tried to ascertain if those countries with similar levels of unemployment, inflation, and income inequality share the same public policies. Of course, factors other than fiscal or monetary policies may influence economic conditions. In some cases, policy variables may exert a weaker impact on economic effects than do variables not subject to such direct policy control. For instance, at least in the short run, policy officials can more effectively control interest rates, increases in the money supply, levels of government expenditures, and taxes than change individual expectations, weather conditions, or the actions of multinational corporations. Yet expectations about future price rises, shortages of food caused by droughts, and the pricing decisions made by concentrated industries may better explain rising inflation. In this analysis, we consider the impacts of nonpolicy variables, especially the effects of concentrated industries on both inflation and on public policies designed to lower price rises.

In sum, the complexity of economic and political life creates difficulties in assessing all the variables that may affect certain outcomes, like inflation, unemployment, or inequality. Many social scientists hence remain skeptical about the possibilities of developing a "policy science" that accurately specifies the precise impact of public policies. Aaron Wildavsky points out the dilemma faced by analysts seeking theoretical explanations for policy impacts: "If predictive variables are too few, the theoretical models are too simple; and if there are too many, it is extremely difficult to understand their interaction."[2] Thus, to understand economic complexities, we need theoretical simplicity; yet by concentrating on a few variables, especially ones linked to policy decisions, we ignore other relevant factors that may explain the effects.

Because of the complex operation of economic systems, economists have failed to reach widespread agreement about the causes of unemployment, inflation, and income distributions and the effects of public policies. Analysts use diverse techniques for measuring such variables as income equality. The time periods and countries studied may differ.

Not all economists use the same models for explaining inflation or unemployment. Some models give priority to monetary policies, welfare expenditures, and wage increases as causes of rapid price increases; other models focus instead on tax policies, military expenditures, and profit rates. Since diverse models assume different patterns of interaction among the specific variables, all economists may not reach identical conclusions even when studying the same factors. The contradictory, ambiguous findings of economists, as well as the difficulties of specifying the complex interaction among variables, mean that generalizations about the impacts of public economic policies must remain tentative.

Notes

1. According to Morris Zelditch, Jr., "A sentence is *explanatory* if it asserts a relation between two or more variables," and he gives the following statement as an example: "A democracy is stable if its wealth is equally distributed." Democracy, stability, wealth, and equal distribution are all general terms. See his "Intelligible Comparisons," in Ivan Vallier, ed., *Comparative Methods in Sociology: Essays on Trends and Applications* (Berkeley: University of California Press, 1971), p. 270.

2. Aaron Wildavsky, *Science* 182 (December 28, 1973):1335. Quoted by Amitai Etzioni, *Social Problems* (Englewood Cliffs, N. J.:Prentice-Hall, 1976), p. 62.

The Impact of Public Policies on Unemployment

For the last fifty years unemployment rates in Western societies have fluctuated widely. At the time of the Depression during the 1930s, between 10 percent and 25 percent of the work force in the United States, England, and Sweden was unemployed. The Second World War greatly reduced jobless levels, as young men joined the armed forces and those remaining at home found work in the war industries. After the war ended, unemployment rates continued to remain fairly low. The demand for consumer goods and the need to replace industries destroyed during the war stimulated expansionary, job-creating economies on the European continent. Throughout the 1960s most European states experienced unemployment rates ranging between 1 percent and 4 percent. However, the 1970s once again saw a rapid growth in the jobless rolls. For example, in Great Britain 2 percent of the work force was unemployed in 1961; that figure rose to over 6 percent in 1976. Between 1961 and 1973 the jobless rates in West Germany averaged less than 1 percent a year; however, in 1975 and 1976 they approached 4 percent. In the United States, where unemployment rates since World War II exceeded those of most Western European countries, the percentage of unemployed workers in the labor force escalated in 1975 to 8.5 percent, the highest figure since the Depression days of the 1930s.

Although before the 1930s most national government officials in Western countries left unemployment problems to the uncontrolled, impersonal forces of the marketplace, today political leaders choose activist government policies as a key mechanism for trying to reduce

Chapter Four

the jobless levels. Especially outside the United States and England, the ideology of the "free market" has declined. The impacts of the war and the growing strength of the corporate state have discouraged government officials from tolerating the high unemployment rates that existed during the Depression. Yet, despite the intentions of political leaders, during the mid-1970s European and North American societies succumbed to severe recessions; jobless rates rose to the highest levels in twenty years. This chapter analyzes these problems by examining the impacts of public policies on unemployment rates. What specific policies did different nations use? How successful were government policies in actually reducing unemployment? Most importantly, in what ways did the content and the impact of the policies relate to theoretical assumptions about the causes of unemployment?

Levels of Unemployment

National Rates

Before exploring the assumed causes of unemployment, we need to ascertain the jobless rates in the seven Western nations. Obviously, published levels of unemployment depend partly on the ways of defining "unemployment" and on the specific techniques for measuring joblessness. These definitions and techniques vary somewhat from nation to nation. From a general perspective, levels of unemployment indicate the number of persons out of work as a percentage of the total labor force. Whom should we count among the unemployed? Those who work part-time or only those who used to be employed full-time? Should we include among the unemployed those workers who have become so discouraged that they no longer seek a job? What groups are included in the labor force? Fifteen year olds? Sixteen year olds? Military personnel? As we can see, the official unemployment rates will depend on the accuracy of the techniques used to measure the total labor force and the number of people unemployed, as well as on the similarity of the definitions applied to these groups. The Bureau of Labor Statistics of the U.S. Department of Labor has attempted to overcome measurement problems by adjusting the official jobless rates in the seven countries to make them comparable crossnationally.[1] We use these data in our analyses.

According to table 4–1, between 1961 and 1975 the United States and Canada had higher unemployment rates than the five Western European societies. Whereas the two North American countries averaged over 5 percent unemployment, the figures for Germany and Sweden, especially during the 1960s, were far lower—below 1 and 2 percent unemployment, respectively. Although the proportion of the labor force unemployed in England, France, and Italy exceeded German and Swedish levels, unemployment rates in those three countries were still lower than in Canada and the United States.

During the 1970s nearly every nation experienced a significant rise in the jobless rate. For instance, the German figures escalated from 0.8 percent in 1973 to 1.7 percent in 1974 to nearly 4 percent in 1975 and 1976. Between 1973 and 1976 the jobless level in Britain doubled from 3.2 percent to 6.4 percent. Between 1961 and 1975 four countries—Britain, West Germany, Sweden, and France—showed a successive increase in unemployment for each five-year period. Neither Canada nor the United States escaped this pattern of growing joblessness. Although during the second part of the 1960s their unemployment rates declined, the 1970s saw a dramatic rise to figures above the 1961–1965 levels. Here, as in other Western societies, specific groups, particularly young people under twenty-five years old, suffered the most from the recession.

Table 4–1   Unemployment Rates as a Percentage of the Civilian Labor Force

	Average Annual Figures		
Country	1961–1965	1966–1970	1971–1975
United States	5.5	3.9	6.1
Canada	5.4	4.6	6.1
Britain	2.6	3.0	3.8
West Germany	0.4	0.8	1.6
Sweden	1.5	1.9	2.3
France	1.5	2.3	3.3
Italy	3.3	3.8	3.6

SOURCE: Joyanna Moy and Constance Sorrentino, "An Analysis of Unemployment in Nine Industrial Countries," *Monthly Labor Review* 100 (April 1977):15; U.S. Department of Labor, Bureau of Labor Statistics, *Handbook of Labor Statistics, 1975—Reference Edition* (Washington, D.C.: Government Printing Office, 1975), p. 437; *Handbook of Labor Statistics, 1976* (Washington, D.C.: Government Printing Office, 1976), p. 332.

Unemployment Rates for
Different Groups

Looking only at the unemployment rate for the whole nation tends to obscure the severe impact suffered by specific groups within a national territory. Generally, across most nations, women, young people, minority ethnic groups, and the less skilled workers within manufacturing and service occupations experience the highest unemployment. Let us briefly examine the different impacts borne by men and women, diverse age groups, ethnic groups, and occupations.

In all the countries except Britain, women experienced higher unemployment rates than did men during the mid-1970s. Women overseas, like those in the United States, hold jobs mainly in the service sector, particularly as teachers, nurses, salespersons, clerks, and office personnel. Most of these jobs cluster in the competitive areas of the economy, where wages are lower, unions are less powerful, and part-time work is more available. In contrast, men receive higher wages, work in more unionized industries, and hold more full-time jobs. Thus, when a recession hits the economy, employers are less likely to lay off male employees.[2] Why does Britain stand as an exception to this tendency? Perhaps the reasons stem from the rapid decline of the British manufacturing sector between 1962 and 1975 and the growth of the service sector, especially teaching, health, and local government. Everywhere men comprise by far the highest proportion of manufacturing workers; the difficulties faced by British firms in selling their manufactured goods overseas have brought severe economic problems to Britain, including rising male unemployment.[3]

Throughout the Western world youth face even bleaker employment prospects than do women. For example, in 1976 the jobless rates of people under 25 years were two to three times higher than the unemployment rates of those over 25. In Italy the ratio between age groups was nearly nine times higher—that is, 1.6 percent of people over 25, compared with 14.3 percent of those under 25, were out of work. In most countries teenagers experience the highest jobless rates; people between 20 and 24 find it easier to secure a job. Those in the prime adult years between 25 and 54 have the lowest unemployment. Although after 55 employment opportunities tend to decline, older persons in any Western country certainly do not face the high unemployment experienced by youth.[4]

In the United States, ethnic minorities—blacks, native Americans, and Spanish-speaking citizens—have higher unemployment rates than do Americans with European ancestry. During the postwar period, the economic situation for black teenagers between 16 and 19 has particularly deteriorated. For example, in 1950 black and white male teenagers had about the same unemployment rate—15 percent and 13 percent, respectively. However, in 1975 the black rate escalated to nearly 40 percent, while the white level increased to 18 percent. A similar pattern holds for black and white female teenagers aged 16 to 19. As the teenage unemployment picture shows, since World War II the black unemployment rate has usually been double that for whites. Spanish-speaking people of both sexes and of all ages face higher unemployment than whites but lower than blacks. Usually the jobless rates for workers of Spanish origin more closely approximate the black rate than the white rate. For instance, in 1975 the rate for whites was 7.8 percent, for blacks 14.7 percent, and for the Spanish-speaking 12.2 percent. Among all ethnic groups, the native Americans (Indians) experience the highest unemployment—over three times the white rate in 1970.[5]

Although European societies are more ethnically homogeneous than the United States, they employ a larger percentage of foreign migrants in their labor force. Turks, Yugoslavs, Greeks, and Italians have migrated to Germany to find work. Algerians and Portuguese have come to France. Finns have entered Sweden. Irish, West Indians, Pakistanis, and Indians have sought employment in Britain. During the recession that hit most of these countries during 1974 and 1975, the migrant workers, who generally held less skilled positions, lost their jobs faster than did members of the indigenous population. Especially in London, the young, unskilled blacks from the West Indies faced higher unemployment rates than did young whites.[6]

The concentration of youth and minority ethnic groups in the less skilled sectors of the economy partially explains their higher unemployment rates. In most Western industrial societies, people filling lower positions in the occupational system experience more joblessness. Data from the United States, Canada, England, West Germany, and Sweden suggest that individuals holding managerial and professional jobs face the lowest unemployment rates. Clerks and salespersons are more likely to find themselves out of work. Service employees have higher jobless rates. Unskilled manufacturing workers face the bleakest employment prospects; generally, a higher skill level within the manufacturing sector means lower unemployment. Thus skilled craft workers experience less joblessness than do unskilled laborers.[7]

Particularly in the United States and Canada, the decline of job opportunities in the agricultural and manufacturing sectors, combined with the growth in the service sector, has created severe unemployment problems. Agriculture no longer needs so many workers. As industries become more capital intensive, fewer unskilled workers can obtain manufacturing jobs. The service occupations in commerce, finance, education, health, and government require advanced formal education, which unskilled individuals lack. Therefore, we expect that those countries where a smaller percentage of the labor force is engaged in manufacturing will experience higher unemployment. Table 4–2 indicates that this expectation held true during 1975. In the United States and Canada, the lowest proportions of workers are employed in manufactuing (including mining, electricity, gas, water, construction), and the highest percentages are in the services: wholesale and retail trade, finance, insurance, real estate, government, transportation, communications, and recreational activities. The two North American countries had the highest unemployment rates. As the proportion of manufacturing jobs declines, unskilled workers thus become more vulnerable to unemployment.

Table 4–2   Unemployment and Civilian Employment by Economic Sector, 1975

| Country | Percentage of Civilian Labor Force Employed in | | | Unemployment Rate (%) |
	Agriculture[a]	Manufacturing[b]	Services[c]	
United States	4.0	29.0	67.0	8.5
Canada	6.1	29.3	64.6	6.9
United Kingdom	2.7	40.9	56.4	4.7
France	11.3	38.4	50.1	4.3
West Germany	7.3	46.0	46.7	3.8
Italy	15.8	44.1	40.1	3.7
Sweden	6.4	36.5	57.1	1.6

[a]Hunting, forestry, and fishing.

[b]Mining, electricity, gas, water, construction, and manufacturing in the narrow sense.

[c]Wholesale and retail trade, restaurants, hotels, transportation, storage, communications, financing, insurance, real estate, business, and community, social, and personal services.

NOTE: The Pearson correlation coefficients between unemployment rates in 1975 and percentage of labor force engaged in the three economic sectors are as follows: (1) agriculture: −.37, (2) manufacturing: −.68, (3) services: .65. As a greater percentage of the labor force works in the services and a smaller proportion finds employment in the manufacturing sector, unemployment rates increase.

SOURCE: Data on civilian employment by economic sector from OECD *Labour Force Statistics: Quarterly Supplement to the Yearbook* (November 1976).

In sum, we have seen that between 1960 and 1975 unemployment rates varied across nations and among specific groups within the same nation. Whereas the United States and Canada experienced the highest unemployment, West Germany and Sweden had much lower jobless rates. Within each nation, women, youth, ethnic minorities, and the occupationally unskilled generally faced bleaker employment opportunities than did men, adults between twenty-five and fifty-four, ethnic majorities, and those workers with demanded skills. What theoretical assumptions explain both the national and the group differences?

Explanations of Unemployment

Economists have formulated two complementary explanations to account for the levels of unemployment among nations and specific groups. The neoclassical explanation, which focuses on the supply of labor, assumes that certain rigidities in the labor market create unemployment problems. Although jobs are available, individuals lack the skills or the mobility opportunities to fill these occupations. If government ensures that individuals gain highly demanded skills, receive information about jobs, experience no hiring discrimination based on ascriptive characteristics (sex, age, ethnic origin) and enjoy opportunities for geographic mobility to areas where jobs lie waiting, then unemployment will be low.

In contrast to the neoclassical view, Keynesian economists assume that unemployment derives primarily from insufficient aggregate demand (spending) by government, private businesses, and consumers. In their view, the government should expand spending for both consumption and investment to lower the jobless rates. If the government promotes higher wages and larger expenditures for social services, like social security payments, then consumer expenditures will probably rise. When the government spends money for such projects as electric power machinery, transportation equipment, communications, and plants, it will directly raise spending on investment. More indirect ways of expanding demand include lowering taxes and increasing the money supply.[8] To what extent are these two assumptions valid in the seven economies? Let us examine each explanation in turn.

Rigidities in the Labor Market

According to neoclassical economists, the most cogent explanation of unemployment stems from rigidities in the labor market. Although jobs are available, the unemployment rate will decline only when government and other agencies, such as schools and private employment firms, succeed in matching qualified people with jobs. Government thus has a prime responsibility to create a more flexible labor market.

What are the main sources of rigidity in the labor market? Two seem especially important. First, as technologically advanced new plants, equipment, and machinery make possible vast increases in production, unskilled workers find greater difficulties securing jobs. In this view, one main cause of unemployment arises from individuals' lack of skills, which decreases their likelihood of obtaining a job in a technologically advanced, automated, and computerized economy. To increase the supply of skilled labor, government needs to provide advanced education in the new demanded skills, as well as to institute training and retraining programs for the unskilled.

Second, some features of an economy may hinder opportunities for labor mobility. Even if people have the requisite skills, they may lack needed information about available jobs. Additionally, groups with high jobless rates often suffer from discrimination. Regardless of their marginal productivity (the degree to which each additional worker increases the output of goods and services), those at the bottom of the social stratification system have less political and economic power to gain and retain a job. Compared with men, middle-aged employees, ethnic majorities, indigenous workers, and managerial and professional personnel, the following groups—women, youth, ethnic minorities, foreign workers, and unskilled labor—are less likely to see their economic preferences taken into account by government agencies, labor unions, and business corporations. Rather than hiring people according to their occupational skills and job performances, employers and union leaders may base their recruitment decisions on such ascriptive characteristics as an individual's age, sex, and ethnic origin. Such hiring practices interfere with job mobility. Finally, certain individuals and groups may lack opportunities for geographic movement from areas where employment prospects are bleak to places enjoying economic booms. In this case, housing and transportation opportunities become especially important. Faced with these rigidities in the labor market, governments can create a more flexible employment situation by supplying information about available jobs, by ending discrimination based on ascriptive qualities, and by implementing housing and transportation policies that would expand geographic mobility.

The market rigidity assumption better accounts for unemployment rates of specific groups than for variations in joblessness across nations. Look first at the employment status of women. Throughout the West-

ern world, women hold jobs primarily in the service sector as nurses, elementary schoolteachers, librarians, social workers, office personnel (bank tellers, bookkeepers, secretaries, typists, cashiers), private household servants, and waitresses. In all seven nations, fewer women than men gain a formal higher education; partly for this reason, women may lack the skills and educational background needed to fulfill managerial and technical jobs; these occupations have experienced lower jobless rates. Like ethnic minorities, women also suffer from discrimination. Men in business, government, and labor unions have the major responsibility for hiring personnel. Their notions about "appropriate" jobs for women may lead employers to select workers on criteria other than their abilities or productivity. Not only in the crafts and manufacturing but also in medicine, corporate finance, and higher education, ascriptive biases have influenced employment practices. Since men dominate labor unions, women may lack the bargaining strength to enforce their wills on the employers. Married women in particular also lack the mobility opportunities enjoyed by their husbands. By custom, a wife has been willing to accompany her husband across country when a new job opens for him. Men, however, have traditionally shown greater reluctance to give up their jobs and move to a place where their wives can find employment.[9]

The higher jobless rates experienced by youth stem more from discrimination and lack of skills than from lesser opportunities for geographic mobility. Individuals under twenty-five obviously do not possess the greater work experience and the longer on-the-job training enjoyed by the middle aged. Many employers perceive that young persons lack the motivation, emotional stability, dependability, and conformity needed for effective job performance. As a result, even if youths have gained the required occupational skills, they may not be hired.

In both the United States and Europe, ethnic minorities and foreign workers confront higher unemployment because they lack advanced skills. For instance, in 1970 American blacks were more likely to hold jobs as unskilled laborers (e.g., garbage collectors) and skilled "operatives" (e.g., busdrivers, smelters) than as craftsworkers (e.g., carpenters) and managers. Spanish-speaking workers are more concentrated in farming and blue-collar manufacturing, which have higher jobless rates, than in white-collar professions and skilled occupations. Many Spanish-speaking people lack fluency in English, which may hinder their prospects in managerial and professional pursuits. On the European continent, most foreign workers find employment as skilled or semi-skilled laborers. Lacking advanced formal education, they obtain jobs in construction, machine tool production, electronics, and the automobile industry. Women immigrants, who constitute about 30 percent of the foreign work force, are employed mainly as textile workers, retail salespersons, nurses, and service personnel in hotels and restaurants. [10]

Discrimination and limited mobility opportunities also plague ethnic minorities in the United States and overseas. Since the end of World War II the educational gap between American blacks and whites has drastically narrowed; yet during the 1970s the jobless rate for blacks remained double that for whites. In March 1972 blacks with some college education experienced the same unemployment rate as did white high school graduates. [11] Discrimination also confronts black residents in England and immigrants on the continent who serve as "guest workers."

Housing and transportation policies interfere with geographic mobility. In the United States, for example, the Federal Housing Administration's mortgage policies stimulated the construction of single-family homes for middle-income persons living in the suburbs, which are populated mainly by the white middle class. Local government zoning regulations restricted the supply of housing for the poor, especially the black poor. Political leaders have failed to build public housing projects in places of high employment opportunities. Since the Second World War, transportation policies have encouraged the growth of freeways and discouraged the construction of public mass transit. As a result, poor citizens find it far more difficult than the wealthy to take jobs far away from their residences. Similarly, in England local government leaders have been reluctant to build public housing for West Indians, Pakistanis, and Indians; as a result, they cluster in segregated residences. Although London has a far more extensive public transportation system than do most U.S. cities, the rise in bus and subway fares in 1976 curtailed the opportunities for unemployed West Indians and Asians, as well as the poor in general, to take jobs far away from their homes. [12]

Finally, whatever their sex, age, or ethnic origin, unskilled persons experience higher unemployment. As we have noted, the agricultural and manufacturing sectors have declined throughout most industrial nations. New technologically advanced equipment has greatly increased productivity in these sectors, making it possible to produce more goods with fewer workers. Even within the service sector, automation and computers threaten to reduce the need for unskilled personnel; for example, a few automatic typewriters can replace many typists. Although spending on capital investment for new plants, machines, and equipment may stimulate the economic growth rate, this investment usually benefits skilled more than unskilled workers. Generally, the unskilled have more part-time jobs and receive lower wages; of all employees, they are the lest likely to belong to unions. As a result, particularly where governments provide low unemployment compensation, unskilled workers lack the money to search for new jobs when they become unemployed.

Assumptions about labor market rigidities also offer some clues into the variations in unemployment rates across nations. One reason that European countries have experienced lower jobless rates since World War II than the United States and Canada stems from the stronger European efforts to create more flexible labor markets. Of course, these societies are geographically smaller, politically more centralized, and ethnically more homogeneous than either the United States or Canada. Perhaps for these reasons, European governments can establish more extensive job training programs for helping the unemployed learn marketable skills. Certainly, through labor bureaus and employment exchanges, public officials in Europe provide more comprehensive information about available jobs. Although some discrimination takes place against "foreign" workers, the labor shortage during the 1960s made ethnic discrimination less feasible or desirable. European governments take special efforts to expand labor mobility. The Swedish government pays individuals to move from areas of low employment to areas of higher employment to find jobs. Although housing is scarce, European leaders sponsor more public housing projects where both middle- and lower-income people live; these projects are often built near places of high employment. The mass public transportation system facilitates access to jobs for those without private automobiles.[13]

In contrast, Canada and the United States are geographically vast areas. The federal system decentralizes power to the provincial and state levels. A variety of ethnic groups populate the two countries. For these reasons, North American leaders have more difficulty than their European counterparts in reducing the rigidities of the labor market. For example, Canadian unemployment is lowest in the prairie province of Alberta but highest in Newfoundland and the Maritime provinces of Nova Scotia, New Brunswick, and Prince Edward Island. Because of closer geographical proximity and easier access to transportation, a Swedish citizen in the northern part of Sweden can more easily move southward toward greater employment prospects than can a resident of Newfoundland move west to Alberta.[14] Furthermore, North American private business firms, especially automobile manufacturers, banks, and real estate agencies, have stimulated the building of freeways but have discouraged the construction of mass public transportation systems and public housing projects located near employment opportunities. Automobiles still serve as the dominant means of transportation; the privately owned home represents the ideal housing pattern. North American governments thus have less power than their European counterparts to implement public policies expanding geographic labor mobility.

Lack of Sufficient Total Demand

Although assumptions about the supply of skilled labor and about opportunities for mobility may partially explain varying levels of unemployment among different *groups* within a nation, Keynesian notions that focus on the lack of sufficient total demand more clearly explain diverse unemployment rates among *nations*. When a country faces an economic recession, the problems lie less with the lack of skilled labor or mobility opportunities than with the lack of jobs. Even if people have learned certain skills, when the demand for these abilities remains low they will fail to find jobs. Economists interpret "aggregate demand" not as psychological preferences but as the total spending by government, private business, and consumers. Many poor people may prefer more consumer goods, higher quality housing, and more nutritious food; but if they lack the money to spend on these products, then their preferences will register no impact on the market. Business firms increase demand when they spend more money for production of consumer goods and for capital investment in new plants, equipment, and machinery. Government, in turn, can stimulate demand by raising expenditures, cutting taxes, and increasing the money supply. According to Keynesian economists, these expansionary policies should lead to lower unemployment rates. Increased government expenditures will presumably encourage the hiring of additional personnel to meet the orders. Higher annual increases in the money supply should encourage greater lending and investment. Tax reductions will supposedly give consumers and business enterprises more money to spend. How valid is the assumption that increased demand leads to lower unemployment rates?

According to table 4–3, between 1965 and 1975 fiscal policies exerted a stronger impact on unemployment than did monetary policies. During each five-year period, countries with higher government expenditures as a percentage of the gross national product generally had lower unemployment rates. At all government levels, the U.S. and Canadian governments spent the lowest proportion of total national income; they experienced the highest unemployment. In contrast, Sweden's total public expenditures during the early 1970s were much higher; yet the Swedish unemployment level was one-third lower.

Faced with the fiscal policy option of either increasing spending or reducing taxes, U.S. public officials have stressed tax reductions as the main tactic to stimulate the economy; yet the data for the seven countries reveal that higher taxes were associated with lower unemployment. As chapter 2 pointed out, most governments, except the U.S. and the Italian, have avoided fiscal deficits; instead, until 1975 they managed to secure rather high fiscal surpluses. A rise in taxes accompanied the growth in government expenditures. Evidently, the growth in public spending stimulated demand more than the tax raises led to decreased demand. Why? According to Keynesian economists, government expenditures generally exert a deeper impact on the economy than taxes—that is, the "multiplier" effect is greater for expenditures. (For

Table 4–3 Public Policies and Unemployment Rates

Policy Variables	Pearson r
Government Expenditures as a Proportion of GNP	
1965–1969	−.72
1970–1974	−.63
Taxes as a Proportion of GNP	
1965–1969	−.69
1970–1974	−.65
Annual Percentage Increase in the Money Supply	
1965–1969	.22
1970–1974	−.21

NOTE: The Pearson r expresses a correlation between government policies (e.g., the average annual rate of government expenditures as a proportion of the gross national product) and the unemployment rate (the yearly jobless rates during two periods: 1966–1970 and 1971–1975). The values of r range between −1 and +1. The closer the Pearson r is to +1 or −1, the higher the association. A minus r indicates an inverse statistical relationship; for instance, as government expenditures as a proportion of the GNP *increase,* unemployment rates *decrease.* A positive r shows a positive correlation. Between 1965 and 1970, for example, as annual percentage increases in the money supply rose, unemployment rates also rose slightly. With only seven countries under study, Pearson correlation coefficients should reach at least .75 to be statistically significant at the 5 percent level; that is, in only five instances out of 100 would we expect to obtain an r of .75 or larger by chance.

SOURCE: Data calculated from tables 2–1, 2–4, and 4–1.

example, if a $10 billion rise in government expenditures leads to a $50 billion increase in national income, then the multiplier is 5.) Relative to increased government expenditures, tax reductions represent an *indirect* way to stimulate aggregate demand. Since the poor and the unemployed pay relatively low income taxes or none at all, lower taxes benefit mainly middle-income and wealthy people. They may choose to save, rather than spend, their additional income. If the additional money is placed in savings accounts, it may not generate jobs for the unemployed, especially if banks decide to increase cash holdings, rather than invest in labor-intensive projects.[15]

As table 4–3 shows, government actions to raise expenditures exert a much greater effect on reducing unemployment than policies that increase the annual growth in the money supply. Like tax reductions, increases in the quantity of money operate indirectly through the banking system. Faced with rising unemployment, elected government leaders usually have difficulty forcing banking officials to release more money for expanding credit. Even if banks increase their investments, the additional money may not be spent on programs that require a vast number of workers. For example, a bank may realize a higher rate of return by investing overseas or by lending money for space research at home. In these instances, unemployment rates among unskilled blue-collar workers will probably not decline. Thus, as the next chapter indicates, monetary policy exerts a greater impact on lowering inflation than on reducing unemployment. Whereas monetary policy acts more effectively to constrain economic expansion, fiscal policy better accelerates total spending.[16]

Not just total government spending but also the specific types of goods and services preferred by public officials affect national unemployment rates. Compared with U.S. leaders, Europeans have given higher priority to spending for both capital investment and labor-intensive activities. Between 1965 and 1974 U.S. spending on construction projects, equipment, and machinery constituted less than 20 percent of the gross national product. In the four continental European countries, however, capital investment averaged from 20 to 25 percent of GNP. The government's share of total capital investment was also higher in continental Europe than in the United States. For example, from 1970 through 1974, U.S. governments at all levels financed each year around 13 percent of the total value of gross fixed capital formation; in France and Italy that figure amounted to 14 percent, in Germany 15 percent, and in Sweden 23 percent.[17] This type of spending created more jobs for skilled blue-collar workers in the manufacturing sector.

European political leaders stressed not only capital investment spending but also the implementation of spending policies to create new jobs, maintain old jobs, and reduce the labor supply.[18] While North American government officials have concentrated on tax reductions and tax credits as the major means to lower unemployment, European governments have placed a somewhat higher priority on policies that spend money for job creation and job maintenance programs. True, both Canada and the United States have instituted public service jobs for the unemployed. In the United States, the Comprehensive Employment and Training Act has expanded the number of jobs available at the local level. Similarly, the Canadian Works Program has granted federal funds to local governments and private firms to hire the unemployed for nonprofit community service activities. European governments, however, have instituted a wider variety of spending programs to create jobs. For example, the Swedish government has financed community projects initiated by the unemployed themselves. When a recession has begun to appear, the Swedish National Labor Market Board has released funds for public works projects. Similarly, in an effort to provide jobs to unemployed youths, the British Manpower Services Commission has established labor-intensive programs that improved the environment and expanded community services. The French government has reserved jobs in the postal service for unemployed young people.

Both in North America and Europe, governments also hope to lower unemployment rates by providing extensive subsidies to private business firms. Especially during recessions, political leaders release investment subsidies to encourage new jobs. They purchase output from private firms and grant loans to failing businesses. Unlike U.S. officials, West European leaders show greater reluctance to subsidize private corporations engaged in defense and space research; these programs do not directly benefit the three groups facing high unemployment—youth, women, and the unskilled. In West Germany and France the central governments pay wage subsidies to private firms. The German federal government supplies 60 percent of the gross wage for six months to industries that hire permanent workers from the ranks of the unemployed. The French government also gives wage subsidies to firms hiring unemployed people for at least a year.

Besides creating new jobs for the currently unemployed, European governments have also enacted numerous programs designed to maintain the job security of the employed worker. Among the modified market economies of the West, the highest paying and most secure jobs are found in the government sector and in concentrated manufacturing industries. Here, employees are relatively skilled and unions are fairly powerful. However, in the small-scale, competitive part of the economy, especially the nongovernment service sector, the labor force, mainly women and youth, is less skilled. Unions exert less economic influence. As a partial result, wages are lower and employees experience a greater number of permanent layoffs, particularly in Canada and the United States. European political leaders have taken more active steps than North American officials to discourage temporary layoffs and permanent discharges. European governments have pressured managers of nationalized industries to refrain from firing workers when recessions hit the economies. Not only in government and concentrated industries but in the competitive sector as well, European public policies have placed restrictions on discharing employees. For example, before managers can lay off workers, they must give at least one week's advance notice. A French employer must gain approval from the Ministry of Labor before a person is fired for economic reasons. Both managers and workers support work sharing as a superior alternative to layoffs. They also express greater opposition to overtime than do most Americans. The higher rates of European unemployment benefits as a proportion of normal earnings have meant that European employers must bear higher costs if they discharge workers. Especially in the concentrated manufacturing industries, European managers must consult with trade union representatives before layoffs occur. Since the union movement is weaker in the United States than in most European nations, U.S. business firms do not need to cope with this restriction. In sum, the United States and Canada have experienced higher unemployment rates partly because workers have gained fewer rights to job security than in Europe. Government policies in most European countries have discouraged permanent discharges and temporary layoffs from jobs in government, concentrated manufacturing industries, and competitive private firms.

Finally, West European governments have tried to reduce unemployment by spending money to decrease the labor supply. For example, in Germany, France, and Italy, either the firm or the individual worker receives from the government a payment for the proportion of wages lost because of a shortened work week. In these countries, and in Sweden as well, government officials provide educational grants to individuals who want a temporary work leave. The French government provides pensions to employees who want early retirement, pays foreign workers who want to return to their home country, and makes grants to French youth who seek employment in French companies overseas. All these expenditure programs are intended to reduce the labor supply, encourage the hiring of new employees, and thus lower the jobless rates.

In sum, for two major reasons, European countries from 1960 through 1975 experienced lower unemployment rates than did the United States and Canada. First, European governments took more active steps to establish flexible labor markets. Compared with North Americans, Europeans participated in more extensive job retraining programs, enjoyed greater opportunities for geographic mobility, and gained more information about available jobs. Second, until the 1974–1975 recession occurred, European government leaders concentrated on expanding aggregate demand. Government expenditures as proportions of the GNP were higher in Europe than in the United States and Canada. European public officials stressed spending for both capital investment and for labor-intensive programs that created new jobs and maintained jobs held by employed workers. In contrast, U.S. officials emphasized tax reductions as the most appropriate technique for expanding total demand. Yet, crossnationally, low taxes had less effect on reducing the jobless rate than did high government expenditures.

Unemployment and the Business Cycle

Public policies to deal with unemployment certainly met with greater success during the early 1960s than during the decade of the 1970s. As table 4–1 indicated, the overall employment rate in all seven industrial nations was higher from 1961 through 1965 than during the period from 1971 to 1975. To what extent do the changing levels of joblessness over time stem from the peaks and troughs, the booms and busts of the business cycle? Will Western market economies pull out of the current recession and reestablish the relatively low unemployment rates of the 1960s? Or does there now exist a permanent army of unskilled labor that will not find jobs even when the economic growth rate begins to accelerate? Assumptions about the business cycle can explain the changing levels of unemployment during the last twenty years, even if these theoretical notions cannot give us a conclusive picture of the future economic scenario.

In a market economy, entrepreneurs face the following contradiction: To maximize profits in the long run, economic managers need to lower unit labor costs (ratio of hourly labor costs to output per hour). But they must also increase consumer demand for goods and services. One way to reduce labor costs is to decrease wages. Yet that decision will at the same time lead to a declining consumer demand, lower profits, lower investment, and thus higher unemployment. Since the products cannot be sold on the market, a "crisis of overproduction" ensues. This crisis will be met either by further reducing production or by expanding the market for goods at home and abroad. If wages are too low, then the demand for the goods at home will decline. If labor costs are too high, prices will escalate and firms will be unable to sell their products on the domestic or foreign markets. If production declines, then unemployment will probably rise. In turn, the growing joblessness will curtail the domestic market, further reinforcing the trend toward high unemployment.[19]

These theoretical assumptions about the course of the business cycle offer some insights into the unemployment situation confronting Western governments during the 1960s and 1970s. Between 1960 and 1973 most Western societies underwent an economic boom; except in England, where the rate of growth has been relatively slow, the annual increase in the real gross national product or gross domestic product exceeded 4 percent a year. Business fixed investment remained at high levels. Manufacturing plants operated at close to full capacity. Profits, defined as the ratio of gross property income to assets or to capital stock, were fairly high prior to 1973. On the European continent, unit labor costs declined during the last five years of the 1960s in West Germany, Sweden, France, and Italy. Throughout this decade unemployment rates remained relatively low.

After 1973, however, Western economies entered the bust period of the business cycle. Unit labor costs dramatically escalated between 1971 and 1975. During late 1973 the cost of imported oil from the Near East jumped from $2.50 a barrel to over $11.50 per barrel. As the costs of labor and raw materials rose, profits fell. As corporations made fewer outlays for new plants and equipment, business fixed investment declined. At the same time, the decreased production meant that plants were not being used to full capacity. The rising costs for labor and raw materials also stimulated rapid price increases. Attempting to halt the accelerating inflation, most Western governments enacted restrictive policies. Interest rates rose. Taxes as a proportion of the total national income increased. Local government spending declined slightly. As a result of reduced demand and rising costs, production began to decline in 1974 and 1975; only Sweden increased the real growth rate by more than 4 percent a year. In 1975 the United States, Canada, West Germany, and Italy actually experienced decreases in their real gross national products. The declining production and lower purchasing power of employees led to a general rise in the unemployment rate after 1973 and 1974.[20] Along with growing unemployment went comparatively high price increases, at least higher than during the early 1960s. Faced with these severe economic problems, political leaders had difficulty devising appropriate public policies that would simultaneously reduce both unemployment and inflation.

Notes

1. See Joyanna Moy and Constance Sorrentino, "An Analysis of Unemployment in Nine Industrial Countries," *Monthly Labor Review* 100 (April 1977):12–24; U.S. Department of Labor, Bureau of Labor Statistics, *Handbook of Labor Statistics, 1975—Reference Edition* (Washington, D. C.: Government Printing Office, 1975), p. 437 and *Handbook of Labor Statistics, 1976,* p. 322; Joyanna Moy and Constance Sorrentino, "Unemployment in Nine Industrial Nations, 1973–1975," *Monthly Labor Review* 98 (June 1975):9–18; Murray Seeger, "World Jobless: Rate May Depend on System of Keeping Count," *Los Angeles Times,* June 2, 1975, part III, pp. 10–12. The Organisation for Economic Cooperation and Development also adjusts official governmental unemployment rates to make the rates comparable across nations. These adjusted figures are fairly similar to the Bureau of Labor Statistics data. See *OECD Economic Outlook,* no. 21 (July 1977):29.

2. See "How Women Fared during the Recession," *OECD Observer,* no. 83 (September/October 1976):28–31; Moy and Sorrentino, "An Analysis of Unemployment in Nine Industrial Countries," *Monthly Labor Review* (April 1977):17; Barbara Deckard and Howard Sherman, "Monopoly Power and Sex Discrimination," *Politics and Society* 4 (August 1974):475–82; Mary Dublin Keyserling, "The Economic Status of Women in the United States," *American Economic Review* 66 (May 1976):205–12.

3. Tom Forester, "Who, Exactly, Are the Unemployed?" *New Society* 39 (January 13, 1977):54–57; John Hughes, "Employ the Young," *New Society* 37 (October 1976):74–75. According to the *OECD Labour Force Statistics, 1964–1975* (Paris: OECD, 1977), pp. 42–43, in 1962, 47 percent of the English civilian labor force worked in the manufacturing or industrial sector; in 1975 that proportion had fallen to 41 percent.

4. See Moy and Sorrentino, "An Analysis of Unemployment in Nine Industrial Countries," p. 17; *OECD Economic Outlook* (July 1977):32; "Youth Employment and Unemployment," *OECD Observer,* no. 87 (July 1977):31–35.

5. Bernard E. Anderson, "Full Employment and Economic Equality," *The Annals of the American Academy of Political and Social Science* 418 (March 1975):132; Roberta V. McKay, "Americans of Spanish Origin in the Labor Force: An Update," *Monthly Labor Review* 99 (September 1976):3–6; Mary Allen Ayres, "Federal Indian Policy and Labor Statistics—A Review Essay," *Monthly Labor Review* 101 (April 1978):25; Alan L. Sorkin, "The Economic Basis of Indian Life," *The Annals of the American Academy of Political and Social Science* 436 (March 1978):5. If we include both urban Indians (9.4 percent unemployed) and reservation Indians (41.0 percent unemployed), then in 1970 the jobless rate for native Americans was 28.6 percent, compared with 4 percent for whites and 8.2 percent for blacks.

6. See Philip Martin, "Issues in the Evaluation of European Labor Flows," *Social Science Quarterly* 58 (September 1977):255–69; "A Turning Point for European Migration," *OECD Observer*, no. 76 (July/August 1975):13–14; Forester, "Who, Exactly, Are the Unemployed?" pp. 56–57.

7. See International Labour Organization, *Yearbook of Labor Statistics, 1976* (Geneva: International Labour Office, 1976): U.S. Department of Labor, *Handbook of Labor Statistics, 1976,* p. 123; Peter Townsend, "The Neglect of Mass Unemployment," *New Statesman* 94 (October 7, 1977):463–65.

8. For a brief discussion of the causes of unemployment, see Robert L. Heilbroner and Lester C. Thurow, *Understanding Macroeconomics,* 5th ed. (Englewood Cliffs, N. J.: Prentice-Hall, 1975), pp. 247–60. For an analysis of Keynesian assumptions about unemployment, see Richard T. Gill, *Economics and the Public Interest,* 3rd ed. (Pacific Palisades, Calif.: Goodyear, 1976), pp. 79–83; John A. Garraty, *Unemployment in History: Economic Thought and Public Policy* (New York: Harper & Row, 1978), pp. 216–32.

9. In the United States less than 15 percent of women working outside the home belong to a union, compared to one-third of the male labor force who are unionized. See Linda Tarr-Whelan, "Women Workers and Organized Labor," *Social Policy* 9 (May/June 1978):13; "How Women Fared during the Recession," p. 29; Stuart H. Garfinkle, "Occupations of Women and Black Workers, 1962–74," *Monthly Labor Review* 98 (November 1975):32. In most Western industrial countries, over 70 percent of women work in the service sector.

10. Michael P. Johnson and Ralph R. Sell, "The Cost of Being Black: A 1970 Update," *American Journal of Sociology* 82 (July 1976):183–90; Roberta V. McKay, "Americans of Spanish Origin in the Labor Force: An Update," *Monthly Labor Review* (September 1976):5; Philip Martin, "Issues in the Evaluation of European Labor Flows," *Social Science Quarterly* (September 1977):259–61.

11. Sar Levitan, William B. Johnston, and Robert Taggart, *Still a Dream: The Changing Status of Blacks since 1960* (Cambridge, Mass.: Harvard University Press, 1975), p. 68.

12. See Arnold J. Heidenheimer, Hugh Heclo, and Carolyn Teich Adams, *Comparative Public Policy: The Politics of Social Choice in Europe and America* (New York: St. Martin's Press, 1975), chs. 3, 4, 6; Forester, "Who, Exactly, Are the Unemployed?" p. 57.

13. Heidenheimer et al., *Comparative Public Policy,* chs. 3, 4, 6.

14. H. L. Robinson, "Unemployment in 1976," *Canadian Forum* 56 (March 1977):18–21.

15. For discussions of the Keynesian approach to unemployment, see Gill, *Economics and the Public Interest,* pp. 115–32, esp. p. 129; James Tobin, "How Dead Is Keynes?" *Economic Inquiry* 15 (October 1977):459–66.

16. Paul McCracken et al., *Towards Full Employment and Price Stability* (Paris: OECD, 1977), pp. 198, 208.

17. A negative correlation exists between gross fixed capital investment as a percentage of the GNP and unemployment rates. (Capital investment includes spending on buildings, other construction, transport equipment, and other machinery and equipment. For data on capital investment, see *National Accounts*

of OECD Countries, 1975 [Paris: OECD, 1977], vol. 2, table 1 for each of the seven countries.) Between 1965 and 1970 the Pearson *r* was $-.56$; between 1970 and 1975 that correlation was $-.62$. See table 10 for data on governmental investment as a share of total gross capital formation.

18. See *The OECD Economic Observer,* no. 80 (March/April 1976):14–16; *International Economic Report of the President transmitted to the Congress,* January 1977 (Washington, D. C.: Government Printing Office, 1977), p. 108; Moy and Sorrentino, "An Analysis of Unemployment in Nine Industrial Countries," pp. 18–21; Sar A. Levitan and Richard S. Belous, "Work-Sharing Initiatives at Home and Abroad," *Monthly Labor Review* 100 (September 1977):16–20; Anne Corbett, "Job Creation in France," *New Society* 41 (August 11, 1977):287–88; Roger Kaufman, "Why the U. S. Unemployment Rate Is So High," *Challenge* 21 (May/June 1978):40–49; Kenneth D. Walters and R. Joseph Monsen, "The Nationalized Firm: The Politicians' Free Lunch," *Columbia Journal of World Business* 12 (Spring 1977):93.

19. For theories and data that link unemployment rates to changes in the business cycle, see Howard J. Sherman, *Stagflation: A Radical Theory of Unemployment and Inflation* (New York: Harper & Row, 1976), pp. 93–110; Geoffrey H. Moore, "Business Cycles: Partly Exogenous, Mostly Endogenous," *Social Science Quarterly* 58 (June 1977):96–103.

20. For empirical evidence behind the assumptions in these paragraphs see the following sources: (1) *OECD Economic Outlook,* no. 17 (July 1975):13; (2) *OECD Economic Outlook,* no. 21 (July 1977):15–57; (3) *OECD Economic Outlook,* no. 23 (July 1978):1–30; (4) McCracken et al., *Towards Full Employment and Price Stability,* pp. 161–62, 305; (5) Barbara Boner and Arthur Neef, "Productivity and Unit Labor Costs in 12 Industrial Countries," *Monthly Labor Review* 100 (July 1977):11–17; (6) Hanns Maull, "The Price of Crude Oil in the International Energy Market: A Political Analysis," *Energy Policy* 5 (June 1977):147. Between 1961 and 1975 there was a negative correlation between average annual wage increases in manufacturing and profits, defined as the ratio of gross property income to total assets, tangible assets, or gross capital stock. Compared with the five European countries, in the United States and Canada during this period profits were higher but hourly increases in wages were lower. For this reason, higher profit rates and lower annual wage increases were associated with higher unemployment rates.

The Impact of Public Policies on Inflation

Particularly since the end of World War II, inflation has posed a severe economic problem to people throughout the world. In most industrial countries, yearly price increases hovered around 1 or 2 percent during the 1950s. In the next decade inflation rates amounted to about a 4 percent annual increase. During the early 1970s, however, inflationary pressures grew especially acute. For the first time since the Second World War, double-digit inflation affected citizens in the United States, Canada, Britain, Sweden, France, and Italy. Of the seven countries studied in this book, only West Germany managed to escape the trend. For example, whereas Germany's inflation rate reached 6 percent in 1975, Britain and Italy experienced yearly price increases of 24 percent and 17 percent, respectively. In Latin America and the Near East, inflation rates surged to even higher figures. Not surprisingly, the Gallup International Research Institute discovered that, in all areas of the world, samples of adults cited the high cost of living as the most important problem facing their nations.[1]

What is inflation, and what techniques are used to measure it? Robert M. Solow defines inflation as "a substantial, sustained increase in the general level of prices."[2] Inflation thus refers not just to increased prices of a few goods and services but rather to price rises covering a wide variety of items. Although economists disagree about the precise numerical meaning of "substantial, sustained" price rises, most consider that inflation involves greater than 3 percent annual price increases over a period of several years. In short, inflation denotes a decline in the purchasing power of money, which buys fewer goods and services than before.

Chapter Five

Since the consumer price index best reflects the economic experience of consumers purchasing a wide variety of items, we use this index to compare inflation rates across several nations. Throughout the Western world, government economists ascertain the annual price increases for a variety of goods and services, including products purchased at retail stores, and services like medical care, health insurance, education, housing, transportation, water, gas, and electricity, obtained through government agencies, banks, insurance, schools, and hospitals. Officials every month secure information about the prices of between 250 and 900 items in several cities of each nation. These data are then compiled into a consumer price index.[3]

According to table 5–1, in every Western economy between the first five years of the 1960s and the first half of the 1970s, inflation escalated to higher levels. For example, between 1961 and 1965, the U.S. inflation rate averaged only 1.3 percent a year. During the early 1970s prices rose to greater heights until they reached the double-digit figure of 11.0 percent in 1974. Other countries showed a similar trend of steadily rising prices from 1960 through 1975. Only Germany and Italy managed to avoid this pattern; prices actually declined there in the late 1960s but rose again during the 1970s.

Although prices escalated in the United States and Canada during this fifteen-year period, the two North American countries, along with

Table 5–1   Rates of Inflation

Country	Rises in Consumer Prices (average annual % change)		
	1961–1965	*1966–1970*	*1971–1975*
United States	1.3	4.2	6.8
Canada	1.5	3.8	7.4
United Kingdom	3.5	4.6	13.2
West Germany	2.8	2.6	6.1
Sweden	3.6	4.5	8.0
France	3.8	4.3	8.8
Italy	4.9	3.0	11.5

SOURCE: *Main Economic Indicators, Historical Statistics: 1960–1975* (Paris: OECD, 1976); *Main Economic Indicators* (January 1977):154; (January 1975):154; (February 1969, supplement):8–9.

West Germany, experienced lower inflation rates than did Britain, Italy, France, and Sweden. As we have seen, inflation has constituted an especially severe problem in Britain and Italy, most notably between 1973 and 1977. In contrast, the German government successfully held price rises to under 7 percent, a better record than engineered by U.S. or Canadian officials.

What are the causes of inflation across both time and space? Economists have suggested two complementary reasons.[4] The *demand-pull* explanation assumes that inflation stems from too many dollars chasing too few goods; the total demand stimulated by consumers, government, and business firms exceeds the supply of goods. Demand-pull theories imply a fully competitive market where the forces of supply and demand operate freely. In contrast, the *cost-push* explanation for inflation assumes the presence of imperfect competition. Three key institutions—concentrated industries, labor unions, and government—have the power to cause prices to rise above existing demand; that is, the actions of these institutions push up the prices of goods and services by raising the cost of supplies. Concentrated industries administer prices so that they do not fall when demand declines or supply increases. Similarly, labor unions secure wage increases that exceed gains in productivity; corporations or government-owned firms pass along these wage hikes in the form of higher prices. Government organizations encourage cost and price increases by institutionalizing certain noncompetitive practices. Fiscal, monetary, regulatory, and income policies pursued by the government fail to check cost-push inflation.

As the analysis of the actual causes of inflation between 1961 and 1975 indicates, the demand-pull and cost-push explanations are complementary, not necessarily contradictory. If wage increases exceed gains in output, then the higher earnings will not only push up the costs of labor supplies but will also pull up demand—that is, workers will have more money to spend. Similarly, if costs of supplies increase, business corporations that need to borrow money for expanded production will pressure the central banking officials to increase the money supply, a sign of accelerated aggregate demand.

Demand-Pull Explanations for Inflation

The classical demand-pull explanation for inflation assumes the existence of a competitive market where prices respond to changes in supply and demand. Under the pure competition model, the price system gives consumers a free choice of goods and the ability to influence production. The prices secured in the market indicate to the producers the value consumers place on particular goods and services. If prices are too high, consumers will not make purchases. Demand (or consumer spending) will decline. When price reductions occur, demand will increase for the lower-priced products. In short, an equilibrium occurs between the consumer demand for goods and the supply of goods by producers at given prices. Scarce, highly demanded goods command higher prices than abundant, undemanded goods. Prices freely respond to both consumer demand and producer supply.

A fully competitive economy encourages downward pressures on costs. To compete effectively with other firms producing goods at lower cost, entrepreneurs must reduce their costs of production or else go bankrupt. To maximize their profits, they set prices that correspond to the marginal costs of producing one additional unit of the good.

Under these competitive conditions, a large number of sellers operate on the market. Oligopolies do not control the market; no concentrated industry restricts the entry of new firms into a market characterized by high demand and low supply. Firms seeking higher profits can move freely from one industry to another. The produced goods have a virtually identical design; people buy them for their favorable prices, not for their style or design. Price competition, rather than product differentiation, guides the purchase of goods. If these conditions prevail, sellers try to secure the highest prices for their goods, and consumers purchase goods at the lowest possible prices. If producers charge overly high prices, then demand falls. To reduce prices and thereby restimulate purchases, producers who experience the problems of overproduction may lower wages. If we assume that no substitutes for a specific product are available on the market, spending should increase for the good now bearing a lower price. However, this "law" of supply and demand holds true only if buyers and sellers expect that prices will return to a previous low level. If they expect prices to continue rising, in the short run purchases may rise rather than fall.[5]

Although the model of pure competition does not posit a major role for government, governments in fact exert extremely important effects on prices in actual economies. In the United States, Canada, and Western Europe, governments at all levels—central, state, provincial, city—provide services to individuals. Many services, like health care and education, are financed through tax revenues. Government agencies also operate as both buyers and sellers; that is, they purchase goods from private enterprises, for example, weapons manufacturers. European governments often sell goods, such as Renault automobiles, on the open market. By its purchases, sales, and provision of services, the government stimulates or reduces demand, thus influencing inflation rates.

In sum, the demand-pull perspective assumes that the main cause of inflation is that the total demand exceeds the supply of goods. Total demand means the sum of spending by consumers, business, and government. What indicators reflect the existence of "excessive" demand— that is, demand that exceeds the total output and growth in productivity? The following indicators seem especially important: First, consumers save a low percentage of their disposable income. Second, government's fiscal policies result in high deficits; expenditures exceed tax revenues. Third, monetary policies produce low interest rates and high annual increases in the money supply. Fourth, business firms spend a high proportion of the national income on capital investment; plants are operated at maximum capacity.[6] The following sections examine the association between each indicator and inflation rates. To uncover the causes of price increases, we need to make crossnational comparisons over time. As we have seen, the United States, Canada, and Germany have experienced less inflation than Britain, Italy, Sweden, and France. From a temporal perspective, inflation has grown worse during the 1970s, compared with the late 1960s. Do countries with high price increases rank higher on the preceding indicators of excessive demand? Have the indicators of excess spending risen during the 1970s? Probes into these questions should offer some clues about the plausibility of demand-pull theories of inflation.

Effects of Consumer Saving

If consumers save a fairly high percentage of their disposable income, then the increased savings should curtail total demand and dampen inflationary pressures. However, if consumers spend, rather than save, their money, total demand will increase, thereby pulling up prices. Decisions about the relative proportions of income allocated for spending and saving depend on individuals' expectations of future price rises and future income. If people believe that prices will increase but their incomes will decline' in the future, then they may decrease their expenditures. Expectations of declining prices may encourage consumers to postpone spending in the hopes of securing more favorable prices in the future. These actions should deflate the economy. But if consumers expect both their incomes and prices to continue rising, their purchases may increase. Such conditions will expand total demand and reinforce inflation.[7]

Despite the importance attached to consumer spending in the pure competition model, the associations between consumer savings ratios and price increases between 1965 and 1975 appear ambiguous. As table 5–2 indicates, during the last half of the 1960s high inflation was indeed linked to low personal savings. Yet during the early 1970s, an opposite relationship emerged. Although the correlation is quite low, countries with high savings ratios experienced slightly higher price rises. Comparisons of countries showed no clearcut pattern. For instance, West Germans, Italians, and French saved the highest proportion of their disposable incomes; yet inflation posed far more severe problems in Italy and France than in West Germany. Although the Americans, Canadians, and Swedes all chose to save a comparatively low proportion of their incomes, Sweden faced sharper price rises than did the United States or Canada. Most important, in all seven countries consumers saved a larger proportion of their income during the period from 1970 through 1974 than they did in the late 1960s. In short, as inflation grew more severe, citizens responded by increasing their savings, rather than their expenditures. Therefore, the surge in prices that developed during the 1970s stemmed primarily from other factors, not from consumer spending practices.

Table 5–2   Inflation and Personal Savings Rates

Country	Personal Savings Rate[a] 1965–1969	Price Rise 1966–1970	Personal Savings Rate 1970–1974	Price Rise 1971–1975
United States	6.5%	4.2%	7.8%	6.8%
Canada	5.9	3.8	7.8	7.4
United Kingdom	8.4	4.6	10.4	13.2
West Germany	12.3	2.6	14.3	6.1
Sweden	4.3	4.5	6.2	8.0
France	11.8	4.3	13.6	8.8
Italy	15.7	3.0	18.1	11.5

[a]Percentages of personal disposable income actually saved. See *Hearings before the Committee on the Budget, U. S. Senate, 94th Session, September 25, 1975, vol. 1* (Washington, D.C.: Government Printing Office, 1975), pp. 142–45.

NOTE: The Pearson correlation coefficient between savings rates and price rises (1965–1970 period) is −.67; the r for the years between 1970 and 1975 is .33.

Effects of Fiscal Policies

If consumer saving decisions do not account for crossnational differences in rates of inflation, can fiscal deficits incurred by governments explain the differences? Do countries where expenditures exceed revenues experience the highest price increases? The demand-pull explanation suggests that high government expenditures and low taxes increase total demand and thereby stimulate inflationary pressures, particularly when plants are used to full capacity (over 90 percent) and unemployment rates are low (under 4 percent). Under these conditions, tax cuts and spending hikes cannot lead to increased production. Rather than increasing output, greater government expenditures result in higher prices. However, when unemployment rates are high and plants do not operate at maximum capacity, government deficits may stimulate greater output of goods and services without raising prices.[8]

Although Keynesian economists assume that high government expenditures, low taxes, and high fiscal deficits all represent signs of excess demand and therefore contribute to inflation, the evidence from seven Western countries between 1965 and 1975 does not substantiate these hypotheses. Table 5–3 points out that during this period the crossnational relationships between fiscal policies and price increases remained quite low. Although high government expenditures accompanied low jobless rates, fiscal policies exerted a weaker impact on inflation than on unemployment. For example, compare Britain and Germany. Throughout this period, taxes and expenditures as a percentage of the gross national product were about the same; yet Germany achieved the lowest price increases while Britain confronted the most severe inflation.

Between 1965 and 1975 government leaders in most nations did not enact fiscal policies that greatly increased aggregate demand. True, in all seven countries expenditures as a percentage of the GNP grew somewhat, but only Canada and Sweden registered sizable increases. Taxes as a percentage of GNP rose in all nations except France, where they remained constant. Therefore, from a temporal perspective, fiscal policies—decisions about total government expenditures and total tax revenues—do not appear the main contributing factor explaining the marked price rises after 1972.

As expected from these tax and spending patterns, fiscal deficits bear only a weak relationship to crossnational inflationary differences. Between 1965 and 1975 few central governments except the Italian and U.S. resorted to deficit financing. Despite this similarity, the United States recorded the second lowest inflation rate, whereas Italy faced the second highest price increases. During the early 1970s the British government attained higher fiscal surpluses than both the U.S. and Canadian governments (federal, state-provincial, local). Yet Britain's inflation rate was nearly twice as high as the two North American societies'. At all government levels, Sweden compiled the largest fiscal surpluses as a percentage of the gross national product; however, throughout this period, the Swedes had to contend with more severe inflationary pressures than those experienced by West Germans, who recorded lower surpluses.

Comparisons across time also cast doubt on the credibility of the fiscal deficit explanation for inflation. If high deficits really did account for inflation, then we would expect that, during the 1970s, fiscal sur-

Table 5–3 Inflation and Fiscal Policies

Country	Fiscal Policies 1965–1969 (% of GNP)			66–70 Price Rises
	Expenditures[a]	Taxes[b]	Surplus[c]	
United States	27.4	26.4	1.32	4.2%
Canada	28.0	30.1	3.62	3.8
United Kingdom	32.3	33.3	3.56	4.6
West Germany	32.0	33.4	4.62	2.6
Sweden	33.1	38.0	9.26	4.5
France	34.2	37.0	4.54	4.3
Italy	31.3	29.8	1.02	3.0

[a]All governmental levels (central, state-provincial, and local).

[b]Revenues actually gathered by all levels of government.

[c]Differences between *receipts* and disbursements. Since current receipts include revenues other than taxes—for example, withdrawals from entrepreneurial income of quasi-corporate government enterprises, property income, compulsory fees, fines, and penalties, unfunded employee welfare contributions, and current transfers received from other resident sectors or from the rest of the world—the fiscal surplus does not amount to the difference between *taxes* and expenditures.

NOTE: The Pearson *r* correlations between fiscal policies and inflation rates are as follows:

pluses as a proportion of the total national income would decline, relative to the figures for the late 1960s. Yet no clearcut pattern emerges. True, as shown by table 5–3, the surplus at all levels of government did fall in the United States, Canada, Sweden, and most notably in Italy, the only country to record an annual average deficit between 1970 and 1974. Generally, however, the drop was quite modest, usually less than 1 percent of the GNP. Contrary to this tendency, fiscal surplus as a proportion of the GNP actually grew in West Germany and France; in England it remained about the same. In most of these nations, only after 1974 did unbalanced budgets become common, especially at the central government level. Yet, as we have seen, price rises preceded, rather than followed, these fiscal deficits. Moreover, deficit spending

		Fiscal Policies 1970–1974 *(% of GNP)*		
Expenditures[a]	*Taxes*[b]	*Surplus*[c]	*71–75* *Price* *Rises*
30.5	28.3	0.38	6.8%
34.0	33.9	3.22	7.4
34.9	34.9	3.54	13.2
34.3	35.8	5.12	6.1
40.3	42.6	8.36	8.0
34.7	37.0	4.78	8.8
35.6	30.6	−1.82	11.5

Fiscal Policies		*Inflation Rates*	*Pearson r*
Expenditures as Percentage	1965–1969	1966–1970	.10
of GNP	1970–1974	1971–1975	.21
Taxes as Percentage of GNP	1965–1969	1966–1970	.28
	1970–1974	1971–1975	−.08
Surplus as Percentage of GNP	1965–1969	1966–1970	.33
	1970–1974	1971–1975	−.31

SOURCE: *National Accounts of OECD Countries, 1975* (Paris: OECD, 1977), vol. 2; *1962–1973* (Paris: OECD, 1975); *1961–1972* (Paris: OECD, 1974); *Revenue Statistics of OECD Member Countries, 1965–1974* (Paris: OECD, 1976), p. 74. Data on gross national product at market prices appeared in *Revenue Statistics of OECD Member Countries, 1965–1974,* p. 98.

arose at a time of growing unemployment and falling use of plant capacity, two signs of contracting demand. When labor and capital resources are not being used to full capacity, then fiscal deficits should not lead to inflation. Hence, the main explanation for price rises during the 1970s must derive primarily from factors other than government fiscal policies. For example, if budgetary deficits stimulate the central bank to increase the money supply, then the greater quantity of money may generate inflationary pressures.

Effects of Monetary Policies

If fiscal policies do not adequately explain the recent inflation, can monetary policies explain the rising price level? According to the monetarist approach to inflation, high annual increases in the money supply constitute the main policy variable stimulating excess demand and therefore high price rises. To economists like Milton Friedman and his associates, fiscal policies, including the size of the government deficit, are less important than monetary policies. For example, William Poole asserts:

> *Except over short periods, significant price level increases do not occur in the absence of monetary expansion; money growth is clearly a necessary condition for continuing inflation. . . . A change in money growth is a sufficient condition for a change in the inflation rate. . . . Budget deficits and interest rate increases not accompanied by monetary expansion do not generate inflation. . . . Monetary expansions not accompanied by budget deficits and interest rate increases do cause inflation.* [9]

By this reasoning, if the government increases the amount of money available for spending and lending, then total demand will rise, with inflation the result. Looking at the United States, Poole finds his assumption confirmed. Between 1958 and 1966 the money supply grew by 3 percent a year; prices averaged a 1.5 percent increase. Between 1966 and 1974 the money supply increased by nearly 6 percent annually; as a consequence, the consumer price index rose 5.4 percent a year. [10] Poole has examined American data. How valid are his assumptions crossnationally? To test the validity of the monetarist explanation, two questions are crucial: First, do countries with high increases in the money supply experience high rates of inflation? Second, across all seven countries, have the central banks drastically increased the money supply between the early 1960s and the early 1970s?

By looking at tables 5–3 and 5–4, we see that monetary policies seem to exert a stronger impact on inflation than do fiscal policies. Throughout each five-year period from 1960 to 1975, the crossnational correlations between the annual increases in the money supply and price rises were substantially greater than the correlations between fiscal policies and inflation rates.[11] Despite the greater effect of monetary policies, the correlations between the money supply and price increases remain somewhat ambiguous. Germany and Britain provide interesting contrasts. During the 1960s Germany showed a higher average annual growth of money than did Britain; yet, compared with the British, the Germans faced less acute inflation. Furthermore, although Canada and the United States had similar inflation rates between 1961 and 1975, the Bank of Canada pursued a more expansionary monetary policy than did the U.S. Federal Reserve System. In short, even if monetary policies do explain some of the crossnational variations in inflation rates, the monetary impact is not as clearly evident as suggested by Poole.

The consequences of changes in the money supply also tend to vary over time. Between 1960 and 1965 the association between inflation and money was quite high and in the predicted direction. Throughout North America and Western Europe, those countries that experienced the highest annual growth in the money supply generally wound up with the highest price increases. However, from 1965 to 1969 the relationship reversed direction, with increased money actually correlated with *lower* price rises. Britain, Germany, and Italy accounted for this unexpected finding. Although the British government engineered the lowest relative increase in the quantity of money, Britain faced the highest inflation. Italy and Germany pursued the most expansionary monetary policies yet faced the two lowest inflation rates. During the early 1970s the association between money supply and inflation returned to moderately high levels in the expected direction; that is, once again, countries with more rapid growth in the quantity of money had to contend with higher price increases. In sum, the monetary explanation for inflation holds the most credence during the first half of the 1960s and the 1970s; however, from 1965 through 1969, higher increases in the money supply were actually associated with lower price rises.

Except in Germany and Italy, inflation rates rose during each five-year period from 1960 through 1975; did the money supply show a similar rise? If we compare two periods—1960–1964 and 1970–1974—we see that all nations except France registered a higher increase in the money supply during the early 1970s. A comparison of the two halves of the 1960s, however, reveals a different picture. The German, Swedish, and French banking officials decreased their money supplies between 1965 and 1969, compared with 1960 to 1964. Despite these actions, inflation grew worse in Sweden and France while declining only slightly in West Germany. In short, although the monetary approach to inflation retains some plausibility, other variables obviously affect crossnational variations in price increases over time.

If we control for the growth in productivity, then the monetarist explanation of inflation appears slightly more credible. According to this logic, the quantity of money exerts a large inflationary effect mainly when additions to the money supply exceed the growth in total output of goods and services. The assumption rests on the premise that inflation stems from too many dollars (pounds, marks, kroner, francs) chasing too few goods. If the quantity of goods rapidly increases, it will come into balance with the money supply, thereby reducing inflationary pressures.[12] As indicated by table 5–5, during the early 1960s and 1970s, a slightly larger correlation between the money supply and price rises emerges when we control for rates of increase in the real gross national product. That is, the relationship of price rises, on the one hand, to the difference between increased money and a nation's economic growth rate, on the other, is higher than the correlation between

Table 5–4 Inflation and Increases in the Money Supply

Country	Money[a] 1960–1964	Price Rise 1961–1965	Money 1965–19
United States	2.5%	1.3%	5.0%
Canada	5.1	1.5	6.6
United Kingdom	2.9	3.5	3.2
West Germany	9.1	2.8	6.7
Sweden	6.0	3.6	5.7
France	13.9	3.8	6.0
Italy	13.6	4.9	14.5

[a]Averages of the annual increases in the supply of money (M1, the sum of currency outside banks and demand deposits disposable by checks and transfer orders).
SOURCE: *Main Economic Indicators, Historical Statistics: 1960–1975* (Paris: OECD, 1976); *Main Economic Indicators, Historical Statistics: 1955–1971* (Paris: OECD, 1973); *Rates of Change in Economic Data for Ten Industrial Countries: 1956–1975* (Federal Reserve Bank of St. Louis, October 1976).

inflation and growth in the quantity of money. Inflation is thus most likely to ensue when increases in the money supply outstrip the production of goods and services.

Another monetary variable, interest rates (the price of borrowing money), also affects inflation. Keynesian and monetarist economists disagree about the relation of money supply to interest rates. On the one hand, monetarists like Milton Friedman and William Poole believe that large increases in the money supply produce an expanding economy that leads to a stronger demand for credit; *higher* interest rates thus result. A restricted supply of money causes less expansion in the total output of goods and services; as a consequence, the lower demand for credit produces lower interest rates. On the other hand, Keynesians assume that increases in the money supply stimulate lower interest rates; these two monetary policies should expand total demand, particularly spending on capital investment. Compared with the monetarists, Keynesian economists assign greater significance to interest rates as a cause of inflation. They perceive low interest rates as a stimulus to higher spending and thus to stronger inflationary pressures.[13] How valid are these competing explanations?

Price Rise 1966–1970	Money 1970–1974	Price Rise 1971–1975
4.2%	6.3%	6.8%
3.8	10.8	7.4
4.6	10.9	13.2
2.6	9.9	6.1
4.5	9.5	8.0
4.3	12.3	8.8
3.0	19.6	11.5

NOTE: The Pearson correlation coefficients between changes in the money supply and price increases are as follows:

Dates	r
1960–1965	.69
1965–1970	−.65
1970–1975	.57

Table 5–6 suggests that neither explanation holds completely true. During the 1960s countries with high increases in the money supply had lower interest rates. Between 1965 and 1975 inflation showed a similar or higher association with interest rates than with changes in the money supply. Particularly from 1965 to 1969, the impact of interest rates, compared with the money supply, became crucial. Countries with higher annual increases in the quantity of money experienced lower interest rates and less acute inflation. For example, while at this time the German central bank set the second lowest discount rates (the price of money charged to member commercial banks), the Bank of England charged the highest rate for borrowing money. Germany wound up with the lowest inflation; Britain faced the highest price rises. Similarly, during the early 1970s, more severe inflationary pressures occurred in nations with higher interest rates. Rather than dampening total demand, these high interest rates increased costs, which generated upward price movements.

In all countries except Sweden, interest rates have successively increased during each five-year period from 1960 through 1974; yet inflation has become more acute. Why? Rising interest rates probably constituted both a response to inflationary pressures generated from other

Table 5–5   Inflation, Increases in the Money Supply, and Economic Growth Rate

Country	1960–1964			1961–1965	1965–1969		
	Money[a]	Growth Rate[b]	Difference	Price Rise	Money[a]	Growth Rate[b]	Difference
United States	2.5%	4.0%	−1.5%	1.3%	5.0%	4.3%	0.7%
Canada	5.1	4.9	0.2	1.5	6.6	5.6	1.0
United Kingdom	2.9	3.8	−0.9	3.5	3.2	2.3	0.9
West Germany	9.1	5.7	3.4	2.8	6.7	4.8	1.9
Sweden	6.0	5.1	0.9	3.6	5.7	3.8	1.9
France	13.9	6.2	7.7	3.8	6.0	5.4	0.6
Italy	13.6	4.8	8.8	4.9	14.5	2.5	12.0

[a]Annual increases in M1.

[b]Annual rates of change in the real gross national product. (For Sweden, the growth figures indicate changes in the real gross *domestic* product.)

SOURCE: *Rates of Change in Economic Data for Ten Industrial Countries: 1956–1975* (Federal Reserve Bank of St. Louis, October 1976); *International Financial Statistics* 30 (May and October 1977):362, 334.

sources and a cause of the continuing inflation. As inflation grew worse, interest rates tended to rise. Instead of restricting total spending and causing a drop in prices, interest rates raised costs incurred by consumers, business firms, and local governments. As the price of borrowing money escalated, the increased business costs of securing a loan became expressed in higher prices for the consumer.[14] Higher interest rates thus pushed up costs more than they restrained demand.

Effects of Spending for Capital Investment

Expenditures made by government and private business firms for capital investment stimulate total demand and thereby pull up prices. In this regard, two signs of excess demand include a high level of spending for capital investment and use of capital resources at full levels of capacity. If firms spend a high amount of money for construction, machinery, and equipment, the prices of these producers' goods may escalate, thereby constributing to inflation. Despite this short-run result, over the longer range capital investment stimulates greater productivity

1966–1970	1970–1974			1971–1975
Price Rise	Money[a]	Growth Rate[b]	Difference	Price Rise
4.2%	6.3%	2.4%	3.9%	6.8%
3.8	10.8	5.1	5.7	7.4
4.6	10.9	2.7	8.2	13.2
2.6	9.9	3.5	6.4	6.1
4.5	9.5	3.2	6.3	8.0
4.3	12.3	5.3	7.0	8.8
3.0	19.6	3.9	15.7	11.5

NOTE: The Pearson correlation coefficients between (1) price increases and (2) the difference between increases in the money supply and increases in the real GNP are as follows:

Dates	r
1960–1965	.73
1965–1970	−.54
1970–1975	.66

and increases the supply of demanded goods. Under the latter condition inflationary tendencies may subside.

As shown in table 5–7, the correlation between gross fixed capital formation and price rises from 1965 to 1975 seems negligible. Apparently, the short-run and long-run effects of capital investment cancel each other. The evidence reveals only a modest tendency for prices to decline as capital investment as a percentage of the GNP grows. Moreover, no clear pattern of rising capital investment emerges during the 1970s, relative to the late 1960s. Although the United Kingdom, West Germany, France, and Italy all experienced a slight growth of capital investment in the 1970s, capital formation fell in the United States, Canada, and Sweden. For these reasons, capital investment showed no tendency in all seven nations to stimulate aggregate demand and thereby raise the general level of prices.

Another indicator of excess demand, high use of plant capacity, played a limited part in explaining the severe inflation which developed after 1973. Manufacturing firms actually operated at fuller plant capacity before 1973 than after that year. Not only in the United States but in other Western countries as well, manufacturers began to operate at

Table 5–6 Inflation and Interest Rates

Country	Interest Rate[a] 1960–1964	Price Rise 1961–1965	Interest Rate 1965–1
United States	3.3%	1.3%	5.0%
Canada	3.8	1.5	6.1
United Kingdom	5.3	3.5	7.2
West Germany	3.2	2.8	4.2
Sweden	4.6	3.6	5.9
France	3.7	3.8	4.9
Italy	3.5	4.9	3.6

[a]Official discount rates, percent per year.

NOTE: The Pearson correlation coefficients between interest rates and price rises are as follows:

Dates	r
1960–1965	.25
1965–1970	.76
1970–1975	.56

lower levels of plant capacity in 1973 and 1974.[15] Although demand fell and business production declined, prices escalated at this time. Therefore, high plant capacity use could hardly have acted as a primary factor pulling up demand and contributing to more acute inflation.

In sum, we have seen in this section that the demand-pull approach to inflation neither adequately explains crossnational differences in price increases nor accounts for the surging inflation during the early 1970s. We have explored several indicators of excess demand supposedly associated with inflation: (1) low levels of consumer saving; (2) high government expenditures, low tax revenues, and consequent high fiscal deficits; (3) low interest rates and high annual increases in the money supply; (4) high capital investment and high use of plant capacity. The crossnational relationships between inflation, on the one hand, and fiscal deficits, consumer saving, and capital investment, on the other hand, were all quite low. Compared with the late 1960s, the early 1970s saw consumers increase their savings and manufacturers operate their plants at lower levels of capacity. Although the money supply increased, so did interest rates. From 1965 through 1975 high interest rates accompanied high price increases. The relationship between infla-

Price Rise 1966–1970	Interest Rate 1970–1974	Price Rise 1971–1975
4.2%	6.0%	6.8%
3.8	6.3	7.4
4.6	9.1	13.2
2.6	5.5	6.1
4.5	5.8	8.0
4.3	9.0	8.8
3.0	5.7	11.5

The correlation coefficients between interest rates and changes in the money supply are −.42 (1960–1964); −.75 (1965–1969); and .00 (1970–1974).

SOURCE: *Main Economic Indicators, Historical Statistics: 1960–1975* (Paris: OECD, 1976).

tion and the money supply displayed a more ambiguous pattern. During the first part of the 1960s, a sharp growth in the money supply did go along with higher prices. However, from 1965 to 1969 the relationship reversed direction, with increased money correlated with lower price rises. Then, during the first half of the 1970s, a rapid growth in the quantity of money once again became associated with more severe inflation. Finally, fiscal deficits appear a less important reason for inflation than do monetary policies. Between 1965 and 1974 only two societies—Italy and the United States—experienced any fiscal deficits at all government levels. Despite this similar fiscal pattern, Americans lived under less severe inflation than Italians. Compared with the United States, where unbalanced central government budgets were common throughout the 1970s, the central governments in other countries maintained higher fiscal surpluses. Yet, except for Germany, these societies confronted more severe price increases than did the United States. In most countries a fiscal deficit occurred only in 1974 or 1975, when rising unemployment and declining use of plant capacity indicated lower demand. In short, factors other than excessive demand are needed to explain the rising inflation after 1972 and crossnational variations in price changes.

Table 5–7 Inflation and Spending for Capital Investment

Country	Gross Fixed Capital Formation[a] 1965–1969	Price Rises 1966–1970	Gross Fixed Capital Formation 1970–1974	Price Rises 1971—1975
United States	18.1%	4.2%	17.9%	6.8%
Canada	23.3	3.8	22.4	7.4
United Kingdom	18.5	4.6	19.1	13.2
West Germany	24.5	2.6	25.3	6.1
Sweden	23.8	4.5	22.0	8.0
France	23.5	4.3	23.9	8.8
Italy	19.5	3.0	21.2	11.5

[a]Domestic expenditures at current prices on buildings, machinery, and equipment as percentages of the gross national product.

NOTE: The Pearson correlation coefficients between spending on capital investment and price increases are −.25 (1965–1970) and −.40 (1970–1975).

SOURCE: See *National Accounts of OECD Countries, 1975* (Paris: OECD, 1977), vol. 2.

Cost-Push Explanations for Inflation

Unlike the demand-pull approach to inflation, the cost-push explanation assumes that prices do not necessarily fall when demand remains constant or declines. Rather, powerful institutions, such as concentrated industries, labor unions, and government agencies, create market imperfections and thereby push up prices. Large corporations administer prices that do not respond to changes in aggregate demand. Rather than stemming primarily from excess total demand, increased prices reflect the higher costs of supplies, including labor, raw materials, capital, interest rates, and taxes. The desire to maximize long-range profits encourages corporations to fix their prices at a certain level above these costs. Where fully competitive markets do not operate, inflation partly represents a profit-push phenomenon. Similarly, powerful labor unions seek to maximize their own economic interests, such as higher real wages and more favorable fringe benefits. Under wage-push conditions, unions secure annual wage settlements that greatly exceed increases in labor output per hour. Corporations pass on these wage hikes to the consumer in the form of higher prices. In combination with unions and especially corporations, government agencies push up costs by restricting competition. Although wage and price controls or administrative regulation of private business activities may temporarily restrict price rises, over the long run they may curtail the competitive market and thereby accelerate inflationary tendencies. Finally, high taxes and interest rates raise both business and labor costs.

In short, all three institutions—concentrated industries, labor unions, and government—propel costs upward beyond total demand and increased productivity. Through their impact on the market, they also restrict supplies of goods and services. The relative insensitivity of prices to changes in demand, combined with the reduced output, produce severe inflationary trends. Under oligopolistic conditions, prices no longer so readily respond to the changes in supply and demand associated with a competitive market.

Although the demand-pull explanation assumes a fully competitive market where supply and demand come into an eventual equilibrium, the cost-push explanation asserts that imperfect competition characterizes the most important sectors of the economy. According to the model of perfect competition, the following four conditions exist: (1) Each firm controls only a small part of the market. (2) A business enterprise has complete freedom to move to areas of the market where demand for a product is high and supplies of that good are low. (3) Each product, like a car or television set, produced by different firms has a similar design and style; consumers purchase the product solely because of price considerations. (4) Prices respond to changes in demand and quantities of the good supplied. When demand for the product declines, the firm lowers both wages and prices.

In contrast, cost-push explanations of inflation assume that the economies of contemporary Western societies are not fully competitive. Instead, the following conditions of imperfect competition generate upward price movements: (1) Concentrated industries dominate key sectors of the whole economy as well as a large part of each product market. (2) Large corporations restrict the entry of new firms into markets where high demand and low supply exist for a good or service. (3) The same product produced by different firms differs in style and design; these features, not just price alone, guide consumer purchases. (4) Prices respond not only to changes in demand but more importantly to changes in the costs of supplies. Government policies and labor union actions exert powerful upward pressures on these costs. As a consequence, when demand falls the concentrated industry cuts production, rather than wages or prices.[16] In the following sections, we elaborate on the impacts of concentrated industries, government, and labor unions on cost-push inflation.

The Impact of Concentrated Industries

The oligopolistic market power of an industrial firm denotes both extensive control over the whole economy and high concentration within a particular product market, such as steel, oil, electricity, automobiles, furniture, and food. Several measures are used to assess a concentrated industry's power over the whole market, including the percentage of the gross national product or total output produced by the 100 largest firms, the percentage of the work force employed in the 100 largest firms, and the proportion of sales and assets secured by the top 100 enterprises. Similarly, concentration within a particular product market refers to such indicators as the percentage of total sales or assets earned by the four largest firms, the share of all industry shipments controlled by the top four corporations, and the proportion of the labor force working in the four largest enterprises. According to conventional definitions, a *tight* oligopoly exists when four producers control more than 40 percent of a market. A *loose* oligopoly occurs with a concentration ratio between 20 and 40 percent. When the four largest sellers earn less than 20 percent of sales within a product market, effective competition exists.[17]

Throughout North America and Western Europe, large-scale enterprises, such as government-owned firms, state holding firms, joint private-government enterprises, and privately owned concentrated industries, control the most crucial sectors of the economy, including transportation, communication, electricity, banking, and the manufacturing of capital goods (heavy industry, plants, machinery and equipment). For example, the highest degree of concentration exists within markets for key industrial inputs: transportation equipment, machinery, oil, coal, chemicals, rubber, and electrical equipment. The banking business reveals particularly high concentration. On the European continent, central banks and a few private banks together make most financial decisions.

Although in North America the central banks occupy a less powerful position than they do in Europe, a few privately owned banks exercise considerable economic control in both Canada and the United States. In Canada five private "chartered" banks—the Royal Bank, Canadian Imperial Bank of Commerce, Toronto Dominion Bank, Bank of Nova Scotia, and Bank of Montreal—hold slightly more than 90 percent of all bank deposits. U.S. data indicate that the 100 largest commercial banks retain nearly 50 percent of all deposits. More important than this modest concentration ratio is the extensive control exercised by the six biggest banks over nearly one-third of the largest 200 nonfinancial corporations. Through buying stock, supplying credit (loans, bonds), and providing directors to serve on company boards, such financial institutions as Chase Manhattan Bank and the Morgan Guarantee Trust can effectively influence the decisions taken by nonfinancial corporations. This financial control has grown in recent years. As a result, reduced competition, vertical integration (one firm controls all stages of the productive process), and conglomerate mergers (one corporation operates several different industries) have occurred. These tendencies toward growing financial concentration have encouraged higher price increases.[18]

Concentrated industries not only control the most important product markets but also exert a profound effect on the entire economy. All Western market economies contain three different sectors—the government sector, the private nonprofit sector (schools, hospitals, churches), and the private profit-seeking sector. The private profit-oriented sector includes both competitive industries (such as those in light industry, consumer goods, retail sales, and some personal services) and privately owned concentrated industries (e.g., banks, manufacturing, and heavy industry). Although analytically distinct, competitive and concentrated industries are functionally interdependent. Because concentrated industries, either government-owned or privately owned, manufacture so many capital goods—tools, equipment, machinery—as well as vital materials—coal, oil, chemicals, metal, and rubber—competitive industries must purchase these industrial inputs from concentrated firms. For this reason, the prices charged by the oligopolies will raise the costs incurred by competitive firms, thereby increasing their prices as well. Since oligopolistic banks also regulate the interest rates charged to all firms that want to borrow money, these interest charges and other banking techniques for controlling the money supply raise the costs and prices of competitive enterprises.[19] Under these conditions, we cannot easily isolate the separate effects of concentrated and competitive industries on general inflation.

What specific impacts have concentrated industries exerted on prices? Although economists have reached somewhat contradictory conclusions, concentrated industries seem to push up the costs of production and thereby accelerate price rises. Higher profits and higher wages reinforce the general upward movement of prices. When demand for a product declines, the concentrated industry decides to cut production, rather than wages or prices. As a result, inflation continues.

First, concentrated industries operate less efficiently than competitive firms yet still receive higher and more stable long-run profits. According to the theory of pure competition, firms attempt to maximize efficiency by reducing costs and encouraging technical innovations that expand production. The most efficient industries receive the highest rewards or profits. However, under imperfect competition economic rewards do not necessarily spring from technical efficiency but rather from control over a market. Although small firms may lack economies of scale, very large bureaucratic enterprises are also inefficient. The administrative, supervisory, and clerical personnel needed to operate the hierarchical structures do not contribute to efficiency. Lacking such a wasteful hierarchy, medium-sized plants probably have the greatest economies of scale.[20]

If tight oligopolies are inefficient, how do they manage to receive higher long-term profits than more competitive industries? The substantial economic power wielded by concentrated industries enables them to transfer the costs to the consumer. By controlling the entry of new firms into a market, oligopolies can prevent competitors from charging a lower price for a highly demanded good. Compared with competitive firms, concentrated industries spend more money on advertising; these expenditures are associated with higher profits. The large-scale corporations also possess the economic power to purchase goods from competitive firms at a relatively low price and then to sell industrial inputs to them at a higher price. Furthermore, concentrated industries tend to receive the largest share of government contracts, especially in the areas of defense, manufacturing, and space research. Since many government contracts are made through noncompetitive bidding, manufacturers have little incentive to cut costs; hence, prices increase fairly rapidly. Finally, one type of concentrated industry, the multinational corporation, dominates foreign investment. Access to markets overseas enables them to obtain labor and raw materials at a lower price than in the industrial West.[21] Through all these economic advantages, concentrated industries can obtain higher, more stable profits than competitive firms. The profit-push accelerates inflationary pressures on the whole economy.

Second, workers in privately owned concentrated industries tend to receive higher aggregate wages than those employed in the more competitive industries. For instance, during 1976 in every one of seven nations—the United States, Canada, the United Kingdom, West Germany, Sweden, France, and Italy—workers employed in the competitive enterprises (textiles, footwear, and apparel) earned lower hourly wages than those in the more concentrated industries (automobiles, primary metals, chemicals, nonelectric machinery, and electrical equipment). Since these concentrated industries use expensive, complex capital equipment, they hire skilled, well-educated laborers to operate the machines. Compared with unskilled laborers, skilled workers usually command higher wages. Extensive control of the market gives oligopolies the power to pass wage increases on to consumers in the form of higher prices. Because concentrated industries generally earn higher long-term profits, they can grant larger annual wage settlements than more competitive firms. Generally, too, in North America and Western Europe labor unions are strongest in big companies and government. For instance, unions wield greater power in the auto and steel industries than in textile plants, retail sales, or personal services. Rather than opposing the efforts of industrialists to secure higher profits, labor union officials now work closely with corporate heads to increase sales and preserve jobs for workers. Recently, U.S. union leaders supported business lobbies campaigning for low taxes on business, quotas on foreign imports, and cessation of government regulations over corporations. All these actions reinforce the long-range profits of concentrated industries, thus adding to inflationary pressures.[22]

Third, concentrated industries administer prices so that they fail to drop when demand falls. In the more competitive industries prices respond more readily to changing demand; when spending for a particular good drops, the price also declines. Concentrated industries, however, may raise prices even when demand falls, as occurred during the early 1970s, when the U.S. demand for cars and steel dropped while auto and steel prices rose. As a corollary, when demand rises the prices of competitive firms show a faster increase than do prices set by concentrated industries.[23] Nevertheless, the post–World War II period has seen rising prices predominant over falling prices. Relative to the prewar period, since the late 1940s the gap between price increases and marginal costs has grown.

Why do prices keep rising? When demand rises and production approaches full capacity, shortages of materials result; wages also increase with the growing labor shortage. Since production costs rise, so do prices. Yet why do prices fail to decline when demand falls? When demand declines, the producers of a good fear a price war within a particular market. If their rivals lower prices when demand decreases, then all firms will suffer lower profits. The largest producer usually sets the prices for other firms in the same field. The oligopolist also controls a wide range of products, industries, and markets. The growing power of conglomerates (firms manufacturing more than one product) enables them to subsidize losses in one area from gains in other markets. Therefore, when sales begin to decline and an oversupply of a good results, the concentrated industry will probably cut production rather than prices. To maximize long-range profits and gain the funds needed to finance future capital investment, it may choose to raise the price and sell the product to fewer customers. For example, General Motors, Volvo, Renault, or Volkswagen can realize similar profits either by charging $3000 for a car bought by 100 people or by selling the car for $4000 to seventy-five customers. The latter strategy represents a larger "markup" of price over the costs for labor, raw materials, and capital. The effect of the higher markup is to accelerate the overall upsurge of prices.[24]

Despite the tendency of concentrated industries to administer prices so that they fail to respond to falling demand, we should not underestimate the contraints on price-setting that face oligopolies in Western economies. Although inflationary pressures have become more acute since the early 1970s, some price competition still occurs. If consumer purchasing power declines, too rapid a price escalation will cause a drop in sales; at some price peak above costs, the reduced demand will produce lower revenues than those obtained from the higher price. Furthermore, to gain new customers and maximize long-range profits, even the oligopolists at times engage in price cutting. They resort to this strategy if consumers can buy a substitute for the highly priced good. For example, when the retail price of refined fuel oil increased dramatically after 1973, many Europeans switched to solid fuel or gas. Threats by government officials to establish price controls or to regulate more effectively the oligopolies can also encourage lower prices when demand declines. Finally, free trade leads to price competition. The movement of imports into a domestic economy deters home manufacturers from excessive price markups over costs. Before President Nixon devalued the dollar in 1971, an action that raised the price of imported goods, most small foreign automobiles sold at a lower price than those produced in the United States. The presence of foreign competition held down the prices of American cars made by such concentrated industries as General Motors and Ford Motor Company.[25]

The preceding assumptions about the effects of concentrated industries help explain the inflationary pressures plaguing the Western world during the postwar era. We assume that (1) countries with more acute inflation display a higher extent of economic concentration, (2) during the last ten years the economic power of concentrated industries throughout the Western world has increased. These two assumptions raise the following questions: What is the degree of concentration found in the seven economies? Do concentrated industries in the United States and abroad exercise greater market power now than they did twenty years ago? Let us explore the first question first.

Measuring the degree of concentration within either the whole economy or a particular product market is difficult for the comparative investigator who tries to estimate the relative strength of oligopolistic tendencies. The most widely used indicator of industrial concentration—the concentration ratio or share of the output accounted for by the four largest firms in a product market—is a rather imperfect measure of the power exercised by oligopolies. The concentration ratio applies to national markets; yet consumers must purchase goods in local markets. Although a few corporations may not control the whole national market of a good or service, they may effectively monopolize sales in a particular area. Within a country local concentration ratios exceed regional ratios, which in turn are higher than national concentration figures. Among different nations, concentration ratios are higher for smaller than for larger countries. Furthermore, concentration ratios for a particular product market conceal the massive economic power wielded by conglomerates over the whole economy. For example, in the United States the baking industry has a low concentration ratio, less than 25 percent. However, Hostess Bakery is owned by the conglomerate International Telephone and Telegraph. Therefore, the prices set by Hostess Bakery reflect the resources and preferences of the ITT conglomerate. Finally, concentration ratios do not take into account the degree of vertical integration or joint activities within an industry. For instance, the oil industry shows a modest concentration ratio; the four largest U.S. corporations share about 30 percent of the markets for crude oil production, transportation, refining, and distribution to consumers. Despite this low figure, the largest seven oil companies also reveal high vertical integration and extensive joint activities, as evidenced by interlocking directorates and by joint ownership of oil reserves, production, and pipelines. All these structural features increase interdependence among several oil companies, expand their power over the market, and thereby reduce price competition.[26] Because of the difficulty of accurately estimating the market power of corporations, economists have reached divergent conclusions not only about the extent of industrial concentration in the United States but also about the different strengths of oligopolies in the United States compared with Western Europe.

Economic concentration in most product markets is probably higher in Europe and Canada than in the United States. The Swedish and Canadian economies seem especially dominated by concentrated industries; in Sweden a few domestically owned private firms employ a high proportion of the labor force and control large shares of output. In Canada multinational corporations headquartered in the United States employ over 50 percent of all manufacturing workers. The French and Italian economies are split into two divergent sectors, with very low (under 20 percent) and very high (over 60 percent) concentration ratios. Small-scale family businesses contend with larger-scale private oligopolies, nationalized industries, and state holding companies. Perhaps Britain and West Germany, with their stronger commitment to private enterprise, have concentration ratios similar to those in the United States.[27]

Regardless of the general patterns, some parts of the U.S. market reveal stronger concentration than comparable product markets in Europe. For example, the U.S. automobile and steel industries show less competition. In 1972 General Motors manufactured around 45 percent of the total number of cars produced in the United States. That year in West Germany, however, the largest manufacturer, Volkswagen, produced only 26 percent of the total. Other corporations—General Motors (21%), Ford (12%), Daimler Benz (8%), Renault (7%), and Fiat (5%)—gained over half the remaining share of the market. Defense industries, which consume a far larger part of the total national wealth in the United States than they do abroad, are the most concentrated U.S. industries.[28]

Certain international economic patterns, especially the relationship between foreign trade and overseas investment, suggest that oligopolistic tendencies may be stronger in the United States than abroad. Most

European countries place greater reliance on foreign trade; imported goods provide greater price competition in European than in U.S. markets. For instance, during 1974 total imports as a percentage of the gross domestic product amounted to 26 percent in Sweden, 23 percent in the United Kingdom, 22 percent in Italy and Canada, 18 percent in Germany, 17 percent in France, but only 6 percent in the United States.[29] Particularly within the European Economic Community established after World War II, free trade policies encourage price competition among different national firms.

In contrast to European corporations, U.S. industries have concentrated more on investment overseas than on foreign trade. Although small-scale firms can gain considerable economic advantages from foreign trade, only concentrated industries have the technological capabilities for extensive overseas investment. Therefore, international investment encourages the growth of oligopolies; world trade, however, facilitates market competition and hence reduces inflationary pressures. By encouraging overseas investments through tax incentives, the U.S. government has strengthened the economic power held by the concentrated industries. Many multinational corporations—Coca-Cola, Gillette, Hoover, IBM, National Cash Register—now secure more than 50 percent of their earnings from foreign operations. The largest industrial corporation in the United States, Exxon Oil Company, in 1972 made over two-thirds of its sales abroad.

What are the consequences of overseas investment on the U.S. economy? Oligopolies become more economically powerful. U.S. plants become more inefficient as corporations spend little money for research and development on civilian industrial technology. Americans become vulnerable to foreign states controlling the supplies of needed resources like oil. The resulting concentration of industry leads to severe inflation.[30]

U.S. overseas investment also increases inflationary pressures in Europe. During the early 1970s American banks began to make extensive investments in Europe to earn higher interest rates. The Eurocurrency market expanded in 1973. Eurodollars constitute currency deposits held outside the United States in foreign commercial banks. The largest U.S. banks—Bank of America, Chase Manhattan, Citibank—hold these deposits in their subsidiaries in London, Geneva, Frankfurt, and Paris. The national governments in Europe cannot easily control this Eurocurrency market.[31] The expansion in the supply of Euromoney has partly intensified the inflationary pressures.

In conclusion, economists have found it difficult to draw valid conclusions about the overall extent of concentration in the United

States and European nations. Inflationary tendencies counterbalance trends toward price competition. On the one hand, in the United States the absence of extensive import competition, the reliance on overseas investment rather than foreign trade, and the high percentage of the gross national product allocated to defense industries all strengthen the oligopolies, thus stimulating price rises. On the other hand, historically most European states have not adopted policies committed to price competition. Until the establishment of the European Common Market after World War II, cartels flourished. Even today concentrated industries probably dominate a larger share of particular product markets in Europe than they do in the United States; automobiles and steel are perhaps exceptions. Price fixing and price controls interfere with the competitive market. Compared with the United States, the European state bureaucrats cooperate with private entrepreneurs in setting prices, and thereby reinforce inflationary pressures caused by higher costs, increased aggregate demand, and restricted production.

Even if disagreements exist about the extent of economic concentration across different market economies, most economists do agree that throughout the Western world economic concentration has increased during the last two decades.[32] The growing power of concentrated industries over the whole economy stems mainly from the historical development of technology. Technological advancements have led to vastly expanded production. By increasing communication and transportation capabilities, advanced technology has also integrated national markets. World trade has grown in importance. Large-scale corporate enterprises have the economic power to control most effectively these expanding markets, as well as to purchase the capital equipment needed to expand production. As the market grows larger, mass media advertising becomes more important; the costs of buying the time to advertise on national television and in the written media give concentrated industries greater opportunities than less profitable competitive industries to advertise their products. Rather than stressing price competition, commercials focus on product differentiation—for example, the nonprice differences between a Mustang and a Monza or a Renault and a Volkswagen Rabbit. Buyers are encouraged to purchase an automobile for reasons other than its low price.

During the last twenty years, both the United States and Western Europe have experienced the growing power of concentrated industries. Although U.S. oligopolies may not have expanded their control over particular product markets, they have gained greater power over the whole economy, especially the manufacturing sector. The 1960s in particular saw the 200 largest corporations strengthen their economic power. In 1955 the 200 top enterprises controlled 48 percent of manufacturing sales, held 53 percent of assets, and employed 40 percent of workers; by 1974 these three figures had increased to 63 percent of sales, 67 percent of assets, and 61 percent of total manufacturing employment.[33] Mainly through mergers and the formation of conglomerates, oligopolies enlarged their ability to administer prices throughout the economy. Conglomerates manufacture more than one product; ITT, Gulf and Western, Tenneco, and Litton are among the best known examples. For instance, ITT owns a hotel chain (Sheraton), an insurance company (Hartford), a baking enterprise (Hostess), a grain company (Continental), a car rental agency (Avis), and several other types of business. Through ownership of several different firms, conglomerates can affect prices of various products. One firm within the conglomerate can temporarily lower its price for a product to drive a small-scale competitor out of business. Conglomerates possess the resources to gain control over both the suppliers of raw materials and the retailers selling the finished good. By dominating large sectors of the economy, conglomerates can restrict output and charge higher prices, even when demand falls. As the gap between costs and the consumer price for products widens, inflation becomes more severe.

Just as in the United States, throughout Western Europe the 1960s represented a period of growing economic concentration. More mergers, acquisitions, and conglomerate formations occurred. Within the European Economic Community, industries were more competitive before 1965; the corporate mergers that took place between 1965 and 1968 reinforced the pressure toward price increases. During this period Britain, France, and Germany all experienced increasing industrial concentration, mainly deriving from corporate mergers. The concentrated industries showed less responsiveness to changes in demand than did the more competitive firms. As a result, prices began to soar during the early 1970s.

The Impact of Government

Not only big business but also big government has taken actions that have strengthened cost-push inflation. Government officials work in conjunction with heads of corporations to formulate public policies; their joint decisions often raise the costs of supplies and accelerate rising prices. Let us examine in this section first the effects of fiscal and monetary policies, then regulatory and public ownership policies, and finally incomes policies setting prices and wages.

The fiscal and monetary policies of government can affect inflation either by expanding demand or by increasing the costs of supplies.

Economists assume that although higher taxes may reduce demand for products, they may also raise business costs. As business firms pay higher corporate income, capital gains, property, value-added, and social security taxes, they charge higher prices for retail goods. In this way, taxes "push up" costs and prices.[34] To what extent does this tax-push assumption hold true for the seven nations between 1965 and 1975? According to table 5–3, the twin impacts of taxes counterbalance each other—that is, the low correlations between taxes and general price increases indicate that higher taxes restrict demand to the same degree that they raise business and consumer costs. If anything, particularly during the late 1960s, the cost-push effect seemed slightly greater than the impact on demand.

On the monetary side of the policy ledger, higher interest rates may also increase business costs and thereby accelerate the inflationary pressures. Compared with the impact of taxes on inflation, the consequences of higher interest rates seem clearer. As table 5–6 indicates, in each five-year period from 1961 through 1975, higher interest rates were associated with higher price increases. Throughout the Western world, interest rates rose between the early 1960s and the early 1970s. As Western economies entered their boom period from 1965 through 1973, large corporations incurred higher and higher debts. For example, in the United States corporate debt rose over 100 percent between 1967 and 1974, when it totaled over one trillion dollars. During the mid-1970s corporate debt comprised about 45 percent of the total debt; the public sector debt for all governmental levels accounted for only 23 percent of all debt. The need to finance these debts magnified the costs of interest payments. Corporate firms were reluctant to borrow more money for investment in plants and equipment. Faced with a lack of cash on hand, banks became more cautious about lending any more money. As a consequence of higher interest rates and greater reluctance to borrow or lend, business firms and banks took few actions to expand the supplies of capital and consumer goods. The reduced supplies for highly demanded goods, such as houses, meant more severe inflation.[35]

By restricting competition to a few firms, government regulatory and nationalization policies may also encourage general price increases. Both in the United States and Western Europe certain regulatory policies have reinforced the trends toward concentrated industries. Governments enact import quotas and tariffs on foreign goods that restrict competition from abroad. Government patents establish monopolies over products. In countries like the United States, Britain, France, West Germany, and Sweden, which dominate the world market for arms exports, giant corporations manufacture the armaments; government regulations ensure that these corporations receive the largest share of military contracts both at home and overseas. Neither the U.S. nor European governments give enthusiastic support to antitrust legislation. Government organizations allocate few funds or staff to enforce laws forbidding noncompetitive practices of concentrated industries.[36]

Particularly in the United States, where governments own few industries, regulatory policies toward most enterprises have failed to restrain price increases. The major exceptions lie with such "public monopolies" as gas, electric, and telephone companies; if these monopolies were not regulated, then their prices would probably rise by a slightly larger amount than at present. However, regulatory agencies until recently have contributed to price rises in transportation industries like trucking and airlines. The Interstate Commerce Commission (ICC) places limits on competition within the trucking industry. New firms find it difficult to gain entry into the market. By granting numerous antitrust exemptions, the ICC establishes higher rates but rarely lowers rates. Indeed, it often forbids truckers from taking the shortest route from one place to another. Since the ICC specifies the routes, trucks often carry less than a full load. The lower-than-capacity usage, combined with higher fuel costs, means higher prices. (In Canada, where the provincial governments, rather than the federal government, decide whether or not to regulate trucking firms, freight rates are slightly higher in the regulated than in the unregulated provinces.) Similarly, until 1977 the U.S. Civil Aeronautics Board (CAB) discouraged open competition between airline companies. The CAB restricted entry of new firms into the airline industry, specified air passenger rates, and set minimum fares. Since the airlines could not compete by offering lower fares, they provided more flights and more amenities, like first-run movies. As a result, planes carried less than full loads, unit costs rose, and airline rates remained high. Where airlines operated only within a state, rather than among several states, they escaped CAB regulations; their fares for the same distance were lower than interstate airlines.[37] Beginning in 1977, the president, Congress, and the CAB moved to deregulate the airline industry. The CAB's decision to open existing routes to new firms and to encourage reduced prices for airline tickets helped bring about lower fares for the passenger.

Throughout Western Europe and North America regulatory policies also affect prices by restricting supplies of a demanded good. In particular, agricultural policies raise the prices of farm products by regulating their prices and supplies. In 1972–1973, a period of surging general inflation, the prices for food showed an even more dramatic rise than prices for nonfood products except oil. Why? One reason stemmed from the growing demand for cereals along with involuntary shortages of cereals; that is, drought caused crop shortages, and a corn blight led to poor harvests. Other factors, however, arose from the actions of policy officials to restrict supplies. For instance, in the United States, government policies have strengthened the food oligopolies. The federal government subsidizes the large corporation farms; it has granted export subsidies to wheat growers shipping grain to the Soviet Union, Japan, and West Europe. Multinational corporations like Cargill and Continental sold wheat at a lower price to the Russians than to Americans; then the government subsidized the difference between the domestic and foreign prices. As a result, temporary shortages occurred, reserves were depleted, and domestic prices increased. Besides granting export subsidies which benefited mainly the multinational corporations, the U.S. federal government restricted import competition by placing quotas on imported wheat, peanuts, and dairy products. Beginning in 1933 the Department of Agriculture has also paid farmers for eliminating "excess" produce and for failing to plant crops. Although this policy helped resolve the problem of overproduction caused by advanced agricultural technology, when demand for food suddenly increased or when poor harvests occurred, consumers faced a shortage of farm products. Prices naturally escalated, as happened during the early 1970s.

Canadian and European agricultural policies have exerted a similar inflationary impact. During the early 1970s the federal government in Canada encouraged farmers to limit production of some farm products. By establishing import quotas and tariffs on agricultural goods, European governments restricted supplies at home. Since the Second World War, European political leaders have generally lowered tariffs on industrial goods to a greater extent than those levied on farm products. Since joining the European Economic Community in 1973, Britain has faced rising food prices. Before entry into the EEC, British consumers could purchase inexpensive farm produce from the Commonwealth countries, mainly Australia, New Zealand, and Canada. However, membership in the EEC raised the prices paid by the British for food, since the Common Customs Tariff established duties on goods imported into Britain from outside the Common Market. Because of price support programs and policies limiting agricultural production in the EEC, farm imports from Europe cost more than food originating from the Commonwealth countries prior to 1973.[38] In sum, throughout both North America and Europe, agricultural policies have restricted supplies and benefited the large-scale mechanized farms more than the small producers. As a result, during the 1970s agricultural competition declined and food prices showed a dramatic increase.

Economists also assume that public ownership policies have strength-ened inflationary trends. Compared with the situation in the United States, nationalized industries abroad control a larger share of diverse markets. Basic industries like oil, steel, gas, electricity, railroads, and airlines often operate under public ownership. Since public corporations in these basic sectors of the economy cannot be allowed to go bankrupt, the officials managing them must either keep wages down or else raise prices. The power of unions and the threat of strikes motivate managers to choose the option of price increases. If the state firms operate at a deficit, then political leaders often choose to finance the operations of these firms through tax increases. If deficits continue, central banks may expand the money supply to repay the debts. If the goods produced by a nationalized firm, like the steel industry, do not sell in the domestic market, the government may raise tariffs on competing imports. All four policies—increased prices charged by the nationalized industries, higher taxes, an expanded money supply, and higher tariffs—may stimulate general inflationary pressures.[39]

Despite the persuasiveness of these assumptions about the inflation-ary impacts of public industries, the evidence remains somewhat ambig-uous. Although few empirical studies have been conducted, one investi-gation analyzed the prices levied by public corporations and private enterprises in Britain between 1949 and 1973. The investigation found that both types of firms showed similar annual rates of price changes. Beginning with the mid 1960s, prices in the private manufacturing industries actually rose slightly faster than prices set by such public corporations as the National Coal Board, British Railways, British Gas Corporation, the Post Office, and British European Airways. After 1973, however, price increases of the nationalized industries exceeded those of private firms.[40] If nationalized firms really do cause price rises, their inflationary impact probably derives less from their direct effect on prices than from their indirect effects on taxes, the money supply, and tariffs.

Like the consequences of nationalized industries, the inflationary impact of incomes policies also remains ambiguous. According to the theory of concentrated industries, policies restraining wage and price increases should curtail cost-push inflation but not inflation deriving from excess demand. When demand declines, concentrated industries tend to cut production, rather than prices or wages. Long-term profits remain higher than those secured by more competitive industries. When formulating an incomes policy, government leaders intend that it will exert the following effects: First, since prices are allowed to rise at only a modest rate, concentrated industries have no incentive to reduce production; thus no shortages should result, as would happen in a demand-pull inflation. Second, competitive firms that purchase industrial inputs from the concentrated industries can also lower their price increases. Third, the incomes policy will curtail wage hikes exceeding increases in production. Fourth, concentrated industries will no longer secure "excess" or "windfall" profits that greatly exceed the costs of production. Fifth, the wage and price controls will lower expectations about future price rises and thus should dampen the inflation originating from excessive spending.[41] To what extent have the incomes policies pursued since 1960 realized these five intended effects?

The evidence suggests that, in practice, incomes policies have exerted only a limited impact on controlling inflation.[42] Because several factors other than wage and price controls influence inflation rates, economists cannot easily isolate the particular effect of incomes policies. The short-term consequences seem more significant than the long-term impact. For instance, between 1971 and 1974 the wage and price controls administered by the Nixon administration did not lead to a long-range price decline. For a short time in 1971 and 1972 the prices of concentrated industries experienced a smaller percentage rise than those of more competitive industries; the Cost of Living Council effectively controlled the prices of the largest corporations. In 1972, one year after the introduction of the program, manufacturing wages increased only 5.5 percent, exactly the figure recommended by the Pay Board. Nevertheless, after the Nixon administration lifted the mandatory controls in early 1973, the prices set by the concentrated industries began to accelerate faster than those of more competitive firms. Wage increases in 1973 and 1974 rose to over 7 percent and 10 percent, as manufacturing workers strove to regain the purchasing power lost in 1973. The controls apparently failed to cause a long-range overall lessening of inflationary pressures; yet the extent to which the wage and price increases after 1972 stemmed from a lifting of the controls remains unclear. A number of inflation-causing events took place in 1972 and 1973, including crop shortages, rising demand for food, and the fourfold increase in OPEC oil prices.

Throughout the 1960s and 1970s incomes policies in Canada and Western Europe also failed to exert a dramatic effect on curtailing inflation. Why? Some countries sought to restrain either wage increases, as in Germany, or price rises, as in France, but not both. Simultaneous controls over both wages and prices appear more effective, mainly because controls on wages only will reduce the purchasing power of the workers and will encounter opposition from unions. A policy to control only prices will increase the costs of production and accelerate cost-push inflation.

In the market economies of the Western world, unions and corporations have independence from the government. Western capitalist economies are more pluralistic than Eastern Europe economies; there the government and dominant party control the unions, and state-owned firms, rather than privately owned corporations, dominate the production and sale of products. Eastern European governments have the effective power to regulate both wages and prices, but democratic governments lack this power. In the West, the enforcement machinery to implement wage and price controls remains ineffective, understaffed, and underfinanced. Rather than controlling unions and corporations, Western governments often seem controlled by them. For example, in Britain the incomes policies implemented by the Labour and Tory governments depend upon securing a voluntary "social contract" with the unions. If the unions decide that a 10 percent annual wage increase no longer seems fair, then they can reject that wage limitation, threaten a strike, or actually go out on strike. Unlike the situation in Sweden, where the central labor federation controls member unions and negotiates directly with centrally organized employer associations, the British collective bargaining situation is more pluralistic. The central Trades Union Congress exercises only limited power over member unions, which negotiate wage agreements and decide when to call a strike. As in Britain, elsewhere in Europe heads of concentrated industries, like unionists, want to retain the autonomy to engage freely in collective bargaining. Under these pluralistic conditions, a mandatory incomes policy imposed by the government becomes difficult to implement. Union members reject wage controls when their purchasing power declines. Corporation executives reject price controls when the costs of production begin to escalate and profit margins fall. Although incomes policies may be desirable in restraining cost-push inflation, they appear difficult to administer effectively over a long-term period.

The Impact of Labor Unions

Particularly since the end of World War II, labor unions in Western countries have gained sufficient market power to influence cost-push inflation. Both unions and concentrated industries seek to maximize their economic returns. Corporations desire higher long-range profits; unions strive to maximize wages and fringe benefits. The search for higher profits leads to profit-push inflation; when wage increases exceed gains in workers' productivity, wage-push inflation results. Often wages in the more efficient, productive, and heavily unionized industries set the pattern for less efficient enterprises. Under these conditions, wages drift upward as the favorable settlements gained in certain industries spill over to other sectors of the economy. Except in the United States, nonunion employees receive the same benefits won by unions in collective bargaining agreements. Of course, unions do not operate in an economic vacuum independent of other variables affecting general inflation rates. Whatever the original cause of price increases, union officials attempt to avert a decline in their members' purchasing power. Workers demand higher wages to maximize their real take-home pay—that is, their wages less taxes and general price rises. Yet, if the wage explosion occurs when the economy faces a recession and high unem-

Table 5–8 Inflation and Manufacturing Unit Labor Costs

| Country | 1965–1969 | | | | 1966–19 |
	Wages[a]	Output per Hour[b]	Differ- ence[c]	Unit Labor Costs[d]	Price Rises
United States	5.1%	2.3%	2.8%	2.9%	4.2%
Canada	7.1	4.5	2.6	2.4	3.8
United Kingdom	7.2	3.8	3.4	3.2	4.6
West Germany	7.9	6.2	1.7	1.7	2.6
Sweden	9.8	7.6	2.2	2.0	4.5
France	8.3	6.7	1.6	1.6	4.3
Italy	7.4	6.7	0.7	0.8	3.0

[a]Annual percentage change in hourly compensation in manufacturing.

[b]Average annual percentage change in output per hour (total output divided by the number of hours worked by all employees in manufacturing).

[c]Difference between the wage increases and labor output.

[d]Unit labor costs in national currency indicate the ratio of hourly labor costs to output per hour performed by workers in manufacturing industries.

NOTE: The Pearson correlation coefficients between price increases and each of three indicators of labor costs are as follows:

ployment rates (a time of decreased demand for labor), wage increases that exceed output reinforce cost-push inflationary pressures.[43] Let us examine the validity of the wage-push assumption by looking first at wage increases for manufacturing workers and then at wage increases secured by government employees.

As table 5–8 indicates, in nations where manufacturing labor costs are high and a large gap separates annual wage increases from the growth in labor output, the most marked inflation rates occur. Indeed, during both time periods—1965–1970 and 1970–1975—the relationships of the two labor variables to price increases are among the highest

	1970–1974				1971–1975
Wages	Output per Hour	Differ-ence	Unit Labor Costs	Price Rises	
7.3%	1.9%	5.4%	5.5%	6.8%	
8.6	3.2	5.4	5.4	7.4	
15.4	3.4	12.0	11.7	13.2	
14.0	5.4	8.6	8.2	6.1	
12.7	5.5	7.2	7.2	8.0	
13.6	5.4	8.2	7.8	8.8	
20.5	6.8	13.7	12.8	11.5	

Variable	Dates	r
Difference between Wage Increases and Output per Hour	1965–1970	.66
	1970–1975	.82
Unit Labor Costs	1965–1970	.63
	1970–1975	.85
Wage Increases	1965–1970	.06
	1970–1975	.67

SOURCE: Barbara Boner and Arthur Neef, "Productivity and Unit Labor Costs in 12 Industrial Countries," *Monthly Labor Review* 100 (July 1977):15–16; U. S. Department of Labor, Bureau of Labor Statistics, *Handbook of Labor Statistics 1976* (Washington, D.C.: Government Printing Office, 1976), p. 333; *Handbook of Labor Statistics 1975–Reference Edition,* (Washington, D.C.: Government Printing Office, 1975), p. 438.

associations we have found. Both unit labor costs and the difference between wage increases and the growth in labor output measure a similar phenomenon; "unit labor cost" means the ratio of hourly labor costs to output per hour. Not surprisingly, then, the relationships among (1) unit labor costs and (2) the difference between hourly compensation and output per hour, on the one hand, and (3) price increases on the other, yield approximately the same correlations. By contrast, between 1965 and 1970, the statistical association between inflation and hourly compensation was quite low, suggesting that if labor output keeps up with wage increases severe price increases should not result.

Crossnationally, the ability of manufacturing workers to secure high wage increases depends partly on the power of their unions. In Canada and the United States, where unions are weaker than in Northern Europe, wage gains from 1965 to 1974 were the lowest for all seven countries. Since output per hour was also relatively low, these two nations demonstrated the lowest unit labor costs and also comparatively small price rises. In contrast, in Britain and Italy unit labor costs were highest, and wage increases most exceeded output per hour. After World War II British unions grew more powerful; they encouraged rising wages in all sectors of the economy. Indeed, between 1949 and 1967, in both unionized and nonunionized industries, employees received roughly equal wage gains.[44] Similarly, during the 1970s Italian unions began to achieve greater solidarity against employers. As a result, wages rose rapidly in both the public and private manufacturing sectors. Like the British, the Italians had to cope with acute inflation. Swedish and German unions have gained moderately high wage increases. Yet, unlike U.S. or British unions, they more enthusiastically supported management efforts to expand labor output per hour. Since unit labor costs were therefore lower in Sweden and Germany than in Britain, inflation posed a less severe economic threat.

Most important, the rise in unit labor costs also largely explains the changes in inflation rates over time. In every one of the seven societies, unit labor costs grew between the last part of the 1960s and the first half of the 1970s; accordingly, inflation became more serious. Particularly from 1972 and 1974, as unit labor costs rose faster during each successive year, prices also showed a higher annual increase.

How have salaries paid to government workers affected inflation rates? Especially during the period after the Second World War, government employment as a percentage of the total civilian labor force rose. Today government employees constitute between 15 percent and 30 percent of the work force in most Western industrial societies. Particularly in Canada and Western Europe, unions of government workers have become politically important. As a consequence of greater union power, government employees have secured high wage increases. Even though most government workers show lower gains in productivity than do employees in the private manufacturing sector, the wages gained by manufacturing workers often set the standards for publicly employed personnel.

The crossnational evidence reveals no consistent trend for all government workers to secure higher earnings than comparable private sector employees. Even though U.S. clerical workers employed by the largest cities' governments earn more than their counterparts in private industry, skilled maintenance workers in city government receive lower wages than do workers in the private sector. U.S. federal government workers earn slightly higher salaries than similarly placed private business employees. In Britain no marked differences separate the wages of workers in the private and public sectors. Especially during the 1970–1972 period, public employees won only slightly higher wage gains than did workers employed by private industries. However slight the wage differential, public wage increases followed, rather than preceded, the increased earnings in the private sector. Perhaps because of the power of German labor unions and their links with the Social Democratic party governing Germany, from 1969 to 1974 German public sector unions obtained larger salary raises than those received by workers in private manufacturing industries.

France and Italy represent contrasting approaches to the issue of compensation for public and private employees. In France most public employees earn less than do their counterparts in private industry. Between 1965 and 1975 they secured lower pay increases than did workers employed by private manufacturing firms. Gaullist officials have governed France since 1968, and they have displayed little inclination to accept the high wage claims pressed by the Confédération Générale du Travail. Dominant in the public sector, this union has close ties with the French Communist party. In Italy, however, Communist party leaders and the governing Christian Democrats have achieved greater rapport since the late 1960s. The Christian Democrats appear willing to accept the pay demands made by public sector employees in the CGIL, the General Confederation of Italian Labor, which is aligned with the Communist party. Unlike government employees in some other European countries, Italian civil servants have even won the legal right to strike. Supported by the government, Italian private manufacturers have resisted union demands for higher wages. As a result of these relationships among government, unions, and private businesses, Italians employed by privately owned firms appear disadvantaged, since they earn lower salaries than those in similar occupations in the public sector. Among the various types of public agencies, workers in the state holding companies, such as the IRI and ENI, obtain the highest compensation, followed by employees in the nationalized industries and state officials working for the post office. Only managers employed by private industries secure higher salaries than any of their counterparts in the public sector.[45] These wage patterns partly account for the severe inflation facing Italians during the 1970s.

Despite the contradictory evidence and the Italian case, wages paid to public employees are not the primary variable behind accelerating price rises. More often than not, wages obtained by powerful unions in private manufacturing industries set the pay standards for government workers. Since labor unions most effectively represent people employed by government and concentrated manufacturing industries, these two groups have generally gained higher pay raises than have employees in the private service sector.

In sum, comparisons across nations and time periods indicate that, especially during the 1970s, the cost-push explanations of inflation accounted for much of the rapid price increase. Labor unions, concentrated industries, and government agencies pushed up costs. In Western Europe, unions and socialist parties exerted more dominant power over the market than they did in the United States or Canada. As a consequence, workers secured high wage increases relative to the growth in labor productivity. The higher unit labor costs meant higher inflation. Because of measurement difficulties, the crossnational impact of concentrated industries on inflation has been more difficult to trace. Although price rises have generally been higher in most European countries than in the United States, we cannot be certain that European concentrated industries are more powerful. The greater import competition in Europe is balanced by the more pervasive presence of nationalized industries, cartels, price controls, and price fixing. Yet the concentration in most product markets is probably higher in Europe than in the United States. In neither North America nor Western Europe do government policies encourage free competition and reduced business costs. Everywhere higher taxes and particularly higher interest rates have increased business and consumer costs. Although the pattern remains somewhat ambiguous, regulatory policies in the United States and public ownership policies in Europe have failed to check rising costs. Because of the economic power exercised by trade unions and concentrated industries over government leaders, incomes polices to control wages and prices have also exerted a limited long-term impact.

Compared with the crossnational impact of big government, big labor, and big business in the short run, the long-term trends seem clearer. Since World War II all three institutions have increased their market power. With the rise of the corporate state, government officials play a more powerful role in the formulation and implementation of economic policy. The stronger postwar power of unions and socialist parties partly explains the upward drift of wages. Contrary to the assumptions of the demand-pull approach, wages no longer fall when demand for labor declines. During the late sixties and early seventies, as the degree of industrial concentration increased in both North America and Europe, inflation grew worse. The greater power of conglomerates and the wave of mergers meant that prices became less sensitive to the competitive market forces of changes in demand. When unemployment grew more extensive and a recession hit the Western economies, prices continued to rise, rather than fall. Cuts in production, not cuts in prices, became the more frequent response to falling demand. The impact of these developments on groups at the bottom of the social stratification system was especially severe.

The Effects of Inflation

During the post–World War II era inflation has exerted a crucial impact on both the economic and political systems. From the economic perspective, how do rapid price increases affect the functioning of the whole economy? Which economic groups gain and lose from severe inflation? From the political standpoint, how do sharp price rises influence the legitimacy of the system, including the leaders holding government office?

Inflation has rather contradictory impacts on the whole economy— that is, on the interaction between aggregate demand and supply. On the one hand, rapid price increases over 5 percent a year will in certain respects *decrease* total demand. As individuals and business firms earn more nominal money, they move into higher tax brackets under a progressive tax system; thus, their "real" tax burden increases. The results are reduced consumption and investment, signs of depressed demand. Higher real taxes encourage support for lower government spending. Even if government officials refrain from reducing existing expenditures, the budget may still decrease demand. Why? Under inflationary pressures, the same amount of money purchases fewer goods and services than before. If high interest rates accompany escalating prices, as they did during the period from 1965 to 1975, these interest rates may also depress spending on consumption and investment. Inflation also brings economic insecurity and uncertainty. Plagued by the difficulties of predictive future prices, individuals may decrease consumption but increase their savings. If businesses choose not to borrow funds for investment, aggregate demand will fall. A recession may result from all these expressions of lower total demand.

On the other hand, especially if rapid price increases are anticipated, expanded demand may result, at least in the short run. For example, if businesses expect that the costs of capital will rise faster in the future, they may accelerate current investment spending. Similarly, consumers who anticipate that future prices will increase more rapidly than current prices will expand their consumer expenditures.

The effects of inflation on aggregate supply also seem unclear. On the one hand, inflation apparently stimulates the production of durable goods, including houses, automobiles, and physical capital (plants and equipment); people perceive that these tangible goods will cost far more in the future yet will retain their use beyond a year. On the other hand, when inflationary pressures become particularly severe, the production of nondurable goods and human services tends to decline.

Inflation also brings greater uncertainty to the production process. Because individual consumers, government officials, and private business executives lack accurate information about future price rises, they fail to plan production for the long-term period. At a time when the purchasing power of money is declining, people engage in short-term speculative activities that will bring them the most money, whether or not their economic activities contribute to greater productive efficiency.[46]

What is the effect of inflation on income distribution? Which economic groups suffer the greatest losses? Although answers to these questions depend on such variables as the inflation rate, the unemployment level, effective tax rates, and allocation of government services, generally the politically powerless bear the greatest burdens. These include the poor, elderly people, workers who do not belong to unions, small-scale entrepreneurs, and owners of small farms.[47] All these groups lack the institutional strength to protect themselves from rising prices. In the emerging corporate state, they cannot rely on powerful labor unions or concentrated industries to press their demands. Government policies may fail to check accelerating prices, especially for food, health care, housing, and fuel. For this reason, inflation accentuates their economic problems.

Specific empirical studies have substantiated these general notions about the consequences of inflation on income distribution. Most research has been carried out in the United States. Let us first compare income groups in the United States between 1950 and 1975. Afterwards, we examine one occupational group, manufacturing workers, in seven different countries from 1961 through 1975.

According to economists studying the United States, whereas the poor and aged suffer the most from rapid price increases, young people and the middle- and upper-middle-income groups undergo fewer losses. Why? Groups with high debts and large holdings of variable-price assets (land, autos, housing) tend to experience the least economic losses during an inflationary period. In contrast, those holding low debts but high shares of their income in monetary assets (bank accounts, currency, bonds) suffer greater disadvantages from inflation. For these reasons, during the period from 1950 through 1972 the very poor (those with less than $3,000 pretax income in 1969) suffered the most; they had few debts but also few variable-price assets. The little money they possessed was held in checking accounts that paid no interest, or else in savings accounts earning a low rate of interest, usually lower than general price increases. Both tax and spending policies failed to cushion the inflationary impact. As their nominal (pretax, preinflation) earnings increased, they paid higher federal income taxes as a proportion of their income. Yet their after-tax spendable income increased less than price rises. The percentage increase in after-tax income was lower for people earning $5,000 than for individuals making between $5,000 and $20,000. Public transfers—payments such as Aid to Families with Dependent Children, unemployment insurance, and general public assistance—generally did not rise as fast as general increases in the cost of living. Even though social security benefits were adjusted upward twice a year when inflation occurred, people over fifty-five and retired people on a fixed income, like a private pension, endured severe hardships during inflation. Creditors, particularly banks and savings associations that failed to anticipate inflation and thus did not raise their interest rates, also suffered losses. In contrast, other groups with either high debts or variable-priced assets endured fewer losses. These groups included young people between twenty-five and thirty-four as well as middle- and upper-middle- income individuals, particularly professionals who earned between $10,000 and $25,000 in 1969. These groups had debts but also owned homes and automobiles. The value of the houses increased faster than mortgage rates.[48] Although property taxes also increased, these professionals still possessed a highly demanded variable-price asset that would bring a high price if sold on the market.

The major difference between the 1950–1972 period and the 1972–1975 period in the United States derives from the different impacts of inflation on wage and salary earners. During the fifties and sixties, periods of moderate inflation, corporate businessmen and farmers suffered more hardships than did wage and salary earners. Wealthy bondholders lost money. Corporate profits as a percentage of the national income fell at the same time that wages and salaries as a share of the national income rose. Particularly between 1960 and 1964, unemployment began to decline while prices remained fairly stable. The unskilled, skilled, and white-collar workers hence benefited the most. After 1964, professionals—engineers, chemists, accountants, attorneys—increased their purchasing power faster than did the skilled, unskilled, and white-collar workers.[49] However, between 1972 and 1975 the economic situation of wage and salary earners declined. Their share of the national income decreased as wages rose less than prices. As we have observed, food and fuel costs escalated after 1972. Since wage and salary earners spent a large share of their incomes for food, housing, and energy, their purchasing power particularly declined. In contrast, some farmers, especially the large-scale agribusinesses, and some corporations, mainly oil companies, experienced considerable gains from the severe inflation. Unlike the earlier period, between 1972 and 1975 their profits as a percentage of the national income increased.

In short, unless unemployment drops to around 1 percent of the labor force and transfer payments increase, the very poor suffer the most from inflation. The impact of inflation on other economic groups tends to vary, depending on the specific rate of price increases, the level of unemployment, interest rates, and the returns from bonds and common stocks. Certainly the conjunction of high inflation and high unemployment that became more pronounced during the early 1970s brought severe disadvantages to wage and salary earners.

From a crossnational perspective, between 1961 and 1975 U.S. manufacturing workers endured greater economic losses from inflation than did European workers. Table 5–9 shows the gains in average real hourly earnings obtained by wage workers in manufacturing; "real" earnings mean the increases in disposable income or purchasing power after deductions for price increases but before tax deductions. According to the table, in each of the three five-year periods, U.S. workers secured the lowest increase in hourly earnings. Although Italian workers earned a lower real wage than did Americans, the Italians won the largest pay raises. Over time the average increase in Americans' real wages, adjusted for inflation, tended to decline from the early 1960s through the first half of the 1970s. In contrast, the real wages earned by Canadian, French, and Italian workers showed successive rises. During the 1970s, U.S. manufacturing workers made fewer economic gains, compared with both their economic position ten years earlier and with the benefits secured by workers in other countries, especially Canada, France, Italy, Germany, and Sweden.

Inflation influences not only the economic performance of a society but also its political stability. Especially in Western democratic societies, rapid price increases may undermine the popular support granted to incumbent government officeholders, and may even threaten the legitimacy of the whole political system, as happened in Germany during the 1920s. An individual evaluates political leaders partly on the basis of their success in securing concrete economic benefits, including price stability and full employment. When government officials fail to obtain these goals, their popularity may begin to wane. For example, in the United States between 1953 and 1975, both inflation and unemployment affected the president's popular support. As the unemployment rate increased by one percentage point, the president's popularity decreased by 4 percent in the Gallup poll. As prices rose 1 percent a year, presidential popularity declined by one-half to one percentage point. In Britain, from 1962 through 1974, similar effects resulted. For each one percentage point rise in the unemployment rate, the popularity of the

Table 5–9 Real Hourly Earnings of Wage Workers in Manufacturing

Country	Annual Percentage Change in Real Hourly Earnings[a]		
	1961–1965	*1966–1970*	*1971–1975*
United States	1.6	0.9	0.7
Canada	1.8	3.3	3.6
United Kingdom	2.4	3.6	2.6
West Germany	6.5	5.2	4.3
Sweden	4.4	4.3	3.6
France	3.3	5.3	5.4
Italy	6.1	6.8	8.6

[a]Figures refer to the percentage changes in the average hourly earnings of wage workers in manufacturing; the earnings have been adjusted for changes in purchasing power since the base period (1967).

SOURCE: U. S. Department of Labor, Bureau of Labor Statistics, *Handbook of Labor Statistics 1976* (Washington, D.C.: Government Printing Office, 1976), p. 337; *Handbook of Labor Statistics 1975–Reference Edition* (Washington, D.C.: Government Printing Office, 1975), p. 441.

party controlling the government fell by 6 percent. As the inflation rate increased by 1 percent, the party holding government office lost about 0.6 of a percentage point in the British Gallup poll.[50] To the extent that neither the Labourites nor the Conservatives could cope effectively with economic problems, popular alienation from both major parties grew.

Inflation also contributed to the Swedish Social Democrats' fall from power in the 1976 election. Between 1932 and 1976 they governed Sweden, usually in a coalition with other parties. During the 1968 election the Social Democratic party won 50 percent of the popular vote, the highest plurality since the close of World War II. That year the inflation rate was only 2 percent; only 2 percent of the work force was unemployed. However, as prices began to rise after 1968, support for the Social Democrats declined. In 1970 they obtained only 45 percent of the total vote and in 1973, just 44 percent. Between 1974 and 1976 annual price increases escalated to the highest levels of the postwar era, around 10 percent a year. Although jobless rates were under 2 percent and most Swedes favored the social service programs implemented by the Social Democratic government, they resented the high taxes and the government's failure to restrain rising prices. As a consequence, popular support for the Social Democrats declined to 43 percent in 1976. Their inability to form a coalition with any of the three major nonsocialist parties—Conservatives, Liberals, and Center—meant that for the first time in 44 years the Socialists no longer controlled the executive.[51]

As the case of Weimar Germany (1919–1933) illustrates, when high inflation and high unemployment occur during the same ten-year period, the backlash against the existing democratic government may lead to the disintegration of the entire political system, not just to the downfall of the incumbent leaders. Between 1922 and 1923 Germany experienced a hyperinflation; in July 1922 the wholesale price index was 101, and by November 1923 it had jumped to 750 billion. By the end of 1923 over one-fourth of the German labor force was unemployed. The double impact of inflation and unemployment brought economic devastation to most German people. Purchasing power drastically declined. Savings disappeared. Which groups bore the greatest burdens? Skilled and unskilled workers, small shopkeepers, lower-ranking civil servants, and professionals like lawyers and doctors endured the greatest sacrifices. Groups that held tangible property and possessed the money to purchase bankrupt businesses tended to profit from the hyperinflation. Unfortunately for German democracy, the economic gainers were industrialists (for example, the steel magnates), financiers, and speculators; all these groups strongly opposed the Weimar Republic. Partly because of the inflationary conditions, the Nazi party won 6.5 percent of the popular vote in the May 1924 elections to the Reichstag, the lower house of the German parliament. An economic recovery brought temporary political stability to Germany between 1924 and 1929. When the Depression hit the country in 1929, however, the Weimar Republic was doomed. By 1932 unemployment had surged to 44 percent of the labor force, nearly double the figure in the United States, Britain, and Sweden. Whereas the Nazi party gained only 2.5 percent of the popular vote to the Reichstag in 1928, its support increased to 18 percent in 1930 and to 37 percent in the July 1932 election. It then formed the largest party in the Reichstag. The following January Adolf Hitler became Chancellor.

Although nationalistic and anti-Semitic appeals partly accounted for Hitler's support, the economic conditions plaguing the Weimar Republic certainly contributed to the Nazi success. The groups hurt the most by the earlier inflation and current unemployment provided the strongest popular backing behind the Nazi movement. They included medium- and small-scale Protestant farmers, the self-employed lower middle class (artisans, craftsmen, shopkeepers, traders), minor civil servants, elementary school teachers, unskilled nonunionized blue-collar workers in small-scale manufacturing, retired people, and pensioners. Industrialists and financiers supplied the economic resources needed for the Nazis to gain power. In contrast, economic groups allied with the two parties that upheld the Weimar Republic, the Social Democrats and the Catholic Center party, showed the least tendency to vote for the Nazis. Instead, factory workers and urban wage earners who belonged to unions supported the Socialist, Center, and Communist parties, which gained a combined total of nearly 52 percent of the popular vote during the July 1932 election.[52] Bitter ideological disputes among these three parties prevented them from forming a coalition government to preserve the democratic regime. In sum, if a parliamentary government can restrain neither rising prices nor joblessness and if few nonmaterial bases of legitimacy prop up the existing political institutions, the resulting loss of popular support can undermine the democratic political system.

After World War II West German leaders achieved greater success in maintaining price stability and full employment. Yet even though the Bonn political system has retained stronger legitimacy than did the Weimar Republic, inflation and unemployment still have threatened the governing parties with a loss of popular support. Between 1951 and 1974 a 1 percent rise in both unemployment and inflation rates meant a 1.7 percentage point drop in the government's popularity, according to national sample surveys.[53] Despite the drastic change in political regimes, economic performance still contributed to political legitimacy.

Notes

1. See *International Financial Statistics* 30 (May 1977):52–53; *World Opinion Update* 1 (November 1977):27.

2. Robert M. Solow, "The Intelligent Citizen's Guide to Inflation," *The Public Interest* 38 (Winter 1975):31.

3. Charlotte Vannereau, "Comparability of Consumer Price Indices in OECD Countries," *OECD Economic Outlook: Occasional Studies* (July 1975):35–56.

4. For analyses of the general causes of inflation, see Abba P. Lerner, *Flation* (Baltimore: Penguin Books, 1973), pp.23–72; Abba P. Lerner, "From Pre-Keynes to Post-Keynes," *Social Research* 44 (Autumn 1977):387–415; James E. Meade, *The Intelligent Radical's Guide to Economic Policy: The Mixed Economy* (London: George Allen and Unwin, 1975), pp. 18–22; John Kenneth Galbraith and Nicole Salinger, *Almost Everyone's Guide to Economics* (Boston: Houghton Mifflin, 1978), pp. 107–08.

5. Robert L. Heilbroner, *Between Capitalism and Socialism: Essays in Political Economics* (New York: Random House Vintage, 1970), p. 175; Peter Wiles, "Cost Inflation and the State Economic Theory," *The Economic Journal* 83 (June 1973):377–98, esp. pp. 383–84; Richard T. Gill, *Economics and the Public Interest,* 3d ed. (Pacific Palisades, Calif.: Goodyear, 1976), pp. 27–32.

6. G. L. Bach, *Making Monetary and Fiscal Policy* (Washington, D. C.: The Brookings Institution, 1971), p. 38; Erich Spitäller, "Prices and Unemployment in Selected Industrial Countries," *International Monetary Fund Staff Papers* 18 (November 1971):529.

7. Lerner, "From Pre-Keynes to Post-Keynes," p. 391; Burkhard Strumpel, "Saving Behavior in Western Germany and the United States," *American Economic Review* 65 (May 1975):210–16.

8. Gill, *Economics and the Public Interest,* pp. 182–93; Ansel M. Sharp and Phyllis Smith Flenniken, "Budget Deficits: A Major Cause of Inflation?" *Public Finance Quarterly* 6 (January 1978):115–27.

9. William Poole, "Monetary Policies in the United States, 1965–74," *Proceedings of the Academy of Political Science* 31, no. 4 (1975):94–95.

10. Ibid., p. 93. Data on increases in the money supply and increases in consumer prices are from *Rates of Change in Economic Data for Ten Industrial Countries: 1956–1975* (Federal Reserve Bank of St. Louis, October 1976).

11. Using different indicators and methods of analysis than mine, Karl Brunner and Allan H. Meltzer reached similar conclusions in their study of the United States, West Germany, France, Italy, and the Netherlands between 1952 and 1974. They found that monetary policies (changes in the monetary stock, usually M1) in all five countries exerted a significantly stronger impact on price increases than did fiscal policies (changes in government expenditures and tax revenues). See Karl Brunner and Allen H. Meltzer, "The Explanation of Inflation: Some International Evidence," *American Economic Review* 67 (February 1977):148–54; Karl Brunner and Allan H. Meltzer, "Explaining Inflation," *Society* 14 (March/April 1977):35–39.

12. Anna J. Schwartz, "Inflation in the United States," *Current History* 69 (November 1975):171–72.

13. Poole, "Monetary Policies in the United States, 1965–74," p. 97; Richard Gill, *Economics and the Public Interest*, p. 163; Robert L. Heilbroner, *The Economic Problem*, 3d ed. (Englewood Cliffs, N. J.: Prentice-Hall, 1972), pp. 370–75.

14. For an analysis of U.S. data, see Anne Draper, 'Soaring Interest Rates: A Trigger to Inflation," *AFL-CIO American Federationist* 82 (December 1975):15–21.

15. For data on plant capacity utilization, see *OECD Economic Outlook*, no. 21 (July 1977):35–42.

16. See Wiles, "Cost Inflation and the State of Economic Theory," pp. 384–86; Gardiner C. Means, "Simultaneous Inflation and Unemployment: A Challenge to Theory and Policy," in *The Roots of Inflation: The International Crisis* (New York: Burt Franklin, 1975), pp. 1–31; John M. Blair, *Economic Concentration: Structure, Behavior, and Public Policy* (New York: Harcourt Brace Jovanovich, 1972); John M. Blair, "Inflation in the United States: A Short-Run Target Return Model," in *The Roots of Inflation*, pp. 33–67; William G. Shepherd, *Market Power and Economic Welfare* (New York: Random House, 1970); William G. Shepherd, *The Treatment of Market Power: Antitrust, Regulation, and Public Enterprise* (New York: Columbia University Press, 1975).

17. William G. Shepherd, testimony before the Subcommittee on Antitrust and Monopoly of the Committee on the Judiciary, U. S. Senate, 90th Congress, 2nd session, April 1968, part 7, *Economic Concentration* (Washington, D. C.: Government Printing Office, 1968), pp. 3691–92; William N. Leonard, "Mergers, Industrial Concentration, and Antitrust Policy," *Journal of Economic Issues*, 10 (June 1976):355–56; Jerry E. Pohlman, *Inflation Under Control?* (Reston, Va.: Reston Publishing Company, 1976), pp. 102–03; Lloyd G. Reynolds, *Microeconomics*, rev. ed. (Homewood, Ill.: Richard D. Irwin, 1976), pp. 203–08.

18. See Frederick L. Pryor, *Property and Industrial Organization in Communist and Capitalist Nations* (Bloomington: Indiana University Press, 1973), p. 206; Howard J. Sherman, *Stagflation: A Radical Theory of Unemployment and Inflation* (New York: Harper & Row, 1976), p. 139; Keith Acheson, "The Allocation of Government Deposits among Private Banks: The Canadian Case," *Journal of Money, Credit, and Banking* 9 (August 1977):477–49; Daniel M. Kotz, *Bank Control of Large Corporations in the United States* (Berkeley: University of California Press, 1978), esp. pp. 85, 111, 133–46.

19. Amitai Etzioni, *Social Problems* (Englewood Cliffs, N. J.: Prentice-Hall, 1976), pp. 105–17; Blair, "Inflation in the United States," pp. 56–65.

20. For the impact of concentrated industries on economic efficiency in the United States, see the following studies: Blair, *Economic Concentration*, pp. 98, 160; Shepherd, *Market Power and Economic Welfare*, pp. 167–89; James V. Koch, *Industrial Organization and Prices* (Englewood Cliffs, N. J.: Prentice-Hall, 1974), p. 153; F. M. Scherer, *Industrial Market Structure and Economic Performance* (Chicago, Ill.: Rand McNally and Co., 1970), p. 400; James A. Dalton and Stanford L. Levin, "Market Power: Concentration and Market Share," *Industrial Organization Review* 5, no. 1 (1977):34. Taking an opposite view, Steven Lustgarten asserts that concentrated industries are more capital-intensive and therefore more productive. See his *Industrial Concentration and Inflation* (Washington, D. C.: American Enterprise Institute for Public Policy Research, 1975). For the most general account of the effects of concentrated industries throughout Eu-

rope, see *Mergers and Competition Policy* (Paris: Organisation for Economic Co-operation and Development, 1974), pp.5–13. For the effects on inefficiencies in France, see F. Jenny and A. P. Weber, *Concentration et Politique des Structures Industrielles* (Nancy: Le Documentation française, 1974).

21. For data on the profits received by concentrated industries, compared with more competitive industries, see Reynolds, *Microeconomics,* pp. 194–98; Leonard, "Mergers, Industrial Concentration, and Antitrust Policy," pp. 371–72; Sherman, *Stagflation,* pp. 143–53; Michael Reich, "Does the U. S. Economy Require Military Spending?" *American Economic Review* 62 (May 1972):296–303; Alexis P. Jacquemin and Henry W. de Jong, *European Industrial Organisation* (New York: John Wiley, 1977), pp. 109–11, 126, 142–44, 151, 156; T. Hitiris, "Domestic and Foreign Competition and the Degree of Monopoly—A Note," *Journal of Economic Studies* 4 (May 1977):45–51; Kathleen Pulling, "Cyclical Behavior of Profit Margins," *Journal of Economic Issues* 12 (June 1978):287–305; J. C. H. Jones, L. Laudadio, and M. Percy, "Profitability and Market Structure: A Cross-Section Comparison of Canadian and American Manufacturing Industry," *Journal of Industrial Economics* 25 (March 1977):195–211; James A. Dalton and David W. Penn, "The Concentration-Profitability Relationship: Is There a Critical Concentration Ratio?" *The Journal of Industrial Economics* 25 (December 1976):133–42; William James Adams, "International Differences in Corporate Profitability," *Economica* 43 (November 1976):367–79. Dalton and Penn discovered that below a concentration ratio of 45 percent, profit rates are lower than at a ratio above 45 percent. According to Jones, et al, the higher the seller concentration ratios in *producer* goods, but not consumer goods, the higher the profits.

22. *International Economic Report of the President, January 1977* (Washington, D. C.: Government Printing Office, 1977), pp. 100–01; Jacquemin and de Jong, *European Industrial Organisation,* pp. 145, 156; James Dalton and E. J. Ford, Jr., "Concentration and Labor Earnings in Manufacturing and Utilities," *Industrial and Labor Relations Review* 31 (October 1977):45–60; Alfred E. Kahn, "Market Power Inflation: A Conceptual Overview," in *The Roots of Inflation,* p. 247; B. J. Widick, "Labor 1975: The Triumph of Business Unionism," *The Nation* 221 (September 1975):169–73; Scherer, *Industrial Market Structure and Economic Performance,* p. 410; Leslie Hannah and J. A. Kay, *Concentration in Modern Industry* (London: Macmillan Press, 1977), p. 24.

23. See Howard M. Wachtel and Peter D. Adelsheim, "How Recession Feeds Inflation: Price Markups in a Concentrated Economy," *Challenge* 20 (September/October 1977):6–13; Howard Sherman, "Monopoly Power and Stagflation," *Journal of Economic Issues* 11 (June 1977):269–84; Lloyd G. Reynolds, *Macroeconomics,* rev. ed. (Homewood, Ill.: Richard D. Irwin, 1976), pp. 156–58; Means, "Simultaneous Inflation and Unemployment," pp. 7–25; Blair, "Inflation in the United States," pp. 36–48; Blair, *Economic Concentration,* pp. 409–11; Shepherd, *Market Power and Economic Welfare,* pp. 184–85; Koch, *Industrial Organization and Prices,* pp. 153, 333; Scherer, *Industrial Market Structure and Economic Performance,* pp. 288–89, 303, 400–10; Bennett Harrison, "Inflation and Unemployment: Jobs Above All," *Social Policy* 5 (March/April 1975):40; Pulling, "Cyclical Behavior of Profit Margins," pp. 302–03. Not all economists agree that the prices of concentrated industries fail to respond to changes in demand. For example, Steven Lustgarten argues that between 1958 and 1970

demand had an "equal impact on price changes regardless of the levels of industry concentration." See his "Administered Inflation: A Reappraisal," *Economic Inquiry* 13 (June 1975):205. See also a longer analysis in Lustgarten, *Industrial Concentration and Inflation*. Lustgarten believes that concentrated industries reveal greater gains in productivity—"economies of scale"—than less concentrated firms. For a critique of Lustgarten's position, see Emile Benoit, "The Inflation-Unemployment Tradeoff and Full Economic Recovery," *The American Journal of Economics and Sociology* 34 (October 1975):340–41.

24. Sherman, *Stagflation*, pp. 135, 164–72; Jerry E. Pohlman, "Wages, Unions, and Inflation: The Concept of Market Power," *Wage-Price Law and Economics Review* 1, no. 1 (1975):26–27; Reynolds, *Microeconomics*, p. 199; Jacquemin and de Jong, *European Industrial Organisation*, pp. 146–48; Peter Kenyon, "Pricing in Post-Keynesian Economics," *Challenge* 21 (July-August 1978):43–48.

25. See Blair, "Inflation in the United States," pp. 56–65; John M. Blair, *The Control of Oil* (New York: Pantheon Books, 1976), p. 303; Sherman, *Stagflation*, p. 69; Wachtel and Adelsheim, "How Recession Feeds Inflation," pp. 10–12; Reynolds, *Microeconomics*, pp. 209–11.

26. Shepherd, *Market Power and Economic Welfare*, pp. 15, 104–06; Kahn, "Market Power Inflation," p. 258; David Schwartzman and Joan Bodoff, "Concentration in Regional and Local Industries," *Southern Economic Journal* 37 (January 1971):343–48; Lustgarten, *Industrial Concentration and Inflation*, p. 46; Wachtel and Adelsheim, "How Recession Feeds Inflation," pp. 11–12; Jacquemin and de Jong, *European Industrial Organisation*, pp. 44–46; Theresa Ann Flaim, *The Structure of the U. S. Petroleum Industry: Concentration, Vertical Integration and Joint Activities*, unpublished Ph.D dissertation, Department of Economics, Cornell University, Ithaca, N. Y. 1977, esp. pp. 229–52. According to Jacquemin and de Jong, industrial concentration ratios tend to be higher in enterprises rather than plants, in a narrowly defined product market instead of a broadly defined one (for example, in the market for glass containers, rather than all types of containers), and in small industries and countries rather than in larger ones.

27. See Pryor, *Property and Industrial Organization in Communist and Capitalist Nations*, pp. 201–05; Reynolds, *Microeconomics*, p. 210; Richard Scase, "Images of Progress, 1: Sweden," *New Society* 38 (December 23/30, 1976):614; *The OECD Observer*, no. 86 (May 1977):8; Jacquemin and de Jong, *European Industrial Organisation*, pp. 165–67.; Frédéric Jenny and André-Paul Weber, "The Determinants of Concentration Trends in the French Manufacturing Sector," *Journal of Industrial Economics* 26 (March 1978):193–207.

28. Helmut Arndt, "The German Experience: Inflation without Unemployment and the Effect of Competition," in *The Roots of Inflation*, pp. 143–44; *Economic Concentration*, hearings before the Subcommittee on Antitrust and Monopoly, part 7, p. 3811.

29. For data, see the appendix to *OECD Economic Surveys: Sweden* (Paris: OECD, 1977).

30. See Shepherd, *Market Power and Economic Welfare*, pp. 105–14; Robert Gilpin, "An Alternative Strategy to Foreign Investment," *Challenge* 18 (November/December 1975):12–19; Ronald E. Muller, "Globalization and the Failure of Economic Policy," *Challenge* 18 (May/June 1975):57–61.

31. Gerd Junne, "Euromoney, Multinational Corporations, and the Nation

State," *Instant Research on Peace and Violence* 3, no. 2 (1973):74–83; Richard James Sweeney and Thomas D. Willett, "Eurodollars, Petrodollars, and World Liquidity and Inflation," in Karl Brunner and Allan H. Meltzer, eds., *Stabilization of the Domestic and International Economy* (New York: North-Holland Publishing Co., 1977), pp. 277–310, argue that in 1974 the Eurocurrency market contained a gross of 220 billion dollars. Yet, in their view, most of this amount functioned like U.S. certificates of deposit. Only 31 billion dollars resembled demand deposits.

32. See *Mergers and Competition Policy*, pp. 6–9; H. W. de Jong, "Industrial Structure and the Price Problem: Experience within the European Economic Community," in *The Roots of Inflation*, pp. 195–96, 210; Jacquemin and de Jong, *European Industrial Organisation*, pp. 55–57, 71, 78, 98–114; P. Sargant Florence, "Stagflation in Great Britain; The Role of Labor," in *The Roots of Inflation*, pp. 85–87; Joel B. Dirlam, "The Process of Inflation in France," in *The Roots of Inflation*, p. 115; Sherman, *Stagflation*, pp. 138–43; Wachtel and Adelsheim, "How Recession Feeds Inflation," p. 12; Reynolds, *Microeconomics*, pp. 205–16; Pohlman, *Inflation under Control?*, pp. 102–03; Scherer, *Industrial Market Structure and Economic Performance*, pp. 63–65; Koch, *Industrial Organization and Prices*, p. 152; Shepherd, *Market Power and Economic Welfare*, pp. 117–18; Blair, *Economic Concentration*, pp. 22–24, 59, 71; Jenny and Weber, "The Determinants of Concentration Trends in the French Manufacturing Sector," p. 196; Göran Ohlin, "The Changing Role of Private Enterprise in Sweden," in Karl H. Cerny, ed., *Scandinavia at the Polls: Recent Political Trends in Denmark, Norway, and Sweden* (Washington, D. C.: American Enterprise Institute for Public Policy Research, 1977), pp. 259–60; Hannah and Kay, *Concentration in Modern Industry*, pp. 83–96.

33. Leonard, "Mergers, Industrial Concentration, and Antitrust Policy," pp. 355–64.

34. See Robert J. Gordon, "Recent Developments in the Theory of Inflation and Unemployment," *Journal of Monetary Economics* 2 (April 1976):212; John Pitchford and Stephen J. Turnovsky, "Some Effects of Taxes on Inflation," *The Quarterly Journal of Economics* 90 (November 1976):523–39; Christopher Green, "Recent Inflation: Its Causes and Implications for Public Policy," *Canadian Public Policy* 2 (Winter 1976):45–46; D. A. L. Auld, "Taxation and Inflation: A Survey of Recent Theory and Empirical Evidence," *Public Finance Quarterly* 5 (October 1977):403–18.

35. Draper, "Soaring Interest Rates: A Trigger to Inflation," pp. 15–21; "Corporate Debt: Obstacle to Recovery," *Dollars and Sense*, no. 27 (May–June 1977):2–3, 15.

36. Blair, *Economic Concentration*, pp. 256, 385; Koch, *Industrial Organization and Prices*, pp. 361–62.

37. For surveys of the literature on regulatory agencies, see Reynolds, *Microeconomics*, pp. 223–27; Martin Staniland, "Breaking the U. S. Airlines' Cartel," *New Statesman* 94 (August 19, 1977):236–37; Thomas K. McGraw, "Regulation in America: A Review Article," *Business History Review* 49 (Summer 1975):159–83; Paul Sabatier, "Social Movements and Regulatory Agencies: Toward a More Adequate—and Less Pessimistic—Theory of 'Clientele Capture'," *Policy Sciences* 6 (September 1975):301–42. The classic study is Grant McConnell,

Private Power and American Democracy (New York: Random House Vintage Books, 1970). See too Peter H. Schuck, "Why Regulation Fails," *Harper's* 251 (September 1975):16–29; Shepherd, *The Treatment of Market Power,* esp. pp. 139–82, 225–69. According to Shepherd, because the Federal Trade Commission and the Antitrust Division of the Justice Department lack the time and the information to prosecute violations of the antitrust laws, their activities have been ineffective. Similarly, the federal and particularly the state regulatory commissions rarely effectively control the performance of utilities.

38. See Jim Hightower, *Eat Your Heart Out* (New York: Crown Publishers, 1975), chapter 8; *Review of Agricultural Policies: General Survey,* OECD Agricultural Policy Reports (Paris: OECD, 1975).

39. Robert J. Gordon, "The Demand for and Supply of Inflation," *The Journal of Law and Economics* 18 (December 1975):820–21; Kenneth D. Walters and R. Joseph Monsen, "The Nationalized Firm: The Politicians' Free Lunch?" *Columbia Journal of World Business,* 12 (Spring 1977):94–95.

40. Richard Millward, "Price Restraint, Anti-Inflation Policy, and Public and Private Industry in the United Kingdom, 1949–1973," *The Economic Journal* 86 (June 1976):226–42; *OECD Economic Outlook: Occasional Studies* (July 1978):25.

41. Pohlman, *Inflation under Control?* pp. 152–58.

42. See Pohlman, *Inflation under Control?* pp. 177–231; Gardiner C. Means, "How to Control Inflation in the United States: An Alternative to 'Planned Stagnation'," *Wage-Price Law and Economics Review* 1, no. 1 (1975):54–56; Sherman, *Stagflation,* pp. 201–05; Blair, "Inflation in the United States," pp. 52–56; Bennett Harrison, "Inflation by Oligopoly," *The Nation* 221 (August 30, 1975):41; Michael Parkin, Michael T. Sumner, and Robert A. Jones, "A Survey of the Econometric Evidence of the Effects of Incomes Policy on the Rate of Inflation," in Michael Parkin and Michael Sumner, eds., *Incomes Policy and Inflation* (Toronto: University of Toronto Press, 1973), p. 25; Frank P. R. Brechling, "Some Empirical Evidence on the Effectiveness of Prices and Incomes Policies," in *Incomes Policy and Inflation,* pp. 41, 47; T. D. Sheriff, "Some Empirical Evidence on the Effectiveness of Incomes Policy in the U. K.," *Applied Economics* 9 (September 1977):253–63; Richard Portes, "The Control of Inflation: Lessons from East European Experience," *Economica* 44 (May 1977):109–30.

43. See Nicholas Kaldor, "Inflation and Recession in the World Economy," *The Economic Journal* 86 (December 1976):708–10; John Hicks, "What Is Wrong with Monetarism," *Lloyds Bank Review* no. 118 (October 1975):4–5; M. C. Kennedy, "Recent Inflation and the Monetarists," *Applied Economics* 8 (June 1976):152–54; D. G. Rhys and D. Barry, "The Current Inflation: Causation and Mechanics," *International Journal of Social Economics* 3, no. 1 (1976):56; Pohlman, *Inflation under Control?* pp. 109–29; Ekhard Brehmer and Maxwell R. Bradford, "Incomes and Labor Market Policies in Sweden, 1945–70," *International Monetary Fund Staff Papers* 21 (March 1974):115–19; and several essays in *The Roots of Inflation;* P. Sargant Florence, "Stagflation in Great Britain: The Role of Labor," pp. 69–75; Joel B. Dirlam, "The Process of Inflation in France," p. 129; Helmut Arndt, "The German Experience: Inflation without Unemployment and the Effect of Competition," p. 147; Alfred E. Kahn, "Market Power Inflation: A Conceptual Overview," pp. 246–49; "Collective Bargaining and Government Policies," *OECD Observer* no. 94 (September 1978):3–6.

44. Jean-Paul Courtheoux, "The Public Sector," in *Wage Determination* (Paris: OECD, 1974), pp. 134–36, 141–42; Nicholas Kaldor, "Managing the Economy: The British Experience," *The Quarterly Review of Economics and Business* 14 (Autumn 1974):12; R. F. Elliott, "Public Sector Wage Movements: 1950–1973," *Scottish Journal of Political Economy* 24 (June 1977):133–51; Millward, "Price Restraint, Anti-Inflation Policy, and Public and Private Industry in the United Kingdom," pp. 226–42; B. Burkitt and D. Bowers, "Wage Inflation and Union Power in the United Kingdom: 1949–1967," *Applied Economics* 8 (December 1976):289–300; Luigi Graziano, "La Crise d'un Régime Libéral-Démocratique: L'Italie," *Revue française de science politique* 27 (Avril 1977):269–71; Joel Dirlam, "The Process of Inflation in France," p. 130; Sharon P. Smith, "Pay Differentials between Federal Government and Private Sector Workers," *Industrial and Labor Relations Review* 29 (January 1976):179–97; Charles Field and Richard L. Keller, "How Salaries of Large Cities Compare with Industry and Federal Pay," *Monthly Labor Review* 99 (November 1976):23–28. According to Eli Ginzberg, "The Job Problem," *Scientific American* 237 (November 1977):48, in the aggregate, U. S. federal government employees receive higher salaries than do either private employees or state and local government workers. For example, in 1975 Federal employees earned an average of $12,630 a year; state and local employees, $10,900; and private employees, $10,740.

45. *OECD Economic Outlook: Occasional Studies* (July 1978):25; Margaret Stewart, *Trade Unions in Europe* (Essex, England: Employment Conditions Abroad Ltd./Gower Economic Publications, 1974), pp. 84–85, 136–39.

46. See Gardner Ackley, "The Costs of Inflation," *American Economic Review* 68 (May 1978):149–54.

47. Galbraith and Salinger, *Almost Everyone's Guide to Economics,* p. 105.

48. G. L. Bach, "Inflation: Who Gains and Who Loses?" *Challenge* 17 (July/August 1964):48–55, esp. p. 52; G. L. Bach, "The Economic Effects of Inflation," *Proceedings of the Academy of Political Science* 31, no. 4 (1975):20–33; G. L. Bach and James B. Stephenson, "Inflation and the Redistribution of Wealth," *The Review of Economics and Statistics* 56 (February 1974):1–13; G. L. Bach, *The New Inflation: Causes, Effects, Cures* (Providence, R. I.: Brown University Press, 1973), pp. 19–37; John L. Palmer and Michael C. Barth, "The Distributional Effects of Inflation and Higher Unemployment," in Marilyn Moon and Eugene Smolensky, eds., *Improving Measures of Economic Well-Being* (New York: Academic Press, 1977), pp. 202–28. In Canada people with under $3000 annual income experienced higher price increases than people with more than $15,000 annual income. See Allan M. Maslove and J. C. R. Rowley, "Inflation and Redistribution," *The Canadian Journal of Economics* 7 (August 1975):404.

49. Albert E. Burger, "The Effects of Inflation (1960–68)," *Federal Reserve Bank of St. Louis Review* 51 (November 1969):25–36.

50. See Bruno S. Frey and Friedrich Schneider, "An Empirical Study of Politico-Economic Interaction in the United States," *The Review of Economics and Statistics* 60 (May 1978):177–78; Bruno S. Frey and Friedrich Schneider, "A Politico-Economic Model of the United Kingdom," *The Economic Journal* 88 (June 1978):250–51; Norman H. Keehn, "Great Britain: The Illusion of Governmental Authority," *World Politics* 30 (July 1978):538–62. In "Economic Influences on Presidential Popularity," *Public Opinion Quarterly* 42 (Fall 1978):366,

Kristen R. Monroe found that between 1950 and 1974 inflation exerted a stronger impact on presidential popularity than did the unemployment rate: "An increase of 1 percentage point in the annual rate of inflation which is maintained for one year (for example, a simple annual increase from 6 percent to 7 percent) will result in a decrease in presidential popularity of 3.75 percentage points."

51. Neil Elder, "The Swedish General Election of 1976," *Parliamentary Affairs* 30 (Spring 1977):193–208; Bo Särlvik, "Recent Electoral Trends in Sweden," in *Scandinavia at the Polls,* pp. 73–129, esp. pp. 115–23.

52. See Lewis E. Hill, Charles E. Butler, and Stephen A. Lorenzen, "Inflation and the Destruction of Democracy: The Case of the Weimar Republic," *Journal of Economic Issues* 11 (June 1977):299–313; David Abraham, "State and Classes in Weimar Germany," *Politics and Society* 7, no. 3 (1977):229–66; Thomas Childers, "The Social Bases of the National Socialist Vote," *Journal of Contemporary History* 11 (October 1976):17–42; R. I. McKibbin, "The Myth of the Unemployed: Who Did Vote for the Nazis?" *The Australian Journal of Politics and History* 25 (August 1969):25–40; Birgit Jensen-Butler, "An Outline of a Weberian Analysis of Class with Particular Reference to the Middle Class and the NSDAP in Weimar Germany," *British Journal of Sociology* 27 (March 1976):50–60; M. Rainer Lepsius, "From Fragmented Party Democracy to Government by Emergency Decree and National Socialist Takeover: Germany," in Juan J. Linz and Alfred Stepan, eds., *The Breakdown of Democratic Regimes: Europe* (Baltimore, Johns Hopkins University Press, 1978), pp. 34–79, esp. pp. 52, 70.

53. Bruno S. Frey and Werner W. Pommerehne, "Toward a More Theoretical Foundation for Empirical Policy Analysis," *Comparative Political Studies* 11 (October 1978):327.

The Tradeoff Between Unemployment and Inflation

Can a society enjoy the best of all possible worlds where stable prices accompany low employment? Or does a negative tradeoff occur between inflation and unemployment? Must some groups suffer high unemployment if a society is to experience low inflation? Political economists have formulated two different theories to account for the tradeoff between unemployment and inflation. Keynesian explanations assume a competitive market where changes in demand affect both jobless rates and price increases. Excessive demand is the main source of inflation; restricted demand leads to unemployment. Therefore, this theory suggests that the cure for inflation is less government spending, higher taxes, lower increases in the money supply, or higher interest rates. The Keynesian solution for unemployment is just the opposite strategy: increased government expenditures, reduced taxes, larger increases in the money supply, or lower interest rates. Unfortunately, if government leaders pursue both these diverse policies to regulate demand, a negative tradeoff will probably result between inflation and unemployment. During the early 1960s such a negative tradeoff did occur in most Western societies.

The 1970s saw, however, the emergence of an economic situation characterized by both high inflation and high unemployment. To explain this phenomenon, economists began to pay greater attention to the supply side of the equation. Whereas Keynesian approaches focus on demand as the prime reason for inflation and unemployment, theories of concentrated industries stress reduced supplies. When demand for a

Chapter Six

product declines, heads of concentrated industries can either cut prices or cut production. Whether pursued nationally by an oligopoly or internationally by a multinational corporation and an oil cartel, reduced production brings higher prices and increased joblessness. Restricted supplies may cause increased prices for a good. Since fewer workers are needed to produce the product, unemployment rates in that industry become more severe.

This chapter explores in detail the two competing explanations for the tradeoff. To what extent are these theories valid for the period between 1960 and 1975? In what respects do the reasons for the economic problems of the last two decades stem from historical trends dating back to the late nineteenth century? What variables explain the different patterns of unemployment and inflation in West Germany, Britain, the United States, and Sweden? To answer these questions, this chapter examines the interaction between domestic and international conditions. In this regard, such international factors as trade relations, overseas investments, oil cartels, and currency exchanges provide clues to the paradoxical tradeoff of the 1970s.

Theories of the Tradeoff

Keynesian Theory and the Validity of the Phillips Curve

During the late 1950s the Keynesian economist A. W. Phillips explored the linkages of unemployment to money wage rates in the United Kingdom between 1861 and 1957. As a result of his research, the famous *Phillips curve* emerged. According to this idea, full employment and price stability have a contradictory relationship that depends on specific historical conditions. Full employment raises the total demand for goods and services, while high inflation reflects an excessive aggregate demand; therefore, few societies can achieve a situation of low unemployment (say under 3 or 4 percent) simultaneously with low price increases (under 3 percent a year). Some economists even assert that inflation will be curtailed—that is, prices will show no yearly increases—only if jobless rates escalate to between 10 and 15 percent.[1]

According to the Keynesian assumptions of the Phillips curve, the main difficulty with securing the best blend of inflation and unemployment stems from the contradictory policies used to lower prices and jobless rates. If excessive demand is the primary reason for inflation and if deficient demand leads to unemployment, then the policy solution for inflation lies in curtailing spending by consumers, business firms, and government. In turn, government needs to increase total spending to resolve the high unemployment problem. Specifically, decreased demand may flow from some mixture of lower government expenditures, higher taxes, lower increases in the money supply, and higher interest rates. Government can expand total demand by raising government expenditures, decreasing taxes, increasing the yearly money supply, and lowering interest rates. If they accept the notion that the level of demand explains the tradeoff, policy officials face a dilemma. If they increase demand, then unemployment may fall, but prices will escalate. Reductions in overall demand may curtail inflation but at the expense of rising jobless rates. The goals of price stability and full employment thus appear difficult to realize simultaneously.

To what extent does the Phillips curve give an accurate picture of the relationship between unemployment and inflation from 1960 through 1975? According to tables 6–1 and 6–2, during the early 1960s most Western market economies did experience a negative tradeoff. In every one of the seven nations studied here, between 1961 and 1965 a negative

Table 6–1   The Relationship between Unemployment and Inflation

	1961–1965			1966–1970		
Country	Unemployment[a]	Price Rise[b]	Sum	Unemployment	Price Rise	Sum
United States	5.5%	1.3%	6.8%	3.9%	4.2%	8.1
Canada	5.4	1.5	6.9	4.6	3.8	8.4
Britain	2.6	3.5	6.1	3.0	4.6	7.6
West Germany	0.4	2.8	3.2	0.8	2.6	3.4
Sweden	1.5	3.6	5.2	1.9	4.5	6.4
France	1.5	3.8	5.3	2.3	4.3	6.6
Italy	3.3	4.9	8.2	3.8	3.0	6.8

[a] Yearly averages of the number unemployed as a percentage of the civilian labor force.

[b] Consumer price indices—the average annual percentage changes in prices for all goods and services.

or inverse relationship existed between inflation and unemployment. Particularly in the United States and Canada, as the jobless rates declined each successive year, prices gradually increased. Similar, although less marked, trends, occurred in Italy, Sweden, Britain, and France. Only West Germany failed to show a high negative tradeoff between jobless rates and price rises. Moreover, the aggregate correlations between unemployment and inflation in table 6–1 indicate that the expected negative association did prevail. During the first half of the 1960s, countries with high unemployment rates—Canada and the United States—experienced the lowest price increases. Sweden and France, with relatively low unemployment, confronted comparatively severe inflationary pressures. In short, the Phillips curve appeared especially valid for the period lasting from 1961 to 1965.

After the early 1960s, however, the Phillips curve seemed less able to describe accurately the relationship between unemployment and inflation. Western economies no longer appeared responsive to the "fine tuning" of Keynesian economists who postulated the appropriate mix of fiscal and monetary policies that would secure the best blend of inflation and unemployment. In Britain, Sweden, and France, inflation

1971–1975		
Unemploy-ment	Price Rise	Sum
6.1%	6.8%	12.9%
6.1	7.4	13.5
3.8	13.2	17.0
1.6	6.1	7.7
2.3	8.0	10.3
3.3	8.8	12.1
3.6	11.5	15.1

NOTE: The Pearson correlation coefficients of the relationships between unemployment and inflation are as follows: −.59 (1961–1965); .21 (1966–1970); and −.05 (1971–1975).

SOURCE: See tables 4–1 and 5–1.

and unemployment rose concurrently between 1966 and 1970. During the 1970s this trend accelerated. Leaders of most nations confronted the paradoxical situation of rising prices and growing joblessness. The negative tradeoff had disappeared, and policymakers faced the worst of all possible worlds. As table 6–1 shows, over these fifteen years the tradeoff grew worse. In every country except Italy, the sum of price rises and unemployment levels increased successively over the three time periods. Since the Keynesian strategy of stimulating or lessening aggregate demand no longer seemed so effective an option as in the early 1960s, what other policies should political leaders pursue? In this new historical context, economists began to focus greater attention on imperfect competition and on the supply side of the equation.

The Theory of Concentrated Industries: National Oligopolies, Multinational Corporations, and the OPEC Cartel

Whereas Keynesian theories of a competitive market perceive total demand as the main cause of price rises and joblessness, theories that assume the dominance of concentrated industries stress restricted sup-

Table 6–2 Correlations between Unemployment and Inflation within Nations

Country	1961–1965	1966–1970	1971–1975
United States	−.91	.47	.36
Canada	−.98	−.17	−.06
Britain	−.68	.02	.43
West Germany	−.20	−.55	.09
Sweden	−.68	−.88	−.92
France	−.55	.76	.51
Italy	−.78	−.64	−.54

NOTE: These Pearson correlation coefficients link unemployment and inflation rates. A minus number indicates an *inverse* correlation; that is, low unemployment accompanies high inflation, and high unemployment is linked to low price increases. A *positive* number means that as unemployment goes down, inflation rates also decline; similarly, as jobless rates increase, prices rise.

SOURCE: The correlation coefficients are calculated from information in table 6–1.

plies. According to these theories of oligopoly, inflation and unemployment can increase at the same time. In both the national and the international markets, concentrated industries have become more powerful since the early 1960s. Oligopolies dominate national economies, especially markets for heavy industry, transportation, and communication. Multinational corporations and international cartels like the Organization of Petroleum Exporting Countries (OPEC) wield decisive influence over the world market for industrial inputs. Under conditions of imperfect competition, when demand for a product declines, concentrated industries, including the oil cartel, can either lower the price or restrict production. To maintain their long-range profits, oligopolies have curtailed supplies rather than lowered prices for their goods. In most cases, the restricted production led to rising unemployment. John Blair has explained the phenomenon as follows:

> During economic downswings, concentrated products no longer remain "rigid." They have become flexible—upward. . . . The recession behavior of concentrated products implies a Phillips curve in reverse; the greater the importance of concentrated products in an economy, the greater the likelihood that rising unemployment will be accompanied by rising prices.[2]

Assuming that the inflation of the 1970s stemmed primarily from excess demand, Western leaders resorted to restrictive monetary and fiscal policies—that is, they cut some government spending, increased taxes, and raised interest rates. These policies had a greater impact on unemployment than on inflation. As the economy contracted, recession resulted. The economic growth rate declined. Business fixed investment fell. Between 1974 and 1977 the jobless rates rose each successive year in Canada, Britain, France and Italy.[3] Although inflationary pressures became less severe after 1974 and 1975, double-digit inflation still threatened most Western nations except Germany.

Theorists of concentrated industries who base their ideas on these new economic conditions of the 1970s assume that inflation and unemployment can reinforce each other, rather than exist at the expense of the other. Inflation can stimulate higher jobless rates. In oligopolistic markets, what happens when excessive prices for goods lower demand? Instead of cutting prices to increase spending, concentrated industries choose to lower production. As a result, unemployment increases, because fewer workers are needed to produce the goods. Similarly, unemployment can raise prices. When the jobless rolls expand, spending declines because workers have less income to spend. As demand falls, small companies face growing economic pressures. To remain in business, they must lower costs and prices; yet, since concentrated industries supply most capital goods and other vital industrial inputs, costs for the small firms escalate. Confronted with rising costs, the smaller companies often go bankrupt, thereby increasing the strength of concentrated industries. Particularly if government officials enact no price controls and if other producers can offer no substitute for a good, the concentrated industries raise prices to a point that greatly exceeds demand and costs. If they fail to secure new markets for their products, then they cut production. Lower supplies mean both higher inflation and higher unemployment.

On the international market, concentrated industries, including oil cartels, private banks, and other multinational corporations, have recently strengthened their positions. Their growing dominance affects trade relations, overseas investment, oil supplies, and currency exchanges, as well as, in turn, patterns of inflation and unemployment throughout the Western world. Let us look first at the effects of the OPEC cartel, then examine the influence of governments and private banks on international currency transactions, and conclude with an analysis of the relationship between trade and foreign investment.

During the 1970s the main international reason for the general price rise stemmed from the fourfold increase in oil prices that occurred at the end of 1973. The actions of OPEC resembled at the world market level the price-setting behavior of concentrated industries within a nation. In 1960 five oil-producing countries—Saudi Arabia, Iran, Kuwait, Iraq, and Venezuela—founded OPEC as an intergovernmental agency to control the prices of exported crude oil. Not until the early 1970s, however, did the cartel gain enough economic power to implement large price increases. At that time, nationalism in Third World countries developed greater importance. European and North American governments began to lose their power to regulate international events. Concurrently, the eight major oil companies (Exxon, Mobil, Standard Oil of California, Texaco, Gulf, British Petroleum, Royal/Dutch Shell, and the Campagnie Française de Pétroles) experienced a declining share of the world market for crude oil.[4] More countries joined OPEC; by 1977 the oil cartel included the original five founders, plus Qatar, Abu Dhabi, Sharjah, Dubai, Libya, Algeria, Indonesia, Nigeria, Gabon, and Ecuador. The OPEC countries together accounted for slightly over 50 percent of total world crude oil output. Beginning in the early 1970s, their governments took steps to nationalize or assume 51 percent of the shares of private oil companies, including the eight majors and other smaller independent firms. During the previous decade, these "independents" had gained a greater share of the market, mainly by exploiting oil in Libya. Because of economic deconcentration, rising oil supplies, and increased price competition, the prices of exported oil to European countries had actually declined from 1958 to 1971, even though the demand for petroleum products had successively risen each year. When Near Eastern, Asian, and Latin American governments nationalized several oil companies, however, their actions effectively crippled smaller-scale oil firms and brought reduced price competition. By late 1973 OPEC gained sufficient economic power to raise the posted price of Saudi Arabian crude oil from about $2.60 a barrel to $11.65, a fourfold increase that far exceeded the growth in demand. Less drastic price increases followed thereafter.[5]

Because oil represents a crucial resource for both consumers and industrialists, the fourfold increase in crude oil prices exerted a severe economic impact throughout the world. The higher price for oil meant a decline in disposable income, which reduced spending for other goods. In turn, this decreased total demand led to higher unemployment.

Although the oil price hike contributed to economic stagnation throughout the Western world, European nations experienced more acute consequences than the United States or Canada. Why? Western Europe is far more dependent on imported oil, especially from the Near East. For example, in 1970 the United States imported around 20 percent of its total oil supplies. In Canada imports constituted only 2 percent. In the five West European countries, however, imports accounted for over 90 percent of total supply. Therefore, when the price of Near Eastern oil showed a fourfold rise, these higher energy prices accounted for around half the increase in the European consumer price index. Another reason for the steeper price rise for oil in Western Europe after 1973 stemmed from the greater concentration overseas, compared with the United States. In 1972 the four largest European oil corporations—Exxon, Shell, Texaco, and British Petroleum—produced nearly one-half of the oil sold in Western Europe. In the United States, however, the big four—Exxon, Texaco, Shell, and Gulf—produced less than one-third of the total oil supply.[6] In short, the greater concentration of oil production in Europe led to less price competition.

The dramatic rise in crude oil prices generated somewhat different results in Western Europe and in the United States. More dependent than the United States on oil imports from OPEC countries, European nations had to bear higher marginal costs for energy as a proportion of their total domestic expenditures. As imported prices rose, consumption of crude oil and natural gas declined in 1974 and 1975 by amounts ranging from 3 percent a year in Britain to 19 percent in Italy. Decreased demand led to a fall in the output of refined oil; throughout

Europe most refineries operated at only two-thirds of capacity. Faced with the twin conditions of declining European demand and rising surpluses of refined oil, should not the OPEC nations have reduced their prices for crude oil? Since the world market for both crude and refined oil does not approximate the conditions of pure competition, the OPEC cartel chose to cut production, rather than prices, as European demand fell. Thus in 1975 total OPEC production stood at only 84 percent of the late 1973 level.

Unlike Europeans, Americans responded to the oil price hike by decreasing consumption of crude oil and natural gas by only 1 percent in 1974 and 1975. After 1973 imported oil became more important than it had been during the early 1970s. In 1970 oil imports amounted to 20 percent of total supplies; by 1976 that figure had grown to 43 percent. Between 1973 and 1976, oil imports from OPEC countries as a proportion of total imported oil rose from 45 percent to over 67 percent. As a result of the growing U.S. dependence on imported oil, OPEC gained the power to implement price increases. Because the eight largest U.S. oil corporations strengthened their control over the domestic production of crude oil, they too wielded sufficient economic power to restrict supplies and raise prices. By successfully curtailing supplies, both the OPEC cartel and the largest oil companies contributed to unemployment and inflation.[7]

In conclusion, the operations of both the OPEC cartel and the major private oil companies exemplify the price-setting behavior associated with concentrated industries. Although foreign governments in the Near East and Latin America now control large parts of the production process, the multinational oil corporations still dominate the refining, transportation, and retail sale of oil. Most oil is shipped in tankers owned by the eight major companies. Refining takes place under extensive joint venture partnerships. Several interlocking directorates connect the largest oil corporations with leading banks and industries. The majors have even gained control over the production of other vital energy sources—natural gas, coal, uranium, and tar; therefore, consumers cannot obtain oil substitutes from competitive firms. All these interlocking directorates, joint venture partnerships, and controls over oil substitutes facilitate the administration of prices. Like the OPEC governments, the major oil companies respond to increased demand for oil by curtailing supplies, raising prices, and thereby increasing their revenues. The resulting loss in disposable income felt by European and U.S. consumers decreases total demand and thus contributes to rising unemployment as well.[8]

Besides exerting a direct impact on the economic tradeoff, the fourfold increase in OPEC oil prices indirectly accelerated inflation and joblessness by creating trade deficits and causing devaluation of currencies. Of the seven nations, Italy and Britain experienced the largest trade deficits between 1960 and 1975; that is, each year the value of imports exceeded exports. Difficulties in selling their exports on the world market added to the unemployment rates at home. Attempting to expand their overseas markets for exports, these two governments devalued the lira and pound, respectively. By raising the prices for imports, however, devaluation generated more inflationary pressures. No longer facing import competition, domestic producers, especially the concentrated industries, raised their prices. Overall inflation thus accelerated.

During the 1970s inflationary trends became accentuated, especially in Britain and Italy. These two countries, which had the largest trade deficits, underwent the largest currency devaluations between 1973 and 1977. Powerful institutions, including Western governments, Near Eastern governments, multinational corporations (ITT, General Motors, Mobil), central banks, private banks, and the International Monetary Fund (IMF), intervened in the international exchange markets to keep national currencies either undervalued or overvalued. These institutions provided funds to cover the balance of payments deficits faced by Britain and Italy. By lending and withdrawing money from various countries, they affected the value of national currencies. For example, in 1974 OPEC nations used their financial reserves to maintain the value of the British pound. However, in mid-1975 they withdrew their funds from the pound and caused its rapid devaluation. Concerned by the acute inflation ravaging Britain and Italy, IMF officials insisted that the British and Italian governments must deflate their economies if they were to receive funds to pay for the trade deficit. In response to IMF pressures, the two governments have cut government spending, raised taxes, and increased interest rates. Although these actions have reduced spending for imports and brought about a drop in the general price level, the reduced demand has unfortunately created rising unemployment.

As the United States became more dependent on OPEC nations for oil imports, it faced similar pressures from OPEC governments and European central banks. The trade deficit in 1976 and 1977 stemmed mainly from oil imports from Near Eastern countries; indeed, if oil imports had been curbed, the United States would have had a trade surplus. Instead, the trade deficit resulting from the increased prices for imported oil weakened the value of the dollar on the international market. The devaluation of the dollar meant a general rise in prices for imported goods, which accelerated inflationary pressures. As recipients of billions of dollars paid for oil imports, OPEC nations became concerned when the dollars they held declined in value. In response, they threatened to increase the international prices for crude oil.[9] This vicious circle reinforced the tendencies toward economic stagnation.

Faced with economic stagnation, Western government leaders came under pressure to abandon the free trade policies which have operated since the close of World War II. In both the United States and Europe, many firms found it difficult to sell their exports on the world market. Inexpensive imports from Japan, South Korea, Taiwan, Malaysia, and Hong Kong meant steep price competition for domestic producers. Under these conditions, unemployment hit those industries producing goods for the export market as well as those domestic firms unable to compete with foreign imports. Not surprisingly, concentrated industries, especially the U.S. and European steel corporations, demanded protection from Japanese steel imports. Higher tariffs on imported steel would reduce foreign price competition, curtail supplies, raise steel prices, and thereby expand corporate profits. Yet, as occurred during the 1930s, these protectionist policies would probably also accelerate the trends toward greater unemployment. Although higher tariffs may provide some short-term relief for workers in the U.S. steel industries, for example, in the longer run rising protectionism for a variety of products would stimulate other countries to enact trade barriers against U.S. goods. The reduced overseas demand for exports, combined with high tariffs on imports, would reinforce the trends toward inflation and unemployment.[10]

The growing importance of foreign investment relative to free trade also threatens to increase economic stagflation (high inflation and unemployment). Although large-scale concentrated industries now dominate foreign trade, small-scale competitive firms can gain crucial economic advantages by selling their products overseas. Free trade encourages firms to reduce their costs to sell their goods at low prices on the international market. As we have seen, small- and medium-sized firms can often maximize efficiency better than concentrated industries can; thus they can benefit from free trade policies. However, the recent reliance on overseas investment strengthens the economic power wielded by oligopolies and concentrated industries. As expected, both inflation and unemployment result. Why?

According to Robert Gilpin, foreign investment rewards mainly white-collar managerial and technical personnel in the home country while providing some jobs for skilled manufacturing workers overseas. As a result, blue-collar workers at home face growing unemployment. The impact of foreign investment on inflation stems primarily from the strengthened position of multinational corporations. The vast increase in foreign investment means declining capital investment in the domestic economy, especially for civilian industrial technology, transportation, communications, and public utilities. Decreasing productivity means higher costs for reduced supplies of goods, two conditions that stimulate overall price rises. Foreign investment in such vital economic sectors as oil production also increases a nation's dependence on other countries. Foreign governments, as well as multinational corporations, gain greater power to curtail supplies of crucial resources.[11] Stagflation becomes a more acute possibility.

During the early 1970s the United States and Britain placed the greatest reliance on direct foreign investment; Germany in contrast stressed the expansion of exports. For instance, in 1971 U.S. and British concentrated industries realized greater revenues from foreign production than from exports. German corporations, however, earned nearly three times more from exports than from direct foreign investment.[12] As expected, the United States and Britain suffered higher inflation and higher jobless rates between 1971 and 1975. Until the mid 1970s, when German overseas investment began to rise vis-à-vis exports, West Germany managed to secure the most favorable tradeoff between price stability and full employment.

In sum, of the two theories attempting to explain the relationship between jobless rates and price increases, the theory of concentrated industries provides more satisfactory clues about the economic conditions of the 1970s. As we have seen, Keynesian approaches assume an inverse relationship between inflation and unemployment; because excess demand causes inflation and deficient demand leads to unemployment, political leaders find it difficult to realize the best of all possible worlds—full employment and price stability. Although the negative tradeoff did occur during the first half of the 1960s, after 1973 many Western societies began to experience the worst of all cases—escalating prices and rising unemployment. Why? Theories of concentrated industries, which focus on supply shocks, not just demand shocks, offer some tentative answers. Whereas the Keynesian notions behind the Phillips curve imply the existence of a competitive market, other economists point out that in both the national and international markets, powerful oligopolies control supplies of goods. Concentrated industries have grown more powerful within domestic market economies. At the world level, governments, multinational corporations, private banks, and oil cartels exercise decisive power. They have the ability to control the production of oil, regulate international currency exchanges, shape trading relations, and dominate overseas investment. All these activities affect not only the demand for goods but also the supply of goods. By restricting supplies, national and multinational oligopolies cause both higher joblessness and steeper price rises. Under these conditions, assumptions made by Phillips about an inverse association between inflation and unemployment no longer appear so empirically valid.

The Tradeoff in Germany, Britain, the United States, and Sweden

An examination of four countries also casts doubt on the existence of a negative tradeoff between inflation and unemployment. West Germany, Britain, the United States, and Sweden each illustrates a different tradeoff between unemployment and inflation. Throughout the fifteen-year period from 1960 through 1975 and also within each of the three subperiods, West Germany has consistently combined low inflation and low unemployment. Only after 1973 did unemployment rates begin to rise above 1 percent. In contrast to Germany, Britain has experienced relatively high rates of both inflation and unemployment, especially during the seventies. Over the last fifteen years the tradeoff between the two has worsened. Economic conditions in the United States and Sweden better fit the Phillips curve. Until the 1970s the United States achieved low inflation but high unemployment. Although the pattern is not as clearcut, Sweden combined low unemployment rates with moderately high inflation. By examining the actions of the central government, concentrated industries, and labor unions in each nation, we will better understand the reasons for the particular tradeoff.

West Germany

How did West Germany manage to secure such a favorable tradeoff between inflation and unemployment during the 1960s? First, German political officials pursued moderate fiscal policies. Among the seven countries, Germany ranked third or fourth in expenditures and third highest in taxes. Spending on social services, such as health care and transfer payments, was also relatively high. These spending policies helped to maintain a high level of demand. Monetary policies, including low interest rates and comparatively large annual increases in the money supply, also expanded overall demand. Of all seven nations, Germany spent the highest percentage of the GNP on capital investment; hence blue-collar manufacturing workers could easily find jobs. Like Sweden,

Germany also relied on labor mobility and job retraining programs to channel workers into industries experiencing the greatest demand.

Second, the German trade unions settled for moderate wage increases. For example, between 1960 and 1973 hourly wages in manufacturing increased about 10 percent a year, a higher figure than in the United States or Britain but lower than the wage increases for Swedish and Italian workers.[13] As a result, demand for goods increased by a moderate amount, not high enough to cause severe inflation or low enough to create unemployment.

Third, although during the 1960s several mergers reinforced the power of concentrated industries, German firms have attempted to maintain a competitive posture toward foreign trade. They have strongly supported the European Common Market. Of the seven nations, Germany has consistently realized the largest trade surplus. Until the mid-1970s the large export trade lowered unemployment, because most German exported goods were finished industrial products whose manufacture involved extensive job opportunities. Because the German mark remained strong vis-à-vis other national currencies, imports into Germany were relatively inexpensive. Thus the import competition curtailed inflation.[14]

During the 1970s, however, this favorable economic situation began to deteriorate. Although comparatively low, the annual price increases in 1973, 1974, and 1975 hovered around 7 percent. Even worse, the level of unemployment zoomed to nearly 4 percent in 1976, the highest figure in twenty years. Part of the problem stemmed from the German policy priority placed on inflation rather than unemployment. German political leaders, who recalled the hyperinflation of 1922 and 1923, tried to reduce demand by curtailing the money supply and limiting increases in government expenditures. In accordance with the Phillips curve, the resulting drop in demand did bring lower inflation, but unemployment rates rose. Another reason for the worsening economic conditions lay in the combined recession–inflation experienced by the United States in 1974 and 1975. Because of the U.S. recession, which meant high unemployment and declining production, German exports to the United States fell. The devaluations of the dollar between 1971 and 1973 meant that prices for goods imported into the United States rose while prices of U.S. exports to Europe declined. Since the dollar was devalued and the mark appreciated, German exports became less competitive on the world market. As the export trade declined and the costs of producing goods at home increased, German businesses began to invest overseas, for example, in Mexico and Brazil. The drop in demand for German exports and the rising foreign investment partly

explained the additions to the jobless rolls.[15] The price rise derived
from several factors, including the increase in unit labor costs and the
growing concentration of industries in such diverse sectors as manufacturing, banking, agriculture, and retail trade.

Britain

Throughout the fifteen-year period between 1960 and 1975, the
economic situation of Britain steadily deteriorated; by the early 1970s
the British people had to confront both high inflation and growing
unemployment. Unlike Germany, Britain consistently faced chronic
balance of payments problems, with imports exceeding exports. As the
first country in the world to industrialize, England during the eighteenth and nineteenth centuries achieved an early competitive advantage. Indeed, from 1700 to 1740 England exported both agricultural
produce and industrial goods; of all European countries, England secured the greatest advantages from free trade. By 1873, however, the
worldwide markets for English products began to decline. As Germany, France, the United States, and Japan industrialized, they cap-
tured the markets formerly dominated by Britain. British corporations
therefore began to concentrate on foreign investment rather than on the
domestic production of goods for export. The strategy provided fewer
employment opportunities for British workers. During the twentieth
century, both world wars exacerbated Britain's economic difficulties,
especially the problem of selling exports abroad; after World War II
imports nearly always exceeded exports. The decline in the export trade
partly stemmed from the lack of technologically advanced industry;
most firms operated rather inefficiently. Except for the United States,
Britain spent between 1965 and 1974 the lowest proportion of the GNP
on fixed capital investment. The resulting low productivity dampened
the market for British exports, especially in such vital sectors as chemicals, electrical goods, motor vehicles, and aircraft. In 1953 Britain's
share of world exports of manufactured goods amounted to 23 percent;
by 1973 that proportion had declined to less than 8 percent.[16]

Labor relations within Britain also affected the sale of exports.
Among the seven nations, Britain from 1960 to 1975 experienced the
highest unit labor costs in manufacturing; these costs increased threefold
during the first half of the 1970s. The sharp gap between wage increases
received by manufacturing workers and their gains in output per hour
made British goods less competitive on the world market. Compared
with Germany and Sweden, Britain also faced a comparatively large
number of strikes. For example, the number of strike days lost in 1972

per 1,000 employees was higher in Britain than in any nation among the seven except Italy. In short, one reason for British economic stagnation stemmed from the high wage increases sought by the unions relative to the workers' increase in output. Especially between 1969 and 1973, wage increases exceeded the demand for labor.[17]

The difficulties faced by British firms in selling their exports created a vast employment shift from industry into services. For example, in 1962 about 48 percent of the labor force held jobs in the industrial or manufacturing sector; by 1975, however, this figure had declined to 41 percent. The 7 percent decrease was higher than in any other country. In this period employment opportunities rose dramatically in the service sector, especially in education, health care, public administration at the local level, and insurance, banking and finance. Unfortunately, the rapid shift into the service sector brought both higher inflation and rising unemployment. The decline in manufacturing meant fewer jobs for blue-collar workers. Government officials attempted to expand the sales of exports and thereby provide employment for skilled factory workers by devaluing the pound; yet the rise in import prices reinforced the general inflationary trends. Naturally, workers demanded higher wage increases to maintain their disposable income. As expected, wages and prices went into an upward spiral.[18]

Neither fiscal nor monetary policies succeeded in improving Britain's export position; rather, they tended to bring both high inflation and high unemployment. In particular, the monetary policies pursued by British leaders exerted a deflationary impact on production but did not curtail price rises. During the 1960s only the United States showed a lower annual percentage increase in the money supply. Throughout the fifteen-year period, Britain had the highest interest rates. Restrictive monetary policies impeded gains in productivity, thus placing a damper on the export trade.

Fiscal policies followed a rather erratic course too, as both Labour and Conservative politicians adopted a "stop-go" strategy. To stimulate aggregate demand, they raised expenditures and cut taxes; these policies caused greater consumption of imported goods, thereby exacerbating the balance of payments problems. Since industrial firms experienced difficulties selling their manufactured exports on the international market, balance of payments crises ensued—that is, imports exceeded exports. Under pressure from IMF officials and European bankers, who supplied loans to cover the trade deficits, British leaders took steps to curtail demand. Lacking tax revenues that would accrue to the government if a trade surplus were present, they raised taxes and cut expenditures, especially for domestic services. As consumer purchasing power declined, recessions resulted. Workers went on frequent strikes, which curtailed production. Wage settlements exceeded gains in productivity, not only in manufacturing but to an even greater extent in the service sector of local government, health care, education, banking, and insurance.[19] As a result, inflation became more severe. Like the United States, Britain during the first part of the 1970s faced an inflationary recession.

Despite these dismal conditions, Britain's economic future began to improve during the late 1970s. After several years of double-digit inflation, the government successfully persuaded most unions to accept wage increases of around 10 percent a year. More important, the trade deficits turned into a trade surplus when production of North Sea oil reserves started accelerating during 1976 and 1977. Whereas continental European societies continued to remain dependent on oil imports from the Near East, British reliance on imported oil lessened. As indigenous production of crude oil expanded, imports as a proportion of the total supply declined. For example, in 1970 imports amounted to 95 percent of supply; by 1976 that figure fell to 83 percent.[20] In sum, expanded supplies of indigenously produced oil and decreased dependence on OPEC nations meant fewer trade deficits, a stronger pound, greater investment, declining inflation rates, and the expansion of employment opportunities. Although North Sea oil production seemed unlikely to resolve all Britain's economic problems, it did promise to bring a more advantageous tradeoff between unemployment and inflation.

The United States

Prior to World War II, Keynesian theories of excess and deficient demand effectively explained the inverse relationship between inflation and unemployment. The U.S. market economy operated in a relatively competitive manner. Inflation resulted mainly from excess demand; unemployment rates rose when aggregate demand declined. Boom periods of the business cycle lowered the jobless rolls; when the busts occurred, prices fell as workers lost their jobs.

Because warfare stimulates total demand, the sharpest gap between inflation rates and unemployment rates occurred as an effect of wartime pressures. Between 1770 and 1970 the highest average rates of price increases took place during or right after the Revolutionary War, the War of 1812, the Civil War, World War I, World War II, and the Korean War. In these periods, total government spending rose rapidly to meet wartime needs. Shortages of consumer goods prevailed. To stimulate production, the government increased the money supply. All these policies caused a rapid price rise. For example, between 1862 and 1864 prices annually increased by 11 percent, 23 percent, and 27 percent. At the time of the First World War from 1917 through 1920, inflation rates hovered around 17 percent. During World War II, prices increased 11 percent in 1942; because of price controls, price rises declined to 6 percent in 1943 and to only 2 percent in 1944 and 1945. When the government removed price controls at the end of the war, the inflation rate shot up to 9 percent in 1946 and 14 percent in 1947. In 1951, the year of greatest involvement in the Korean War, price increases were 8 percent. Finally, one cause of the U.S. inflation between 1967 and 1972 was the excessive demand created by the Vietnam War. Although military expenditures grew, President Johnson refused to approve a tax increase until 1968, too late to curtail aggregate demand.

During the twentieth century unemployment rates have declined only during and immediately after a war—that is, at times when prices escalate. Between 1890 and 1976 the average annual jobless rate was 7 percent. As Keynesian theories suggest, the lowest unemployment occurred during wartime: 1.4 percent in 1918 and 1919; under 2 percent in 1943, 1944, and 1945; around 3 percent between 1951 and 1953; and under 4 percent from 1966 through 1969. The growing expenditures to finance the Vietnam War raised prices and lowered the jobless rate. As the number of troops in Vietnam rose, unemployment declined. By 1969 the unemployment level was only 3.5 percent, the lowest figure since 1953, during the Korean War. In short, before the 1970s an inverse relationship (or negative tradeoff) existed between inflation and unemployment. The highest price increases and the lowest jobless rates occurred during war, as government spending dramatically raised total demand.

Beginning in the 1970s, Americans faced a worsening tradeoff. As the Nixon administration withdrew troops from Vietnam, prices rose and the percentage of unemployed also grew. While between 1891 and 1977 a 6 percent unemployment rate was linked to perfect price stability, from 1947 through 1977 the jobless rate associated with no inflation rose to 7.5 percent.[21] How can we explain this worsening tradeoff? Let us first examine the economic conditions of the 1960s, and then look at the different situation of the following decade.

Demand theories associated with a competitive economy account for the low inflation with high unemployment that occurred in the sixties. Compared with European public officials, U.S. political leaders have followed rather deflationary fiscal and monetary policies; the need to curtail inflation has taken priority over attempts to lower unemployment. As we have seen, government expenditures for war and defense have constituted the major fiscal policy expanding demand. Among the seven nations, the United States ranked lowest on the percentage of the gross national product allocated for government expenditures. Relative to Canadian and European governments, the U.S. government spent the most for military and the least for social services, especially income transfers, family allowances, and public health care. This pattern of expenditures maintained a comparatively low aggregate demand; hence, price rises were minimal but unemployment remained higher than in Europe. Taxes as a percentage of the GNP were also lower in the United States. European leaders have preferred to finance government expenditures through increased taxes. Even at the risk of incurring high fiscal deficits, U.S. politicians, both Republicans and Democrats, have placed greater reliance on the more indirect route of tax reductions as the most appropriate method for stimulating demand. Not surprisingly, since lower taxes mean reduced costs, this approach has secured greater price stability but at the expense of full employment.

U.S. monetary policies have also been more restrictive than those pursued by European governments. Between 1960 and 1975 the United States consistently showed the lowest annual percentage increase in the money supply. As a result, prices showed only a moderate increase; yet the restricted monetary demand contracted economic growth and kept the unemployment rate comparatively high.

The behavior of labor unions also contributed to low aggregate demand. Compared with Swedish, German, and British unions, the U.S. labor movement is relatively weak. U.S. unions enroll a lower proportion of the labor force, operate more fragmented organizations, maintain looser ties with the major political parties, and encounter greater hostility from management. Partly as a result of the weak bargaining position of most labor unions, manufacturing workers have managed to win only moderate annual wage increases from their employers. For example, from 1960 through 1973, the annual percentage change in hourly wages amounted to only 5 percent, the lowest increase among the seven countries. Similarly, U.S. workers secured the lowest increase in real earnings after controls for inflation. Partly because unit labor costs remained quite low during the sixties, inflation did not pose a severe problem. However, the low consumer demand associated with modest increases in purchasing power also led to higher unemployment rates than found in Europe.[22]

The actions of private business corporations also help explain the relatively modest price increases during the 1960s. Of the seven economies, the United States featured the lowest spending on capital investment as a proportion of the total national income. This timid approach toward increasing investment expenditures may have reduced employment opportunities for blue-collar workers, the occupational group with the highest jobless rates. Relative to the economic situation during the seventies, the 1960s saw some U.S. business firms engage in greater price competition. For instance, independent oil firms—those not in the major eight—actually increased their share of the worldwide crude oil market; profits of the majors declined.[23] Although supplies of crude oil rose to meet the greater demand, prices did not rise. The competitive forces of the marketplace seemed to work.

During the 1970s, however, the power of concentrated industries grew stronger. The restricted production caused by national oligopolies, U.S. multinational corporations, and the OPEC cartel partly led to the worsening tradeoff between inflation and unemployment. In this period, explanations based on curtailed supplies, not just on changes in aggregate demand, account for the simultaneous occurrence of rising prices and jobless rates. Because prices of goods produced by concentrated industries are excessive relative to demand and costs, oligopolistic firms must either curtail production or find new markets when demand declines. If they fail to secure new markets either at home or abroad, they resort to cutbacks in production. As a result, workers are permanently fired or temporarily laid off. When plant capacity declines to around 70 percent, production costs rise. Inflation thus ensues. Under continuing oligopolistic conditions, both inflation and unemployment rise.

The growing power of concentrated industries has particularly affected unskilled workers, women, and blacks. Concentrated industries are fairly capital-intensive, employing mainly skilled blue-collar employees and skilled managerial and professional personnel. The lack of jobs for unskilled laborers and the tendency for corporation executives to hire fewer workers at higher wages meant that unemployment remained high, especially for blacks. Data from the late 1960s and early 1970s indicate that nonprofit institutions (schools, hospitals, government agencies) and competitive firms (e.g., textile industries, restaurants, hotels, lumber companies) hired more blacks than did larger-scale, oligopolistic industries, such as those engaged in banking, oil extraction, chemical production, and the manufacture of electrical equipment. In short, the more concentrated firms employed lower proportions of black workers.[24]

Between 1973 and 1975 the rise in food and fuel prices explained most of the severe inflationary and recessionary pressures experienced by the United States. Some of the problems stemmed from increased worldwide demand for agricultural products and oil, combined with naturally occurring shortages (for example, the temporary shortage of grains caused by droughts and corn blights). Yet concentrated industries, along with the U.S. government, have taken actions to raise costs, reduce supplies, and thereby cause economic stagflation.

Although the eight major U.S. oil corporations no longer own as many production facilities overseas, their control over the manufacture of U.S. crude and refined oil has increased. In 1955 the eight largest corporations produced 30 percent of total output; in 1970 that figure grew to 42 percent. The production of U.S. refined oil shows an ever higher concentration ratio. In 1960 the top eight oil firms manufactured 46 percent of domestic output; ten years later, they accounted for nearly 60 percent of refined oil output.

The major oil companies also pressured the government to restrict supplies to Americans. In 1959, faced with declining profits and rising competition, the majors encouraged the Eisenhower administration to enact a quota on oil imports. Under this mandatory quota, oil imports into the United States could constitute no more than 12 percent of domestically produced oil. As a result of the oil import quota, U.S. producers felt little incentive to build new refineries in the United States. Domestically produced oil cost more than imported oil. Consumption of U.S. oil increased, thus depleting supplies for use in the 1970s. Naturally, when the price of imported oil began to exceed the price of domestically produced crude oil, the Nixon administration in 1972 abandoned the mandatory quota on imported oil. As Americans became more dependent on imported oil, the major oil companies reduced domestic production. Between 1960 and 1972 domestic production of crude oil and natural gas increased by 3 percent a year, but from 1973 through 1975 domestic production showed over a 4 percent annual decrease. Other government policies, such as the foreign tax credit on overseas exploration of oil, also reduced domestic production. Under this arrangement, mutinational oil companies exploring oil outside the United States earned a credit on foreign taxes that made overseas production more profitable than domestic production.

These public policies, along with the decisions taken by OPEC and the oil companies, meant a sharp growth in profit rates. Since the OPEC-induced price hikes stimulated an increase in price for domestically produced U.S. oil, they brought higher profits to the major oil companies. Whereas between 1963 and 1972 the rate of return on investments made by the six largest oil firms amounted to 11 percent, in 1974 returns nearly doubled to 19 percent.[25] John Blair has summarized the overall impact on general inflation and unemployment rates:

The majors must clearly bear the responsibility for curtailing supplies to the American private branders, for raising prices more than any increase in costs occasioned by the OPEC actions (as indicated by the rise in their profit rates), and for bringing about a curtailment in supply during the subsequent recession sufficient to maintain the price at its new and sharply higher level.[26]

Although before World War II agriculture enjoyed considerable competition among small-scale farms, agribusiness corporations began to dominate various segments of the agricultural market in the 1960s. Competitive farms still grew most of the crops, but they bought their basic industrial inputs or supplies from the oligopolies. During the early 1970s the four largest firms controlled 83 percent of the tractor market, 74 percent of agricultural chemicals (like fertilizers, pesticides), two-thirds of oil products, and a large share of animal feeds. Concentrated industries dominated the supplies of propane, gasoline, diesel fuel, petrochemicals, tractors, combines, and heavy equipment; prices for all these industrial inputs have escalated. After producing their crops, the small-scale farmers had to sell their produce to concentrated industries. Oligopolies like Ralston Purina, Cargill, and Continental Baking (a subsidiary of ITT), dominated the exports of American grain. Powerful supermarkets, such as Safeway, A&P, Kroger, and Lucky, gained control over the retail sale of food.

This growing corporate dominance of the agricultural sector brought both inflation and unemployment. Large-scale corporations pushed up the labor and capital costs incurred to produce, process, package, transport, and retail food. They manipulated demand through extensive national advertising. Since losses in one oligopolistic sector could be balanced by gains in another market controlled by the oligopolies, profits for the agribusinesses soared. However, the small-scale independent farmer who originally grew the crop did not benefit. For example, in 1973 the farmers' share of most fruits and vegetables amounted to only 20 to 25 percent of the retail prices. The processors, packagers, and marketers received the remaining 75 percent.[27] As expected, a larger proportion of small farmers have recently gone into debt. The agricultural sector offers fewer employment opportunities than ever before; yet the consumer pays higher and higher prices for food.

The policies followed by the U.S. government and multinational corporations shaped international as well as domestic economic conditions. In particular, their impact on trade, foreign investment, and the devaluation of the dollar contributed to both inflation and unemployment. During the late 1960s and early 1970s the United States confronted a severe balance of payments problem. The Vietnam War accelerated military expenditure abroad. Foreign aid and the sale of military hardware overseas meant a drain of dollars from the United States. Multinational corporations expanded their foreign investment. Agribusiness corporations produced too much food for sale in the domestic market. U.S. manufacturers experienced difficulties selling their industrial exports on the world market. Attempting to remedy these problems, between 1971 and 1973 President Nixon devalued the dollar, enacted a temporary surtax on most imports into the United States, and abandoned the practice of fixing international exchange rates in terms of gold.[28] Nixon's intentions were to expand U.S. export sales. What were the effects?

The devaluation of the dollar, increased overseas trade, and greater multinational investment failed to lower inflation or markedly reduce jobless rates. The devaluation of the dollar led to rising prices as the cost of imports increased. Between 1970 and 1973 the 20 percent depreciation of the dollar accounted for a 4 percent increase in consumer prices. After 1973 the dollar began to float against other currencies—that is, foreign exchange rates became flexible rather than fixed in value. Trade deficits with OPEC nations and the failure of countries like Germany and Japan to buy U.S. exports led to further devaluations of the dollar after 1973. Since imports into the United States exceeded exports, Americans had to pay for these imports with foreign currency. As the dollar depreciated, imports cost more. Faced with less import competition, U.S. concentrated industries, like the automobile and steel industries, raised their prices, thereby aggravating general inflationary tendencies.[29]

The growth of exports in 1974 and 1975 neither reduced inflation rates nor substantially lowered the unemployment level. During the middle 1960s the European Economic Community had placed import quotas on U.S. agricultural products; therefore, after 1971 most food exports went to the Soviet Union. The expansion of agricultural exports meant higher profits for the agribusinessmen but also reduced domestic supply; as a result, food prices escalated. Growing export sales also did not produce substantially lower unemployment. Compared with West Germany, the United States exported more food and fewer manufactured goods. For instance, in 1976 manufactured products constituted 43 percent of the total monetary value of German exports; however, the value of U.S. manufactures amounted to only 27 percent of the total. Blue-collar workers and the unskilled therefore lacked a variety of employment opportunities. Each year a smaller proportion of the civilian labor force secured employment in the agricultural sector. White-collar workers, such as managers, professionals like scientists and engineers, and skilled blue-collar workers dominated manufacturing industries selling exports overseas. Oligopolies producing aircraft, machinery, chemicals, electric equipment, and refined petroleum employed relatively few ethnic minorities, women, and workers under twenty-five—groups facing the highest jobless rates.

The expansion of U.S. investment overseas mainly benefited the oligopolies, which possessed the resources needed to make the investments and to reap the high profits from foreign investment. White-collar personnel and the owners of capital secured greater benefits from overseas investment than did blue-collar workers, especially unskilled blacks. Foreign investment discouraged domestic spending for new plants, machinery, and equipment. The decline in productivity raised costs of production, which in turn generated inflationary pressures.[30]

In conclusion, the growing strength of concentrated industries during the 1960s and early 1970s partly explains the unfavorable tradeoff between unemployment and inflation. Both in the United States and abroad, the actions of the oligopolies have led to higher prices; yet, because of different government policies, their effects on jobless rates in European countries have varied somewhat from the American situation. For example, although the Swedes have experienced comparatively high price increases, their unemployment levels have fallen far below the U.S. figures. Why? Both Keynesian theories and theories of concentrated industries provide some reasons for the Swedish tradeoff.

Sweden

Compared with U.S. leaders, the Swedish public officials since 1960 have secured a more favorable tradeoff between inflation and unemployment. During the period from 1960 through 1975, only Germany managed to attain a better record of low price increases and low jobless rates. (See table 6–1 for the sums of inflation and unemployment rates.) The West German government accords higher priority to lowering inflation, even at the risk of expanding the unemployment rolls. In contrast, the Swedish leaders fear unemployment more than inflation. Whereas jobless rates rose in Germany after 1974, in Sweden from 1974 through 1977 unemployment remained under 2 percent, the lowest figure for all Europe. Although Sweden scored impressive achievements on the employment front, policies to cope with escalating prices have met with less success. In 1977 the inflation rate soared to just over 11 percent; only Italy and Britain experienced higher price rises. Throughout the period from 1960 through 1975, Sweden ranked below Italy, Britain, and France in severity of inflation. More than any other country, Sweden revealed the expected negative tradeoff between inflation and unemployment. As table 6–2 indicates, comparatively high *inverse* correlations linked these two variables. What policy variables explain this negative tradeoff? Swedish political leaders have probably shown the strongest commitment to Keynesian policies for managing the economy. Government has taken active steps to expand total demand, with low unemployment and moderate inflation the result.

The low jobless rates mainly stemmed from expansionary public policies to stimulate aggregate demand. Of the seven countries, Sweden allocated the highest percentage of the gross national product to government expenditures, especially those for health, education, and social services, that will raise consumer demand. Unlike U.S. or Italian officials, however, Swedish leaders avoided deficit financing to raise demand. Compared with the other governments, the Swedish government collected the highest total taxes and personal income taxes as proportions of the GNP. Indeed, Sweden's budget surplus as a percentage of the GNP ranked at the top. The government's monetary policy was somewhat less expansionary than its fiscal policy. As expected of Keynesian policymakers, Swedish officials concentrated less attention on manipulating interest rates and money supplies as techniques for stimulating demand. In Sweden between 1960 and 1975, the yearly increase in the money supply was higher than in the United States but lower than in Germany. Swedish interest rates were higher than German or U.S. rates but lower than the English discount rates.

Swedish policies toward business and labor represent an active commitment to full employment. In particular, public officials want to preserve the best features of the competitive market economy by encouraging both functional and geographic labor mobility. No other government among the seven spends as much money on manpower training as a proportion of the gross domestic product. In Sweden a higher proportion of the labor force participates in training and retraining programs than in the other six nations. For example, in 1972 1 percent of the Swedish work force took part in manpower programs designed to teach new job skills; the U.S. figure stood at one-half of 1 percent. Public works projects—road construction, sewage treatment plants, industrial workshops, and various outdoor jobs—provided employment for the young, the old, and the handicapped. Throughout the sixties nearly one-half of 1 percent of the labor force found work in these government programs.[31] Political leaders stressed geographic mobility of workers; by granting travel allowances and rent supplements to finance housing in areas with labor shortages, the government encouraged people to move to areas of high employment, mainly in the manufacturing areas of southern Sweden. For those who did not want to move south, regional development projects in northern Sweden, the area of highest unemployment, provided work opportunities. Finally, the investment reserves policy created jobs in the private sector. Under this program, during prosperous times, part of a company's profits were placed in a tax-free investment fund. When a recession occurred, the government released these funds for spending on buildings, machinery, equipment, and supplies; these increased expenditures made additional employment opportunities available when they were most needed.[32]

Although the policies to secure full employment have met with great success since the end of World War II, the policies to cope with the postwar inflation have not been equally effective. The high demand stimulated by the Swedish government, the costs incurred by noncompetitive industries, and the rising oil prices account for the moderate inflation. The high taxes probably add to costs more than they restrain demand; hence the continuing low jobless rates with modest price rises.

The wage increases granted the workers and lack of competition among "sheltered" industries also push up costs and thus prices. Swedish economists distinguish between two sectors in the economy. The *competitive* sector includes industries that manufacture finished goods, produce raw materials, make goods for the export market, and face import competition. The *sheltered* sector comprises the government sphere, public and private services, construction, and industries protected from import competition. About 70 percent of the labor force worked in the sheltered sector; only 30 percent was employed in the competitive sector in 1967. This proportion had declined by 3 percent since 1960. The more competitive industries showed lower price increases; yet they also experienced higher productivity than the sheltered sector. Wages rose by a larger amount in the competitive sector, which set the standard for wages in other parts of the economy. Hence, although the Swedish labor unions attempted to avoid a wage drift upward, they did not attain this goal. Workers in the less productive, less competitive industries wanted to secure the wage gains achieved by their fellows employed by the most productive firms. Between 1960 and 1973 Swedish output per hour in manufacturing rose by an average of 7 percent each year, the highest gain in output shown by any country in our sample. Since wages increased by 10 percent, the difference between wage increases and gains in labor productivity was fairly low. Most manufacturing industries, however, belong to the competitive sector. In the sheltered sector wage increases remained high, due to the trade union policy of uniform wage settlements but productivity was lower. Therefore, the moderate inflation occurring in Sweden stemmed mainly from the higher costs associated with the noncompetitive sectors of the economy.[33]

Because Sweden depends on imported oil for its fuel needs, the escalation of oil prices after 1973 contributed to greater inflation. In 1976, 94 percent of the Swedish supply of crude oil was imported, two percentage points higher than in 1970. Yet, compared with Americans, Swedish political leaders took more active steps to conserve oil and therefore to restrain inflationary pressures. The government encouraged the growth of public transportation and discouraged the use of private automobiles. Higher gasoline taxes and higher taxes on cars reduced gasoline consumption. Public policies also stimulated the conservation of heating fuel; for example, government programs teach householders and apartment managers ways to save energy. Mortgage laws allocated public funds to builders and homeowners who installed energy-saving features. Building codes encouraged more efficient heating designs. Several public policies stressed the need to rely on electricity for meeting future energy requirements. All these policies lowered the costs of imported oil and natural gas, thereby helping to curb inflation.[34]

Despite an impressive postwar economic performance, the Swedish economy began to confront greater problems during the late 1970s. Compared with their German competitors, Swedish businesses found it more difficult to sell their exports on the international market. Rising production costs led to a declining demand for Swedish exports which in turn threatened to expand the jobless rolls. Faced with a growing trade deficit, the government devalued the kroner. As a consequence, imported goods rose in price, resulting in a higher general inflation rate. Regardless of these recent problems, however, the Swedish government has still attained a more favorable tradeoff than most other Western societies.

In conclusion, without resorting to the policies associated with an administered command economy, Swedish officials have reached a beneficial tradeoff between unemployment and inflation. The government has not applied extensive price or wage controls. Politicians do not usually intervene in the collective bargaining process; centralized unions work out settlements with centralized employer groups. More than 90 percent of industry is privately owned. Government ownership is limited mainly to postal services, the telephone system, railroads, electric power projects, tobacco firms, and liquor establishments.[35] Private ownership and a market economy coexist with extensive government provision of social services and active public policies to stimulate demand while attempting to curtail rapid price increases. Although the policies to secure full employment have achieved more success than those to restrain prices, Sweden has nonetheless managed to avoid the severe inflationary pressures plaguing Italy and Britain.

In sum, two general conclusions emerge from this examination of the tradeoff in four economies. First, from 1960 through 1975 the actions of government agencies, concentrated industries, and labor unions reciprocally influenced the specific tradeoff between unemployment and inflation. Germany attained the best tradeoff (the lowest inflation and jobless rates) because labor unions sought moderate wage increases, concentrated industries accepted the need for import-export competition, and the government enacted monetary and fiscal policies that stimulated moderately high aggregate demand—neither high enough to cause rapid price rises nor sufficiently low to produce high joblessness. In contrast, Britain secured the worst tradeoff. Why? Unit labor costs (differences between hourly wage increases and labor output per hour) were higher in Britain than in any other of the seven nations. Privately owned concentrated industries and nationalized enterprises restrained price competition. As a result, inflation ensued. The government implemented comparatively low increases in the money supply and relatively high interest rates. These monetary policies, combined with periodic deflationary fiscal policies, caused high unemployment. Unlike British political leaders, Swedish public officials stimulated high total demand; for example, government expenditures were the highest percentage of the GNP. Therefore, unemployment rates remained low. Both concentrated industries and labor unions exercised considerable market power. Partly for this reason, price increases were moderately high. Compared with Sweden, the United States faced the opposite tradeoff—lower inflation but higher unemployment. Here, unions and concentrated industries exerted weaker power over the market than in Western Europe. Although U.S. oligopolies have recently grown stronger, they still practiced some price competition. Particularly during the 1970s, unit labor costs were the lowest among the four countries. From a crossnational perspective, low increases in the money supply and low government expenditures as a percentage of the GNP produced low aggregate demand. Until 1974 high unemployment thus accompanied relatively low price rises.

Second, because the world market has become more interdependent since World War II, the causes of both inflation and unemployment can no longer be found within a nation itself; instead, the particular tradeoff in a single country depends on international economic conditions. Particularly during the 1970s, oil prices and the foreign trade situation became crucial variables explaining jobless levels and price hikes. The quadrupling of oil prices by OPEC nations in late 1973, combined with restrictions on oil supplies, represented acute external "supply shocks" affecting all Western countries. Escalating oil prices meant higher general inflation. Increased costs for oil also lowered the disposable incomes of consumers, business managers, and government officials. As production and consumption declined, demand fell and unemployment rates rose. Currency devaluations and rising import prices reinforced economic stagflation after 1973. Only in Germany, where the mark appreciated, did citizens escape the effects of higher prices for imported goods. In the United States, Britain, and Sweden, the declining value of the national currency caused import prices to rise, which led to higher prices for most consumer goods. In response, unions demanded larger wage increases. When labor and raw material costs rose, capital investment decreased. This decline in productivity meant that firms, especially in Britain, faced difficulties selling their exports on the world market. The resulting trade deficits led to growing unemployment and inflation.

Notes

1. Although A. W. Phillips, "The Relation between Unemployment and the Rate of Change of Money Wage Rates in the United Kingdom, 1861–1957," *Economica* 25 (November 1958):283–99, analyzed the association between levels of unemployment and changes in wages, contemporary economists now use the Phillips curve to show the relation of unemployment to changes in retail prices. See Lloyd G. Reynolds, *Macroeconomics,* rev. ed. (Homewood, Ill.: Richard D. Irwin, 1976), pp. 149–51. According to Reynolds, p. 145: *"There is an inverse relation between the unemployment rate and the rate of price increase.* When unemployment is high, the rate of price increase tends to be low, while a low unemployment rate means a higher rate of price increase." According to Abba P. Lerner, Milton Friedman believes that a zero inflation rate requires a jobless rate exceeding 10 percent. See Lerner's *Flation* (Baltimore: Penguin Books, 1973), pp. 125–30. See also Abba P. Lerner, "From Pre-Keynes to Post-Keynes," *Social Research* 44 (Autumn 1977):293–94.

2. John M. Blair, "Inflation in the United States," in *The Roots of Inflation* (New York: Burt Franklin, 1975), p. 48.

3. See *OECD Economic Outlook* (July 1977):15–29; (July 1978):14.

4. Raymond Vernon, "An Interpretation," *Daedalus* 104 (Fall 1975):5.

5. John M. Blair, *The Control of Oil* (New York: Pantheon, 1976), pp. 169–320; Hanns Maull, "The Price of Crude Oil in the International Energy Market: A Political Analysis," *Energy Policy* 5 (June 1977):147; George Kouris and Colin Robinson, "EEC Demand for Imported Crude Oil, 1956–1985," *Energy Policy* 5 (June 1977):133; *Petroleum Economist* (August 1977):329.

6. See *Oil Statistics 1976* (Paris: International Energy Agency, OECD, 1977); *OECD Observer*, no. 74 (March/April 1975):3–4; *Daedalus* 104 (Fall 1975):289; *Business Week*, December 20, 1976, pp. 44–50.

7. Maull, "The Price of Crude Oil," pp. 142–57; *Petroleum Economist* (March 1977):107, (August 1977):294–96, 329; *Oil Statistics 1976*; Robert W. Rycroft, "U. S. Energy Demand and Supply," *Current History* 74 (March 1978):101; Robert F. Halvorsen and Judith A. Thornton, "Comparative Responses to the Energy Crisis in Different Economic Systems: An Extensive Analysis," *Journal of Comparative Economics* 2 (June 1978):201.

8. See John W. Wilson, "Market Structure and Interfirm Integration in the Petroleum Industry," *Journal of Economic Issues* 9 (June 1975):319–35; John M. Blair, "The Implementation of Oligopolistic Interdependence: International Oil, a Case Study," *Journal of Economic Issues* 9 (June 1975):297–318; Blair, *The Control of Oil*, pp. vii–ix, 371–81; Vernon, "An Interpretation," pp. 1–14.

9. For data on imports and exports, see *Main Economic Indicators, Historical Statistics: 1960–1975* (Paris: OECD, 1977). For analysis of the devaluation and appreciation (upward revaluation) of currencies, see Henry C. Wallich, "What Makes Exchange Rates Move?" *Challenge* 20 (July/August 1977):34–40; *Business Week*, October 3, 1977, pp. 68–80; John Hicks, "What Is Wrong with Monetarism?" *Lloyds Bank Review*, no. 118 (October 1975):6–12.

10. Reynolds, *Macroeconomics*, pp. 375–79; Daniel Chirot, *Social Change in the Twentieth Century* (New York: Harcourt Brace Jovanovich, 1977), pp. 95–98.

11. Robert Gilpin, *U. S. Power and the Multinational Corporation: The Political Economy of Foreign Direct Investment* (New York: Basic Books, 1975), pp. 198–214.

12. Ibid., p. 15.

13. Barbara Boner and Arthur Neef, "Productivity and Unit Labor Costs in 12 Industrial Countries," *Monthly Labor Review* 100 (July 1977):13.

14. Helmut Arndt, "The German Experience: Inflation without Unemployment: The Effect of Competition," in *The Roots of Inflation*, pp. 137–64, esp. p. 162; Lewis J. Edinger, *Politics in West Germany*, 2nd ed. (Boston: Little, Brown, 1977), pp. 333–34; M. E. Streit, "Government and Business: The Case of West Germany," in Richard T. Griffiths, ed., *Government, Business and Labour in European Capitalism*, (London: Europotentials Press, 1977), pp. 120–31.

15. Gerhard Hirseland, "The West German Miracle Revisited," *Challenge* 18 (May/June 1975):52–56.

16. Nicholas Kaldor, "Managing the Economy: The British Experience," *The Quarterly Review of Economics and Business* 14 (Autumn 1974):7–13; Immanuel Wallerstein, "The Rise and Future Demise of the World Capitalist System," *Comparative Studies in Society and History* 16 (September 1974):410–11; Gilpin, *U. S. Power and the Multinational Corporation*, pp. 15, 87–88; Henry Phelps Brown, "What Is the British Predicament?" *The Three Banks Review*, no. 116 (December 1977):7, 23.

17. U. S. Department of Labor, Bureau of Labor Statistics, *Handbook of Labor Statistics 1976* (Washington, D.C.: Government Printing Office), pp. 339–40. See also M. C. Kennedy, "Recent Inflation and the Monetarists," *Applied Eco-*

nomics 8 (June 1976):145–56; Wynne A. H. Godley, "Inflation in the United Kingdom," in Lawrence B. Krause and Walter S. Salant, eds., *Worldwide Inflation: Theory and Recent Experience* (Washington, D. C.: The Brookings Institution, 1977), p. 468.

18. See Robert Bacon and Walter Eltis, *Britain's Economic Problem: Too Few Producers* (London: The Macmillan Press, 1976), pp. 10–31, 167–68; *Labour Force Statistics, 1964–1975* (Paris: OECD, 1977), pp. 42–43.

19. *International Economic Report of the President, January 1977* (Washington, D. C.: Government Printing Office, 1977), pp. 100–01.

20. *Oil Statistics 1976*, p. xxxix.

21. For historical data on inflation and unemployment rates, see U.S. Department of Labor, Bureau of Labor Statistics, *Handbook of Labor Statistics 1975— Reference Edition* (Washington, D.C.: Government Printing Office, 1975) p. 313; Richard B. Du Boff, "Unemployment in the United States: An Historical Summary," *Monthly Review* 29 (November 1977):11. See too Anna J. Schwartz, "Inflation in the United States," *Current History* 69 (November 1975):170–74, 194–96; Charles L. Schultze, *National Income Analysis,* 3rd ed. (Englewood Cliffs, N. J.: Prentice-Hall, 1971), pp. 110–11; Walter W. Heller, "What's Right with Economics?" *American Economic Review* 65 (March 1975):16–17; Jong Ryool Lee and Jeffrey S. Milstein, "A Political Economy of the Vietnam War, 1965–1972," *The Papers of the Peace Science Society International* 21 (1973):41–63; Otto Eckstein and James A. Girola, "Long-Term Properties of the Price-Wage Mechanism in the United States, 1891 to 1977," *The Review of Economics and Statistics* 60 (August 1968):332.

22. Jack Barbash and Kate Barbash, *Trade Unions and National Economic Policy* (Baltimore: Johns Hopkins University Press, 1972), pp. 168–95; Boner and Neef, "Productivity and Unit Labor Costs in 12 Industrial Countries," pp. 13–14; U.S. Department of Labor, *Handbook of Labor Statistics 1976,* p. 337.

23. See Raymond Vernon, "An Interpretation," *Daedalus* 104 (Fall 1975):4–6; Mira Wilkins, "The Oil Companies in Perspective," *Daedalus* 104 (Fall 1975):162–63. According to Vernon, p. 5: "From 1954 on, the share of the profits retained by the oil companies in the production of crude oil had begun gradually to decline, moving to well under 40 percent by the late nineteen-sixties. As a result, the profits recorded by the majors fell from about 80 cents per barrel of crude oil to about 30 cents. At the same time, the share of the international crude oil market accounted for by the majors also fell, dropping from about 90 percent in the early nineteen-fifties to about 70 percent twenty years later." During the 1960s the greater competition and the increase in the supplies of crude oil resulted in lower prices.

24. William G. Shepherd, *Market Power and Economic Welfare: An Introduction* (New York: Random House, 1970), pp. 213–20; Charles F. Peake, "Negro Occupation-Employment Participation in American Industry: Historical Perspective, Improvements during the 1960s, and Recent Plateauing," *American Journal of Economics and Sociology* 34 (January 1975):67–86, esp. pp. 81–83; William Julius Wilson, *The Declining Significance of Race: Blacks and Changing American Institutions* (Chicago: University of Chicago Press, 1978), pp. 88–143; William J. Wilson, "The Declining Significance of Race: Revisited but Not

Revised," *Society* 15 (July/August 1978):11, 16–21. According to Wilson, college-educated blacks between 25 and 29 experience more favorable employment opportunities than do young blacks with no high school degree who live in the inner cities. Since the early 1970s, government and private corporations have hired the college-educated blacks to fulfill managerial and professional jobs. These middle-class black Americans have especially benefited from government equal opportunity and affirmative action programs.

25. Theresa Ann Flaim, *The Structure of the U. S. Petroleum Industry: Concentration, Vertical Integration and Joint Activities,* unpublished Ph.D dissertation, Department of Economics, Cornell University, Ithaca, N.Y., 1977, p. 119; Robert F. Halvrson and Judith A. Thornton, "Comparative Responses to the Energy Crisis in Different Economic Systems," p. 202; Blair, *The Control of Oil,* pp. 128–31, 169–204, 308; Wilson "Market Structure and Interfirm Integration in the Petroleum Industry," p. 324; Steven A. Schneider, "Common Sense about Energy Policy, Part One: Where Has All the Oil Gone?" *Working Papers for a New Society* 6 (January-February 1978):40–41.

26. Blair, *The Control of Oil,* p. 320.

27. The most comprehensive account of the food oligopolies is found in Jim Hightower, *Eat Your Heart Out* (New York: Crown Publishers, 1975). The data on the farmers' share of food prices appear on page 150. See too Shirley E. Greene and Richard W. Priggie, "The 'Free Market' Myth: Fatal Trap for Farmers," *Christianity and Crisis* 37 (October 31, 1977):249–53; Barry Commoner, "Agrinomics: Lesson of Farm Strike," *Politicks and other Human Interests,* no. 7 (January 31, 1978):18–19.

28. Richard T. Gill, *Economics and the Public Interest,* 3rd ed. (Pacific Palisades, Calif.: Goodyear, 1976), pp. 203–06; Jeff Frieden, "The Trilateral Commission: Economics and Politics in the 1970s," *Monthly Review* 29 (December 1977):2–7.

29. Robert McNown, "The Impact of Currency Depreciation and International Markets on U. S. Inflation," *Quarterly Review of Economics and Business* 15 (Winter 1975):12; E. Ray Canterbery, "The International Monetary Crisis and the Delayed Peg," *Challenge* 21 (November/December 1978):4–12.

30. See James R. Crotty and Leonard A. Rapping, "The 1975 Report of the President's Council of Economic Advisors: A Radical Critique," *The American Economic Review* 65 (December 1975):803–05; Reynolds, *Macroeconomics,* pp. 362–63; Gilpin, *U. S. Power and the Multinational Corporation,* pp. 201–05; *OECD Statistics of Foreign Trade: Monthly Bulletin* (November 1977):37, 39.

31. Edhard Brehmer and Maxwell R. Bradford, "Incomes and Labor Market Policies in Sweden, 1945–70," *International Monetary Fund Staff Papers* 21 (March 1974):114; Morley Gunderson, "Training in Canada: Progress and Problems," *International Journal of Social Economics* 4, no. 1 (1977):2.

32. Beatrice Reubens, "A Foreign Experience: Swedish Active Manpower Policy," *New Generation* 53 (Winter 1971):26–32.

33. See Boner and Neef, "Productivity and Unit Labor Costs in 12 Industrial Countries," p. 13; Brehmer and Bradford, "Income and Labor Market Policies in Sweden," pp. 123–25; Erik Lundberg, "Income Policy Issues in Sweden," in Walter Galenson, ed., *Incomes Policy: What Can We Learn from Europe?* (Ithaca: New York State School of Industrial and Labor Relations, Cornell University,

1973), pp. 41–58; Assar Lindbeck, *Swedish Economic Policy* (Berkeley: University of California Press, 1974), pp. 158–59; Hans Brems, "Swedish Fine Tuning," *Challenge* 19 (March-April 1976):39–42.

34. Steven A. Schneider, "Common Sense about Energy, Part Two: Less Is More, Conservation and Renewable Energy," *Working Papers for a New Society* 6 (March-April 1978):49–58.

35. William P. Snavely, "Macroeconomic Institutional Innovation: Some Observations from the Swedish Experience," *Journal of Economic Issues* 6 (December 1972):27–60.

The Impact of Economic Policies on Income Distribution

A fear of equality is haunting some segments of American society. During the late 1950s Robert Lane interviewed fifteen working-class men living around New Haven, Connecticut. Most of these men did not support government policies to promote greater economic equality; rather, they feared the prospect of a more egalitarian society. For them, inequality of income provided an incentive to rise in the social stratification system. They thought that without the continuation of unequal economic rewards for diverse contributions, Americans would lack the motivation to work harder and achieve upward mobility. Other studies sampling the whole population suggested that most Americans regard public policies to realize extensive economic equality as neither desirable nor feasible.[1]

From a similar perspective, the sociologist Robert Nisbet in 1975 viewed with alarm the trend toward greater equality of condition. Surveying 2,000 years of Western political thought, he found equality associated with uniformity, leveling, regimentation, bureaucratic collectivism, and centralized political power. Individual liberty and group diversity suffer at the expense of equality. According to him, equality is not only an undesirable value but also a growing empirical reality:

> No one will question the fact that a higher degree of equality now exists in Western countries than at any time in the past. This is true not only of

Chapter Seven

equality of opportunity and legal equality . . . but of the more generalized equality of economic, political, and social condition.[2]

How valid is Nisbet's belief about the historical trends toward greater equality, including equality of income distribution? Attempting to calculate the degree of income equality in different nations, social scientists have resorted to both crossnational and longitudinal comparisons. For example, how unequally are incomes distributed in the United States, compared with Sweden, Britain, and France? Within each country, has equality increased, decreased, or remained constant since the end of World War II? As we see below, answers to these questions remain tentative, for they largely depend on the specific methods used to measure income and equality. Unfortunately, the variety of measurement techniques and the lack of accurate sources of information confound attempts to estimate economic equality across both time and nations. Generalizations about the actual prevalence of income equality are therefore difficult to prove. Nisbet's fear of equality may rest on invalid assumptions about the empirical world.

Chapter 7 probes four aspects of income distribution in several Western nations. First, it indicates the specific ways in which measurement techniques influence conclusions about income equality. Then, it assesses the actual degree of economic equality across seven countries. Next, this chapter evaluates the impact of tax and expenditure policies on income distribution. Finally, it explores the reasons for the limited impact of fiscal policies on securing greater economic equality.

Measurement of Income Distribution

The measurement of income distribution involves three basic questions: First, what units (individuals and groups) are compared? Second, how is "income" defined and measured? Third, what specific techniques are used to assess the degrees of equality?

Units for Comparison

Since equality refers to distributional relationships among certain units, the choice of individuals and groups for analysis influences the conclusions. Economists have studied income equality among *individuals, nuclear families* (husband, wife, dependent children), and *households* (members of the nuclear family and other persons living with them).

Inequality among individuals seems greater than among nuclear families and especially among households. Why? Persons in a family and household probably share their income with each other; thus, as the household size becomes larger, income increases. For this reason, if the elderly and young people establish separate households and live by themselves as individuals, the measured inequality will grow larger. By the same logic, if a nation experiences a high divorce rate, then its economic inequality will increase.

When comparing crossnationally, we should measure the income of similar economic and age groups. If we compare full-time workers in Britain with full-time workers in Canada, we discover greater equality than if we analyze full-time British employees and part-time Canadian workers. In addition, controls for age affect conclusions about the extent of income equality. People of the same age group generally have more similar incomes than do individuals of different ages.[3]

Operational Definitions of Income

The operational definitions of income also compound the problems of measuring economic inequality. Economists draw a distinction between income and wealth. Within industrialized societies, *income* includes monetary assets—the money received in the form of wages, salaries, rents, interest, dividends, and the like. *Wealth,* defined more broadly, comprises all assets minus liabilities. Assets include monetary resources as well as personal property: corporate stocks, bonds, life insurance, real estate, home, automobile, and durable consumer goods. Because rich people hold a larger proportion of property assets than do the poor, inequality of wealth exceeds income inequality. Another factor affecting the degree of economic equality pertains to the distinction between cash income and noncash or in-kind income. Both in the United States and overseas, senior and middle-level managers employed by private corporations, as well as high-ranking government civil servants, often receive a number of noncash perquisites: free life insurance policies, low-cost private medical care, inexpensive meals in staff canteens, home loans at low interest rates, free cars, paid vacations at luxurious resorts, free travel, free tickets to football or soccer games, free newspapers, and subsidized tuition to private schools for their children. Although skilled factory workers, especially those in unions, also receive such fringe benefits as subsidized meals, health insurance, and pension premiums, they gain access to fewer noncash perquisites than do the wealthy managers. Therefore, operational definitions of income that exclude these in-kind benefits uncover more equality than those definitions including them. In sum, more inclusive definitions of income reveal greater inequality across nations. If economic equality measures wealth and noncash perquisites, a sharper gap between rich and poor emerges.

Government policies also affect the degree of income equality. Generally, income before taxes and expenditures shows a less equal pattern than posttax and postexpenditure income distribution. Although it is difficult to isolate the independent effects of taxes and expenditures, taxes appear to exert a less egalitarian impact than do expenditures. In most nations, regressive (pro-rich) and proportional taxes, rather than progressive (pro-poor) taxes, tend to prevail. The wealthier classes have more opportunities to engage in legal tax avoidance and illegal tax evasion. Compared with taxes, expenditure policies show more egalitarian consequences on income distribution. Transfer benefits to individuals seem especially important. They comprise both cash and noncash (in-kind) payments. Cash transfers include social security grants, old-age pensions, family allowances, sickness cash benefits, unemployment compensation, and public assistance. The noncash benefits consist of low-rent housing, free health care, education, and job training programs. Since all noncash benefits enlarge people's resources, they increase the income people can spend for other purposes. For this reason, measurements that include both cash and in-kind government benefits show greater equality than operational definitions that exclude the noncash programs. Of course, governments in Western capitalist societies also grant subsidies to business firms as well as to individuals. The inclusion of business subsidies reduces the income equality found across several nations.[4]

The comparison of incomes should consider the effects of unemployment and inflation. Measurements of economic equality refer to *real income*—the degree to which different groups (mainly families and households) possess similar potential purchasing power. If unemployment rates decline as prices remain stable, then income equality increases. However, if growing unemployment accompanies more severe inflation, the purchasing power of low-income citizens falls, thereby reducing income equality. Particularly if food prices show a sharp rise, economic equality decreases, because poor people spend a higher proportion of their income on food than do wealthier people.[5]

The time period for measuring income also influences estimates of economic equality. Generally, measurements taken over long time periods find less inequality. For instance, calculations of yearly incomes yield lower equality figures than do lifetime income estimates. Of course, social scientists cannot easily obtain the data required for appraising people's lifetime incomes; therefore, most studies use yearly measures.[6]

Whatever the operational definition given to income, the extent of income equality found crossnationally depends on the accuracy of the informational sources. Social scientists have gathered data about income equality from two primary sources: tax returns and sample surveys. Both these sources may yield inaccurate information. Although income tax records provide crucial insights into income before and after taxes, they typically underreport the income of the wealthy; often, tax records also exclude many low-income people, especially if incomes below a certain minimum level are not taxed. Persons interviewed in a census or sample survey may fail to answer questions about their incomes or may provide false information. They are more likely to report accurately their wages and salaries than income received as interest, dividends, and capital gains.[7] In short, because of problems associated with false reporting and underreporting, conclusions drawn from both surveys and tax records may obscure the actual degree of economic equality.

Techniques to Measure Equality

The specific techniques used to measure equality influence the patterns of income distribution found across several nations. One of the most widely used techniques for measuring economic inequality has been the Gini coefficient, named after the Italian statistician Corrado Gini. To ascertain the extent of income equality, economists compare two variables: the percentage of families (as measured in tenths or fifths of the population) and the proportion of total income possessed by these families. On the horizontal axis of a graph, families are ranked according to their total income. The vertical axis contains information about the percentage of the total income possessed by them. If 10 percent of all families hold 10 percent of the total income, if 20 percent possess 20 percent of the aggregate income, and if 90 percent receive 90 percent of total income, then a society demonstrates perfect equality. However, if 1 percent of the families possess 100 percent of total income, the distribution pattern approaches full inequality. According to conventions, a 0 Gini coefficient means full equality (zero inequality); a Gini index of 1 refers to complete inequality. When we compare Gini coefficients among different nations, Ginis lower than .30 indicate less income inequality than Ginis above .40.[8]

In sum, table 7–1 summarizes the effects of different measurement procedures on estimations of economic equality. Because of the various

Table 7-1   Effects of Measurement Procedures on Estimations of Income Equality

Variable	More Equality	Less Equality
Unit for Comparison	Household, family	Individual (one person household)
	Full-time workers	Full-time and part-time workers
	Same age group	Different age groups
Operational Definition of Income	Income (monetary assets)	Wealth (monetary assets and personal property)
	Cash income	Cash income and noncash "fringe benefits" received by senior and middle-level managers
	Income after progressive taxes	Income before progressive taxes
	Income that includes government cash transfers	Income which excludes government cash transfers
	Income including noncash government transfers	Income excluding noncash government transfers
	Income which excludes government subsidies to private businesses	Income which includes government subsidies to private businesses
	Income earned under conditions of full employment and low price rises	Income earned under conditions of high unemployment and high inflation
	Lifetime income	Yearly income
	Income data derived from sources where actual amount of income is underreported	Income data derived from sources where actual amount of income (especially from interest, dividends, and capital gains) is accurately reported
Techniques to Measure Equality	Gini coefficient nearer 0	Gini coefficient nearer 1

units for comparison, the diverse operational definitions given to income, and the different techniques for measuring equality, social scientists find it difficult to compare the distribution of incomes across several nations. Sensitive to these measurement difficulties, the next sections probe the extent of economic equality among seven societies and attempt to estimate the impacts of government taxes and expenditures on income distribution. Some tentative conclusions are drawn about the historical trend toward greater equality of economic condition.

Degrees of Income Equality
in Seven Nations

The evidence collected by Malcolm Sawyer on behalf of the Organisation for Economic Cooperation and Development suggests that the Swedish and British citizens live in the most economically egalitarian societies. Canada, the United States, and West Germany have less income equality than Britain and especially Sweden. France and Italy appear the least egalitarian. Table 7–2 presents the data on which these conclusions are based. The information pertains to patterns of income distribution between 1969 and 1973. The posttax yearly income comprises revenues received from (1) wages and salaries, (2) entrepreneurial sources, excluding capital gains, (3) property, and (4) current transfers, including private transfer payments. Whether or not we control for household size (that is, assume that the same proportions of people live in houses with different numbers of residents across all nations), the rankings of income equality are the same. Sweden, with the lowest Gini, has the highest equality, followed by the United Kingdom, Canada, the United States, West Germany, and Italy. At the opposite range of the scale, France reveals the greatest inequality. Research conducted during earlier time periods confirms the rankings made by Sawyer.[9]

Crossnational investigations of one occupational group, however, uncover somewhat different degrees of income equality than do studies taking the whole national population as the unit for comparison. Table 7–3 shows the wages received by manufacturing workers in eight industries. Compared with the type of income measured in table 7–2, these measurements of wages do not control for the effects of taxes or government expenditures. Another limitation is that the wage data do not take into account the effects of inflation and the value of the U.S. dollar vis-à-vis foreign currencies. Nevertheless, the figures do offer valuable insights into the extent of wage inequalities within different countries. In all seven nations, workers employed by firms producing motor vehicles, primary metals, nonelectric machinery, and electrical equipment—all examples of capital goods industries—earned the highest wages. In contrast, workers engaged in lighter industries, such as textiles, footwear, and apparel, received lower hourly compensation. One reason for the wage differential stems from the greater economic power of trade unions in heavy industries. Compared with light industries, firms manufacturing capital goods are also more concentrated and earn higher profits.

What nations show the greatest wage differences between the high-

Table 7–2 Income Equality among Seven Nations

Country	Year	Ginis for Posttax Income[a]	
		No Controls for Household Size	*Standardized Household Size[b]*
Sweden	1972	.30	.27
United Kingdom	1973	.32	.33
Canada[c]	1969, 1972	.35	.35
United States	1972	.38	.37
West Germany	1973	.38	.39
Italy	1969	.40	—
France	1970	.41	.42

[a]Low Ginis indicate low inequality (higher income equality).

[b]Calculations for standardized household size assume the following proportions of households in the six countries:

Persons in household	% of total population
One	23
Two	28
Three	17
Four	16
Five or more	16

[c]Information on Canadian income with no controls for household size pertains to 1969; Gini in the standardized household column refers to 1972.

SOURCE: Malcolm Sawyer, "Income Distribution in OECD Countries," *OECD Economic Outlook: Occasional Studies* (July 1976), esp. pp. 17, 19.

est and lowest paid workers? As indicated by table 7–3, Sweden and the United Kingdom have the highest wage equality. By contrast, the United States and Canada show the greatest wage differences, that is, the sharpest gap between auto workers and persons producing clothes. Although France and Italy demonstrate profound income cleavages within the whole nation, the wages gained by their manufacturing workers reveals fewer differences among industries than do wages in Germany, Canada, and the United States.

These patterns of income distribution among manufacturing workers illustrate the crucial importance of the relationship between income equality and the level of wealth. Swedish workers in eight industries earn the highest mean wage, over $8 an hour. Throughout the different industries, their wages are also relatively equal. By contrast, British workers receive relatively low wages, only $3 an hour. Yet, at least in the manufacturing sector, no sharp income gaps separate the highest paid from the lowest paid employees. Indeed, the United Kingdom ranks first on the wage equality scale. If Sweden exemplifies the equality of wealth, Britain demonstrates the equality of poverty. In both countries, high proportions of the work force belong to trade unions; socialist parties have played a powerful role in the political system. Despite these similarities, the Swedish unions and the Social Democratic government have achieved greater success in stimulating economic productivity than have the British unions or Labour party. North American manufacturing employees live in societies where wages for some are comparatively high, but where sharp income gaps divide the best paid from the lowest paid. For example, auto workers in the United States and Canada earn the highest salaries among the seven nations; yet workers making shoes receive less than half the hourly compensation gained by auto employees. Undoubtedly, the weaknesses of trade unions and socialist parties in Canada and the United States, combined with the powerful role played by business firms in the political system, partly explain the pattern of income inequality within two relatively wealthy countries.

In sum, comparisons of income distribution across several nations and among different groups of manufacturing workers suggest that Sweden and Britain display the greatest income equality. Conclusions about the other five countries depend on the units and variables chosen for comparison. If the investigator compares the wages received by manufacturing workers, France and Italy appear more egalitarian than Germany, Canada, or the United States. If, however, the investigator analyzes income distribution patterns among the whole population and defines income to include revenues after taxes and government expenditures, France and Italy reveal the least economic equality. The power exerted by unions in the manufacturing sector, the relative influence of socialist parties and business firms on economic policy making and the type of government tax and spending policies account for these diverse conclusions. As we shall see below, Swedish political leaders have implemented the most progressive taxes and the most redistributive expenditure policies. Governments in France and Italy, however, administer the most regressive tax policies and possibly the most inegalitarian pattern of expenditures.

The Impact of Taxes

Economists have relied on two methods to assess the effects of tax policies on the redistribution of income. One technique measures the incidence of taxes on specific income groups—that is, the share of their actual incomes that different economic groups pay in taxes. Progressive taxes, which are pro-poor, take a higher percentage of income from the wealthy than from the poor. In contrast, regressive taxes tend to favor the rich, because they cause poorer people to pay a higher percentage of

Table 7–3 Hourly Wages in Eight Manufacturing Industries, 1976 (Wages in Manufacturing Industries in U.S. Dollars)

Country	Motor Vehicles	Primary Metals	Chemicals	Nonelectric Machinery	Electrical Equipment
United States	$10.75	$9.95	$7.80	$7.55	$6.50
Canada	9.35	8.90	7.75	8.30	6.75
United Kingdom	3.65	3.70	3.50	3.15	2.90
West Germany	8.60	7.30	7.60	7.05	6.25
Sweden	8.80	9.40	8.30	8.35	7.85
France	4.80	5.60	5.50	4.90	4.40
Italy	5.10	5.60	5.05	4.60	4.55

[a]Measures the dispersion of wages around the mean wage in each country. The higher the standard deviation, the greater the wage inequality among manufacturing workers.

their incomes in taxes than do wealthier people. Under proportional taxes, all persons, regardless of income level, pay an equal percentage of their income in taxes. Hence, progressive taxes redistribute income in favor of the poor; regressive taxes also redistribute income, but the benefits go to the rich; and proportional taxes have no redistributive effects on income equality. A second method for estimating the effects of tax policies is to measure the distribution of actual income before and after taxes. The greater the extent to which the rich lose income and the poor gain, the more egalitarian is the impact of the tax policies. Before drawing conclusions about these assumed effects, we should remember that government policies affect both pretax and posttax incomes. For example, governments devise policies to deal with inflation and unemployment, including wage and price controls, minimum wages, investment tax incentives, interest rates, changes in the money supply, and government purchases of particular goods and services. Since all these public policies affect income before taxes are levied, it becomes difficult to make valid generalizations about the consequences of tax policies.[10]

By examining tax incidence within each country and by comparing pretax and posttax incomes across nations, investigators have discovered that taxes rarely exert a significant impact on income redistribution that favors the poor. Table 7–4 analyzes the share of total money

Tex- tiles	Foot- wear	Apparel	Mean	Standard Deviation[a]
$4.55	$4.10	$4.15	$6.91	$2.58
5.30	4.55	4.60	6.93	1.93
2.60	2.70	1.90	3.01	0.62
5.50	4.80	4.95	6.50	1.36
7.60	7.25	6.95	8.06	0.81
3.80	3.60	3.35	4.26	0.99
3.50	3.20	2.75	4.29	1.02

SOURCE: *International Economic Report of the President,* transmitted to the Congress January 1977 (Washington, D. C.: Government Printing Office, 1977), pp. 100–01.

income possessed by the poorest and wealthiest 20 percent of national populations both before and after taxes. According to this table, in none of the six countries did taxes increase the share going to the poor by more than 1 percent. For example, in the United Kingdom the poorest 20 percent held 5.4 percent of the total pretax monetary income; after taxes, their share rose to only 6.3 percent. The tax system in most countries also failed to significantly lower the income shares accruing to the wealthiest 20 percent. Only in Sweden did the differences between pretax and posttax income shares of the wealthy exceed 3 percent. Even after progressive taxes, the wealthiest 20 percent of the Swedish population still held 37 percent of the total income, compared with 40.5 percent before taxes. By contrast, in France taxes seemed to exert no influence whatsoever on income distribution. Among both rich and poor, pre- and posttax incomes were virtually identical.

Investigations of tax incidence reach similar conclusions about the minimal effects of taxes on economic equality. In all these societies, the central government income tax is the most progressive. Sales and social security taxes, as well as local property taxes, are more regressive than taxes on personal or corporate income. Since the regressive taxes counterbalance the more progressive ones, the after-tax distribution of income remains about the same as pretax income.

Of all the types of taxes levied by governments in the United

Table 7–4   Effects of Taxes on Income Distribution

		Share of Total Money Income Possessed by Poorest 20%		
Country	Date	Pretax Income[a]	Posttax Income[b]	Differen.
United States	1972	3.8%	4.5%	.7%
Canada	1969	4.3	5.0	.7
United Kingdom	1973	5.4	6.3	.9
West Germany	1973	5.9	6.5	.6
Sweden	1972	6.0	6.6	.6
France	1970	4.3	4.3	.0

[a]Wages and salaries, entrepreneurial income, property income, and current transfers (both public and private).
[b]Direct taxes and social security payments are deducted from pretax income.

States, the federal personal and corporation income taxes exert the most progressive effects. People making over $500,000 paid the highest actual rates in the late 1960s; people with incomes under $3,000 paid the lowest rates. Yet, despite the progressivity of the federal personal income tax, wealthy people still manage to find ways to avoid paying high taxes. The effective rates for individuals making more than one million dollars a year are lower than the rates for those who receive between $100,000 and one million dollars, partly because capital gains, inherited wealth, and interest on state and municipal bonds are taxed at low rates. Furthermore, even the progressive income taxes tend to favor some groups at the expense of other less economically fortunate groups. People who gain include homeowners, married persons, the elderly rich, urban residents, and those who itemize deductions and can thus deduct state income taxes, real estate taxes, and interest on home mortgages. People who earn their income from property—interest, dividends, and capital gains—also benefit from the current federal personal income tax laws. In contrast, the following groups secure fewer economic advantages: renters, single persons, the young poor, rural residents, those who take standard deductions, and individuals who earn most of their income from wages or salaries. For all these reasons, even the most progressive tax—the federal personal income tax—has only a limited effect on the reduction of income inequality.[11]

Wealthiest 20%		
Pretax Income	*Posttax Income*	*Difference*
44.8%	42.9%	−1.9%
43.3	41.0	−2.3
40.3	38.7	−1.6
46.8	46.1	−0.7
40.5	37.0	−3.5
47.0	46.9	−0.1

SOURCE: Malcolm Sawyer, "Income Distribution in OECD Countries," *OECD Economic Outlook: Occasional Studies* (July 1976):14.

The growing importance of social security payroll taxes in the United States means that the government pressures toward greater income equality have weakened. Many low-income individuals pay a higher proportion of their income for social security taxes than for federal personal income taxes. Although taxes on personal income still account for the highest percentage of total government revenue, social security taxes now yield over twice as much revenue as corporate income taxes.[12]

Why are social security taxes so regressive, especially for the working poor? All people, whatever their incomes, pay the same rate; the poor receive no exemptions, as they do for the personal income tax. Above a certain income ceiling, an individual no longer has to pay the social security tax, a provision that obviously benefits wealthier citizens. Only income from wages, not from rents, capital gains, dividends, or interest on investments, incurs the social security payroll tax.[13] As a consequence, this tax increases, rather than reduces, income inequality.

Compared with national income taxes, U.S. state and local taxes have a more regressive effect on income distribution. Most state governments raise their revenues through sales taxes. Particularly if the sales tax includes food, the tax takes a larger percentage of the poor person's total income than that of wealthier individuals. During 1977 only twenty-two of the forty-five states levying a sales tax exempted food from that tax. However, services used primarily by the wealthy and business corporations did not incur a sales tax. These services included credit rating, collection of bills, protection of property, detective work, cleaning, maintenance of buildings, and services provided by lawyers, architects, advertisers, and travel agents. Although poor people spend a high proportion of their total income on food and other consumer goods, wealthier individuals spend more money for those services not subject to the sales tax. Regardless of income, all people pay the same rate of sales tax. This constant rate increases its regressive feature, since the sales tax comprises a large share of a poor person's total income. Lower-income people thus pay a greater proportion of their income in general sales taxes.

Although the evidence is not as clearcut, local property taxes also probably benefit the rich more than the poor. Why? Business corporations have managed to secure special exemptions, abatements, and deductions from the property tax. In some states, profit-oriented enterprises, such as car rental agencies, hotels, and restaurants, operate on state government property (like a port authority) that bears no property tax. Because of business exemptions, the property tax is levied primarily on residential property. Local governments usually exempt stocks and bonds, intangible property possessed mainly by high-income people, from the property tax. Among different states, tax assessments widely vary; the assessor's office in a given locality often has sufficient staff to make assessments only every four or five years, even though the price of land and houses may rise each year. Thus, people residing in similar houses may pay different property taxes. Compared with renters, home-owners receive greater benefits from the property tax, since they can deduct property taxes from their federal income taxes.[14]

In conclusion, if we consider all the types of taxes levied in the United States—federal personal income, corporate income, social security, state sales, and local property—then these taxes taken together seem to exert a proportional effect on income equality. During the late 1960s, all families with incomes between $5,000 and $50,000 paid about the same percentage (15 percent) of their total income in taxes. Taxes had practically no impact on reducing inequality, because the regressive social security and sales taxes counterbalanced the more progressive federal income taxes. Between 1950 and 1970 the U.S. tax system actually became more regressive, since corporate income taxes declined while social security taxes increased as a proportion of total tax revenues.[15]

Except for Sweden, the other five Western countries have not experienced a redistribution of income through the tax system. With a few qualifications, the same generalizations about the effects of taxes in the United States apply to other Western nations.

For most Canadians, the total tax burden is approximately proportional, just as in the United States. Canada's federal taxes are more progressive than either provincial or municipal taxes. Unlike the United States, Canada has a federal general sales tax, which tends to be more regressive than either the federal and provincial income taxes or the federal tax on corporation profits. Provincial sales taxes are proportional. The municipal property tax probably exerts the most regressive impact. In sum, Canadian federal taxes are most egalitarian, provincial taxes are proportional, and local taxes are the most regressive.[16] Hence, the total tax system exerts only a minimal impact on securing greater income equality.

Despite the political power of the Labour party in Britain since World War II, British taxes have failed to change substantially the patterns of income distribution. As in Canada and the United States, the actual rates for all taxes are roughly proportional. National income taxes are more progressive than local taxes, which are usually based on property. The homes of the wealthy bear relatively low tax rates. Social security contributions to the National Insurance Fund are also regressive, although less so than the sales tax.[17] Because the regressive sales, property, and social security taxes offset the more progressive national personal income tax, the overall tax system tends to exert a proportional effect on the distribution of income.

Sweden and France diverge from the proportional tax pattern found in Britain, Canada, and the United States. Whereas Swedish taxes are the most progressive among these nations, French taxes are the least progressive. In contrast to U.S., British, and Canadian citizens, Swedes pay no local property taxes. Instead, Swedish local government officials levy taxes on income, rather than on property. Although the local income tax is less progressive than the national income tax, wealthier people still pay higher rates (larger percentages of their total income) than do very poor people. The value-added tax is far more regressive than the two income taxes. Yet, the national and local direct taxes yield a higher percentage of total tax revenues than the indirect sales taxes. Old age pension fees and health insurance contributions seem neither progressive nor regressive, for they take the highest proportion of income from the middle-class groups, rather than from either rich or poor.[18]

Compared with Swedish taxes, the French tax system tends toward greater regressivity mainly because income taxes comprise such a small percentage of total tax revenues—in 1976 only 18 percent in France but 47 percent in Sweden. Although none of the taxes has egalitarian effects, the income tax is more progressive than the value-added and social security taxes. Yet these two regressive taxes produced nearly 75 percent of total government revenues during 1976. Like Italy, France is plagued by extensive tax avoidance and illegal evasion. French economists estimate that about two-thirds of total income escapes taxation. Only about half the French population pays any income tax. Both the rich and the poor gain special deductions, exemptions, and abatements. In particular, the tax laws benefit company directors and senior executives who purchase real estate, other property, and life insurance contracts. Professional expenses also receive special tax exemptions.[19] For these reasons, French taxes, unlike the Swedish, have failed to lessen economic inequalities.

What conclusions can we draw about the impact of taxes on economic equality? In general, taxes seem to exert a minimal effect on income redistribution. As we have seen, Sweden operates the most progressive tax system, mainly because taxes on income and profits are high as a proportion of total tax revenues whereas value-added taxes are comparatively low. By contrast, the French government levies the most regressive taxes, based primarily on social security contributions and value-added taxes. The tax systems of the three Anglo-American countries—the United States, Canada, and Britain—exercise a generally proportional effect, with the more progressive national income tax counterbalanced by less progressive sales and social security taxes.

The Impact of Government Expenditures

Compared with taxes, government expenditures have a greater impact on the redistribution of income. Although it is difficult to analyze the separate effects of taxes and expenditures, economists studying Western societies since the end of the Second World War have discovered that taxes have reduced income inequality less than have government expenditures. Tables 7–4 and 7–5 illustrate the more significant impact of expenditure policies. According to table 7–5, government transfer programs (for example, social security payments, pensions, unemployment compensation, public assistance, and family allowances) enlarge the share of income going to the poorest 20 percent of the population by margins ranging from 2 percent in France to nearly 9 percent in Sweden. By contrast, the differences between the posttax and pretax income of the poor were far smaller; in no country was the difference greater than a 1 percent growth in the share of total income. In most nations too, government transfers, relative to taxes, secure greater reductions in the proportion of total income accruing to the wealthiest 20 percent. The Swedish government has implemented an especially egalitarian transfer program, with about 8 percent of total income redistributed from the wealthiest 20 percent to the poorest 20 percent. By contrast, France features the least egalitarian income maintenance policies. Despite Britain's reputation in the United States as a profligate welfare state, British transfer programs are not really that beneficent; U.S. government expenditures have actually transferred a slightly larger share of national income from the rich to the poor. British expenditures for health, education, and housing may benefit middle-class individuals more than low-income people. Detailed studies of each society have reached similar conclusions about the more egalitarian impact of transfer payments relative to taxes.[20]

According to research conducted in the United States, during the late 1960s federal expenditures benefited the poor more than did state and local expenditures. Three expenditures in particular—public assistance, health, and social insurance and retirement—provided significant benefits for the very poor (in 1968 those with income less than $4,000) and the aged (over sixty-five). Since social security payments received by the aged poor constituted a higher proportion of their previous earnings than did benefits gained by the retired wealthy, social security expenditures transferred income to elderly, low-income citizens. Without these social security and welfare benefits, the aged and poor would have possessed practically no income at all.[21]

Despite the redistributive effects of national government expenditures, we should not exaggerate their egalitarian consequences. During the 1960s and 1970s government transfer programs benefited mainly the elderly, the very poor, and young mothers with dependent children. In contrast, low-income groups less likely to benefit from government income maintenance policies included the working poor with low paid or part-time jobs, childless couples under sixty-five, partially disabled single people, and young and middle-aged men. Indeed, in 1972 nearly two-thirds of families with less than a $4,275 yearly income received no public cash assistance. Despite the expansion of government income support programs since World War II, during the 1970s private payments, such as those granted older people by their children, exerted about as great an effect on reducing income inequality as did public

Table 7–5 Effects of Government Transfers on Income Distribution

| | | Share of Total Money Income Possessed by Poorest 20% | | |
| | | Pretransfer Posttax Income | Posttransfer Posttax Income | Difference |
Country	Date			
United States	1972	2.4%	6.3%	3.9%
Canada	1969	2.2	6.0	3.8
United Kingdom	1973	2.7	6.3	3.6
West Germany	1969	3.5	7.0	3.5
Sweden	1972	0.7	9.4	8.7
France	1970	2.8	4.8	2.0

NOTE: Government transfers include such payments as social security, pensions, unemployment compensation, family allowances, and public assistance. Since the types of transfers vary across countries, the comparisons remain tentative. The data for pretransfer, posttax income of German citizens are estimates. The income unit is a household.

transfer programs like Aid to Families with Dependent Children (primarily helping children in homes where the father is not present) and the Supplementary Security Income (assisting the aged, blind, and disabled). Significantly, whereas the expenditures for these two programs, along with general public assistance for dependent children and the aged, constituted no more than 10 percent of the funds spent for income support policies, over one-half of expenditures for income maintenance went for social security payments.[22]

Even the social security program, which provides the greatest help to the aged, has a limited effect on raising the income of poor citizens. Why? First, although most poor people are under sixty-five, the social security program reaches mainly those over sixty-five. Other low-income groups, like the working poor, receive minimal benefits. Second, several aspects of the social security program disadvantage the elderly poor. Although the government allows people over sixty-four to collect nonsalary income in the form of dividends, rent, and interest, they are prohibited from earning additional wages or salaries above a specified limit to supplement their social security payments. As a result of ill health and unsafe working conditions, manual workers usually

	Wealthiest 20%	
Pretransfer Posttax Income	*Posttransfer Posttax Income*	*Diff-erence*
51.2%	47.1%	−4.1%
42.8	40.6	−2.2
41.9	38.8	−3.1
43.2	39.1	−4.1
43.7	35.6	−8.1
50.1	46.6	−3.5

SOURCE: Data from Malcolm Sawyer, "Income Distribution in OECD Countries," *OECD Economic Outlook: Occasional Studies* (July 1976):22, 34–45; *OECD Studies in Resource Allocation, no. 3: Public Expenditure on Income Maintenance Programs* (Paris: OECD, 1976), pp. 103–04.

retire earlier than nonmanual workers; early retirement means lower payments. Since whites earn higher wages and live longer than do blacks, white retired people receive higher social security checks for longer periods of time. To a certain extent, the social security program thus transfers income from young black workers holding manual jobs to white retired persons formerly employed in skilled, nonmanual positions. In short, the primary effects of social security expenditures have been to supplement the incomes of the wealthy, bring greater economic security to the middle class, and provide a minimum income for the elderly poor.[23]

Other government expenditure policies probably benefit the American middle and upper classes to a even greater extent than do social security programs. Unemployment compensation primarily helps middle-income working people, rather than the poorest segment of the population who can find no work. Because a smaller proportion of low-income individuals attend high schools, colleges, and universities, expenditures for secondary and higher education help the poor less than do health, public assistance, and social insurance programs. Both the federal and state governments provide many transfer payments to business owners and wealthy farmers. These business and agricultural subsidies to maritime firms, airlines, mineral and oil producers, large corporate farms, and the like benefit the wealthy. Expenditures for constructing houses and highways have granted economic advantages mainly to the middle and upper classes. Under urban renewal programs, construction firms have destroyed the houses of low-income families and replaced them with residences and businesses used by the urban wealthy.[24] A large proportion of redistributed income in the United States thus goes to the middle and upper classes, which exercise the greatest political power.

In the U.S. federal system, affluent middle- and upper-class individuals play an active role at the state and local levels of government; they manage to see their preferences translated into public policies. For example, under the general revenue-sharing program begun in 1972, a program by which the federal government allocates to state and local governments funds not directly tied to specific programs, the poorer citizens have lost at the expense of the wealthier. Why? State and local government officials have shown greater interest in reducing taxes than in spending money for health and social service policies. Most federal revenue-sharing funds have gone to finance police work, fire protection, street and road repair, environmental improvements, building renovation, parks, and recreation facilities, rather than to social services directly assisting elderly and low-income people. The replacement of categorical federal grants tied to health and welfare expenditures by general revenue-sharing programs has thus meant a reduction in public services for less affluent citizens.[25]

The generalizations about the impact of government expenditures on economic equality within the United States also apply to Canada and Western European societies. Transfer payments, such as social security, unemployment compensation, public assistance, and family allowances, help the poor much more than do government spending for education, highways, administration, defense, and justice. These transfer programs are direct methods for enlarging the income shares of the poorer citizens. Malcolm Sawyer estimates that in Canada, the United Kingdom, France, and Germany, transfer payments comprise 77 percent of the income of the poorest tenth of the population. Whereas the richest 10 percent derive nearly one-third of their income from investments and other entrepreneurial sources, the poorest 30 percent depend on government transfers.[26]

National government expenditures in Canada and Western Europe contribute more to equality than do local government expenditures. Historically, local government officials have taken fewer steps than have their national counterparts to implement egalitarian policies. During the nineteenth century local governments in both Britain and Sweden strongly opposed comprehensive welfare benefits for the poor. National civil servants had to assume the major responsibility for initiating more equitable income maintenance programs. Although outside the United States opposition to government expenditures for egalitarian objectives has weakened during this century, national governments still finance more redistributive policies. Generally, class ties and concern for income distribution achieve greater importance at the national than at the local government levels. Representatives to national legislatures must appeal to more heterogeneous constituencies, both rich and poor. Labor unions and socialist parties often exert stronger influence over national political leaders. However, within local communities, noneconomic ties often become more significant. Most candidates who run for local office stress their personal qualities, instead of class issues or redistribution policies. Local political activists try to gain more benefits for their territorial, ethnic, or linguistic groups. For example, in Quebec and Scotland, demands arise for the preservation of ethnic status and linguistic autonomy. If local leaders do favor income redistribution, they seek more economic advantages for their regions or cities, not for all poor people as a class.[27] Moreover, regressive tax systems at the local level may diminish support for income redistribution programs among the citizens who pay the highest taxes yet possess the least ability to pay. The national government, which operates a more progressive tax system than the local systems, can better afford to finance redistributive policies.

The Egalitarian Effects of Government Fiscal Policies

What conclusions can we draw about the joint impacts of government tax and spending policies? As we have seen, Sweden has the most egalitarian distribution of income, followed by the United Kingdom, Canada, the United States, and Germany. French leaders must cope with the sharpest income gap between rich and poor.

Table 7–6   The Effects of Fiscal Policies on Income Inequality

| | | Expenditures (% of GNP) | |
| | | | Social |
Country	Date	Total	Services
United States	1971	30.4	10.8
Canada	1971	33.6	18.6
United Kingdom	1972	34.6	12.4
West Germany	1972	34.1	18.7
Sweden	1971	39.3	21.8
France	1969	34.8	18.6
Pearson *r* between Gini and budgetary variable		−.62	−.21

[a] Old age, survivors, and disability insurance; health insurance; public health services; public assistance; benefits for war victims; pensions for government employees; and family allowances (cash payments for families with children).

[b] Gini coefficients range between 1 and 0; the lower the Gini, the less the income inequality. A high negative correlation between personal income taxes and the Gini, for example, means that countries with high personal income taxes as a percentage of the GNP have lower income inequality.

What public policies are associated with these divergent patterns of income distribution?

According to table 7–6, total government expenditures reduce inequality more than do taxes at all governmental levels—that is, the higher the total government spending as a proportion of the gross national product, the lower the income inequality. For instance, of all six nations, Sweden, which has the greatest income equality, spends the highest proportion of the GNP on government programs. As expected, the correlation between the Ginis and total taxes is lower than the association linking inequality to total public spending. Of the three most important taxes—personal income taxes, social security contributions, and taxes on goods and services—the personal income tax as a percentage of GNP bears the strongest relationship to income inequal-

| | Taxes (% of GNP) | | | | |
Total	Personal Income	Goods and Services	Social Security	Gini[b]	Date
27.4	9.2	4.9	5.7	.37	1972
33.1	11.0	9.6	3.0	.35	1972
34.1	10.9	9.0	5.3	.33	1973
35.8	10.0	9.7	12.1	.39	1973
41.6	17.2	12.4	8.3	.27	1972
37.8	4.1	13.9	14.7	.42	1970
−.35	−.95	−.01	.53		

SOURCE: *National Accounts of OECD Countries, 1975* (Paris: OECD, 1977), vol. 2; *1961–1972* (Paris: OECD, 1974); Max Horlick, "National Expenditures on Social Security in Selected Countries," *Research and Statistics Note,* U.S. Department of Health, Education, and Welfare, Social Security Administration, Office of Research and Statistics, no. 29, Washington, D.C., October 18, 1974, pp. 1–2; *Revenue Statistics of OECD Member Countries, 1965–1974* (Paris: OECD, 1976), pp. 74, 77, 83, 87; Malcolm Sawyer, "Income Distribution in OECD Countries," *OECD Economic Outlook: Occasional Studies* (July 1976):19.

ity. As personal income taxes rise, inequality declines. Thus as a proportion of the GNP, personal income taxes are over four times higher
in Sweden than in France (17 percent versus 4 percent). Taxes on goods
and services, primarily sales, value-added, and excise taxes, show virtually no correlation with the crossnational rankings on income equality.
Countries like France and Germany, which have high social security
taxes, rank the lowest on economic equality.

By combining the effects of taxes and expenditures, we can best
assess the influence of fiscal policies on income redistribution. Table 7–
7 shows the correlations between the Ginis for income inequality and a
measure called the "redistributive impact of government budgets."[28]
This index is based on the assumption that personal income taxes and
social service expenditures grant the greatest benefits to poorer citizens;
it is computed by dividing the personal income tax by the sum of
personal income, social security, and taxes on goods and services and
then multiplying this number by expenditures for social security,

Table 7–7 Income Inequality and the Redistributive Effects of Budgetary Policies

Country	Taxes—1971 (% of GNP)			Social Service Expenditures— (% of GNP)
	Personal Income	Social Security	Goods and Services	
United States	9.2	5.7	4.9	10.8
Canada	11.0	3.0	9.6	18.6
United Kingdom	11.6	5.0	9.4	12.4
West Germany	9.2	11.6	9.6	18.7
Sweden	17.2	8.3	12.4	21.8
France	3.7	14.8	13.0	18.6

[a]The redistributive effect of budgetary policies has been computed according to
the following formula that appears in Christopher Hewitt, "The Effect of Political Democracy and Social Democracy on Equality in Industrial Societies: A
Cross-National Comparison," American Sociological Review 42 (June 1977):454.

(personal income taxes ÷ sum of personal income, social security, and
taxes on goods and services) × (social service expenditures)

NOTE: The Pearson correlation coefficient between the redistributive effect health, public assistance, family allowances, benefits for war victims, and pensions for government employees. As expected, the Swedish government's budget exerted the greatest redistributive impact. Although precise calculations are difficult to determine, during the early 1970s nearly 10 percent of Sweden's gross national product contributed to the reduction of income inequalities. By contrast, only 2 percent of the French government budget redistributed income in more egalitarian directions. According to the table, budgets prepared by U.S., West German, and British officials led to weaker redistributive consequences than did Canadian fiscal policies. Yet, as a proportion of the nation's GNP, the redistributive effects in these four countries ranged between 5 and 8.5 percent. Under these fiscal conditions, since World War II neither expenditures nor especially taxes have produced a marked decline in economic inequality throughout most Western societies. Except in Sweden, public policies have modified, rather than significantly changed, the distribution of income.

Redistributive Effect (% of GNP)[a]	Gini	Date
5.0	.37	1972
8.7	.35	1972
5.5	.33	1973
5.7	.39	1973
9.9	.27	1972
2.2	.42	1970

and income inequality is $-.84$, indicating that in countries where the redistributive effect is higher, economic inequality is lower. In contrast to Hewitt's findings, the strength of the socialist party has only a moderate association with both the redistributive effect (.33) and the Gini coefficient ($-.42$); that is, in countries where the socialist party gained a higher percentage of the popular vote in parliamentary elections during the early 1970s, income equality and the redistributive effect were slightly greater.

SOURCE: Data calculated from sources listed in table 7–6.

The Limits of Economic Policy

Due to the methodological problems of measuring historical changes in income distribution across several nations, not all economists have reached the same conclusions about the trends toward growing economic equality. As we saw at the beginning of this chapter, measurements of income that include government cash transfers, noncash government benefits, and lifetime earnings uncover more pronounced egalitarian trends than those measurements of yearly income that exclude government benefits. Pretax income is usually less equally distributed than posttax income. Furthermore, if more young people and people over sixty-five choose to live alone in single households, the movement toward greater equality will be underestimated. In addition, judgments about egalitarian trends depend on the specific years chosen for comparison. For instance, Germans experienced growing economic equality during the 1950s; yet from 1960 through 1973 this trend reversed direction and income equality lessened. Finally, accurate sources of data on incomes of individuals and families are difficult to locate; therefore, conclusions about the longitudinal patterns of income distribution may rest on a weak empirical base. For all these reasons, not all analysts agree with Robert Nisbet's contention: "No one will question the fact that a higher degree of equality now exists in Western countries than at any time in the past."

Although methodological problems make it difficult to reach definitive conclusions, the evidence gathered by most economists indicates a relatively unchanging pattern of income distribution since the close of World War II. Some economists, however, perceive a slight trend toward more equality; a few contend that income equality has decreased. Most empirical studies suggest that redistribution of income within the middle class appears more widespread than a leveling of economic rewards among different classes. Few Western societies except Sweden have experienced a substantial decline in economic inequality during the last thirty years. For example, in the United States, even though government cash transfers increased between 1950 and 1974, the distribution of income after these transfers has remained constant. Rather than promoting greater equality, the transfer programs have prevented a further widening of the income gap between rich and poor. Indeed, during that twenty-five year period, the distribution of income before transfers became slightly more unequal.[29] Over the same period—1951 through 1974—Canadian citizens have experienced a similar pattern. As in the United States, the distribution of income did not fundamentally change. Longitudinal studies of the United Kingdom and West Ger-

many have reached the same conclusions. In France and Italy the declining proportion of persons working in agriculture, rather than government policies per se, probably better explains a slight reduction of
economic inequalities during the 1960s.[30]

Why have government policies exerted only a marginal impact on
economic equality in most Western nations, despite the growth of the
social service state? The main reasons revolve around the weak political
power of the poorer citizens, compared with middle- and upper-income
groups. Neither the majority of citizens nor political elites have placed
income redistribution at the top of their political agendas. Most rank-
and-file citizens show an ambivalent attitude toward economic equality.
On the one hand, they perceive that too great an earnings gap separates
the highest paid employees from the lowest paid workers. On the other
hand, a majority of citizens believes that workers with special skills
should receive higher salaries than unskilled workers; pay differences
are also viewed as a necessary economic incentive for motivating hard
work. Opportunities for social mobility and the allocation of economic
rewards according to individual achievement hence take precedence
over the attainment of extensive income equality. Compared with the
general public, political leaders place even less emphasis on income
redistribution as a primary government objective. Since individuals
supporting redistributive fiscal policies do not dominate the public decision-making process, tax and expenditure programs have limited effectiveness for securing a more egalitarian distribution of income.[31]

Expenditures policies, especially those for transfer payments to the
poor, certainly influence income redistribution more than do tax policies; yet since the poor lack political power, expenditures have not
significantly changed social stratification patterns. Compared with the
middle and upper classes, poorer citizens show lower rates of political
participation not only in voting but also in other more influential activities, such as electoral campaigning, contacting government leaders, and
working with others to help solve community problems. Throughout
the Western world, the most politically active citizens are mainly prosperous, well-educated, middle-aged men. These groups possess the
motivations, information, and economic resources needed to play an
active role in the political process. Through their advanced education,
they gain the skills to use these resources effectively. Their higher sense
of political interest and effectiveness motivates them to participate in
politics. As a result, these active citizens secure representatives from
their social groups in political institutions, including both the legislature
and the civil service. In the United States, lower-status people, compared with the wealthier and better educated, play a less active political

role than they do in Europe, namely, in West Germany, Italy, Britain, Austria, and the Netherlands.[32] U.S. political life thus demonstrates a sharper status gap in levels of participation. In the European countries, socialist parties provide some channels of participation for non-middle-class groups; socialist ideologies proclaim the need to pay some attention to working-class needs; unions have not established such close ties with business firms as have U.S. unions.

Because of regressive methods for financing income redistribution policies, not only the middle and upper classes but also lower-income groups may oppose the extension of social service programs, especially during times of severe inflation. As a result of rapid price increases, manual workers may gain higher nominal wages and move into a higher tax bracket. Yet, despite the wage increases, their after-tax disposable incomes and purchasing power may decline. If government officials decide to raise taxes in order to dampen the aggregate demand supposedly causing inflation, manual workers will endure even more severe hardships.[33] Partly for these reasons, blue-collar workers have resisted paying taxes to finance programs that fail to realize comprehensive benefits for all. For instance, in Sweden blue-collar members of the LO union, the strongest backers of the Social Democratic party, are the most dissatisfied with taxes; they view their taxes as too high compared with the benefits received. Rather than favoring an increase of unemployment compensation and public assistance for the poor, they prefer an expansion of old-age pensions and health care, universal programs bringing benefits to all, not just to the poor.[34]

Although poor people need government help more than do the wealthy, comprehensive policies benefiting all citizens with certain non-economic characteristics like age, veteran's status, and disability probably realize more egalitarian consequences than do selectively applied policies, such as public assistance and public housing for low-income families. European leaders, unlike U.S. politicians, prefer more comprehensive policies under which everyone will secure some benefits. For example, many European governments have established public housing for middle-income as well as low-income people. The public health systems provide medical care for all, not just for the poor and the aged. Family allowances go to all parents with children, instead of just to low-income women with dependent children. In the United States the prevalence of selective policies that help mainly low-income citizens means that these programs fail to receive sufficient financing and other political support to significantly affect the redistribution of income.[35] The working poor as well as members of the middle class resent the selective programs that seem to help the "undeserving." The administrative costs of discovering those individuals who really are needy requires the establishment of a cumbersome bureaucracy, staffed by middle-class administrators.

In short, political leaders supporting egalitarian expenditures policies face a dilemma. On the one hand, if they enact policies that assist only the very poor, then these programs will probably be underfinanced. The egalitarian policies will lose support from politically influential citizens without ever exerting a significant impact. If programs are financed through regressive taxes, then the working poor will not support them either. On the other hand, if political leaders implement more comprehensive programs, such as social security, unemployment compensation, and health care for all, everyone, not just the poor, will secure some benefits. Yet, because of the comprehensive nature of these policies, the effects will probably not produce significantly greater economic equality.

As we have seen, tax policies have produced even less egalitarian consequences than have government expenditures. The main reasons stem from the proportional tax systems in most countries, the opportunities for legal tax avoidance, and the possibilities of engaging in illegal tax evasion. First, in most Western nations except Sweden, proportional taxes are widespread. Local government officials raise revenues mainly through regressive property and sales taxes. Sales, value-added, and social security taxes, not more progressive taxes on personal income and corporate profits, finance national government expenditures. Between 1965 and 1976 whereas regressive social security taxes as a proportion of total tax revenues rose, corporate income taxes declined in most Western nations except France.[36] Partly for this reason, few Western societies experienced growing income equality during this period.

Second, middle-income and wealthy people have more general opportunities than do the poor to legally exclude part of their income from taxes. Although progressive income taxes give exemptions to poor people, nearly everywhere the low taxes levied on inheritances, estates, and gifts enable the wealthy to reduce the amount of their income subject to taxation. British and U.S. homeowners can deduct mortgage interest payments from their taxes. Interest on some government bonds sold in the United States and Germany is tax exempt. In the United States, Canada, Britain, and Germany, owners of capital pay lower taxes than do people receiving wages and salaries. In particular, U.S., Canadian, German, and British government leaders subject capital gains to lower taxes than do Swedish officials, who regard capital gains as regular income.[37] Because the Swedish government provides fewer legal opportunities for the wealthy to avoid paying taxes, since World War II Sweden has shown the greatest income equality.

Third, upper-income groups resort to more extensive tax evasion than do the poor. Since tax laws and tax forms are complicated, highly educated people find it easier to unravel these complexities and to engage in tax evasion. In all nations individuals who derive their incomes from property and entrepreneurial sources are more likely to underreport their actual income than those who receive mainly wages and salaries. Generally, the wealthiest 10 percent of a nation's population holds nearly one-half of the entrepreneurial and investment income. Particularly in France and Italy, tax evasion runs rampant. The inefficient, corrupt Italian bureaucracy further hinders the collection of tax revenues from those persons with the greatest ability to pay. Even the French, who live under a more efficient, competent civil service, succeed in large-scale tax evasion. Estimates for 1965 suggest that tax evasion in France amounted to less than 5 percent of income earned in wages and salaries but 55 percent of the profits of industrialists and businessmen and 82 percent of revenues secured by farmers.[38] Although tax evasion is less prevalent in other countries, it is still widespread. The West German government has probably achieved greater success in preventing tax evasion than have the U.S., Canadian, British, or even the Swedish governments. Despite the honest, efficient bureaucracy and the withholding system in Sweden, as much as one-third of the Swedish tax-paying population has admitted to tax evasion. The well-educated, the self-employed, and the young were the greatest tax evaders; they claimed excessive deductions and failed to report all their income.[39]

In conclusion, the available evidence for longitudinal trends in income distribution suggests that since the end of World War II government policies have not produced substantially greater economic equality. In most of the seven nations, individuals who support egalitarian expenditure policies exert weak political power over the public decision-making process. Few leaders give top priority to income redistribution as a government objective. Most redistributive expenditures are underfinanced, thus weakening their impact. Compared with expenditure policies, tax policies make a lesser contribution to income equality. Regressive and proportional, rather than progressive, taxes prevail. Since the end of World War II government programs have brought greater economic security to citizens. Yet, except in Sweden, fiscal policies have not produced substantially more equality of economic condition.

Notes

1. See Robert E. Lane, *Political Ideology: Why the American Common Man Believes What He Does* (New York: Free Press of Glencoe, 1962), pp. 57–81, esp. p. 78; L. Richard della Fave, "On the Structure of Egalitarianism," *Social Problems* 22 (December 1974):199–213; Joe. R. Feagin, "God Helps Those who Help Themselves," *Psychology Today* 6 (November 1972):101–10, 129; Sidney Verba and Kay Lehman Schlozman, "Unemployment, Class Consciousness, and Radical Politics: What Didn't Happen in the Thirties," *The Journal of Politics* 39 (May 1977):291–323.

According to Feagin, pp. 109–10, in 1969, 13 percent of a national sample favored a proposal to give every family the same income, about $10,000 a year. Thirty percent supported a guaranteed income for all families. Even during the Depression, when nearly 20 percent of the U.S. work force was unemployed, most Americans did not support public policies to ensure greater income equality. In 1939, 35 percent believed that the government should redistribute wealth through high taxes on the rich. Twenty-four percent favored a law limiting income. Unemployed people who identified with the working class and perceived a class conflict between management and workers gave the greatest support to these egalitarian measures. Yet these people constituted only a small proportion—less than 10 percent—of the sample. See the discussion by Verba and Schlozman, especially pages 302, 308–17.

2. Robert A. Nisbet, "The New Despotism," *Commentary* 59 (June 1975):33.

3. For discussions of the difficulties of making accurate crossnational comparisons about economic equality, see Malcolm Sawyer, "Income Distribution in OECD Countries," in *OECD Economic Outlook: Occasional Studies* (July 1976):11–13, 18–20; A. B. Atkinson, *The Economics of Inequality* (London: Oxford University Press, 1975), pp. 36–45; Morton Paglin, "The Measurement and Trend of Inequality: A Basic Revision," *American Economic Review* 65 (September 1975):598–609; Robert J. Lampman, "Measured Inequality of Income: What Does It Mean and What Can It Tell Us?" *The Annals of the American Academy of Political and Social Science* 409 (September 1973):81–91; and a review of Martin Schnitzer's *Income Distribution* by Harold Lydall in *Journal of Economic Literature* 13 (September 1975):918–20.

4. See Morgan Reynolds and Eugene Smolensky, *Public Expenditures, Taxes, and the Distribution of Income: The United States, 1950, 1961, 1970* (New York: Academic Press, 1977), p. 68; Morgan Reynolds and Eugene Smolensky, "Post-Fisc Distributions of Income in 1950, 1961, and 1970," *Public Finance Quarterly* 5 (October 1977):419–38; Eugene Smolensky, Leanna Stiefel, Maria Schmundt, and Robert Plotnick, "In-Kind Transfers and the Size Distribution of Income," in Marilyn Moon and Eugene Smolensky, eds., *Improving Measures of Economic Well-Being* (New York: Academic Press, 1977), pp. 131–53; Timothy M. Smeeding, "The Economic Well-Being of Low-Income Households: Implications for Income Inequality and Poverty," in *Improving Measures of Economic Well-Being*, p. 157; Edgar K. Browning, "The Trend toward Equality in the Distribution of Net Income," *Southern Economic Journal* 43 (July 1976):912–23; Edgar K. Browning, "How Much More Equality Can We Afford?" *The Public Interest*, no. 43 (Spring 1976):90–110; Larry Sawers and Howard M.

Wachtel, "The Distributional Impact of Federal Government Subsidies in the United States," *Kapitalistate: Working Papers on the Capitalist State*, no. 3 (1975):56–70.

5. Jeffrey G. Williamson, " 'Strategic' Wage Goods, Prices, and Inequality," *The American Economic Review* 67 (March 1977):29–41.

6. Atkinson, *The Economics of Inequality*, pp. 36–40; Edward Steinberg, "Measuring Income Inequality with Extended Earnings Periods," *Monthly Labor Review* 100 (June 1977):29–31; Assar Lindbeck, "Inequality and Redistribution Policy Issues (Principles and Swedish Experience)," in *Education, Inequality and Life Chances* (Paris: OECD, 1975), vol. 2, p. 316.

7. Sawyer, "Income Distribution in OECD Countries," pp. 11–13.

8. Steinberg, "Measuring Income Inequality," pp. 29–30; James B. Hagerbaumer, "The Gini Concentration Ratio and the Minor Concentration Ratio: A Two-Parameter Index of Inequality," *Review of Economics and Statistics* 59 (August 1977):377–79; Atkinson, *The Economics of Inequality*, pp. 45–47; Sawyer, "Income Distribution in OECD Countries," pp. 6–10.

9. For examples, see Martin Schnitzer, *Income Distribution: A Comparative Study of the United States, Sweden, West Germany, East Germany, the United Kingdom, and Japan* (New York: Praeger, 1974), pp. 87, 117, 184; Benjamin A. Okner, "Individual Taxes and the Distribution of Income," in James D. Smith, ed., *The Personal Distribution of Income and Wealth* (New York: National Bureau of Economic Research and Columbia University Press, 1975), p. 71; S. M. Miller and Martin Rein, "The Possibilities of Income Transformation," in *Guaranteed Annual Income: An Integrated Approach*, background papers and proceedings of the Nuffield Canadian Seminar held at Ste-Adele, Quebec, April 12–14, 1972, organized by the Canadian Council on Social Development (Ottawa, 1973), p. 134; Nanak C. Kakwani, "Measurement of Tax Progressivity: An International Comparison," *The Economic Journal* 87 (March 1976):77; Frederic L. Pryor, "The Distribution of Nonagricultural Labor Incomes in Communist and Capitalist Nations," *Slavic Review* 31 (September 1972):645; P. J. D. Wiles and Stefan Markowski, "Income Distribution under Communism and Capitalism," *Soviet Studies* 22 (January 1971):344, 367; Christopher Jencks, "Inequality in Retrospect," *Harvard Educational Review* 43 (February 1973):162.

10. S. M. Miller and Martin Rein, "Can Income Redistribution Work?" *Social Policy* 6 (May/June 1975):6–7.

11. See the data contained in the following studies: Daniel B. Suits, "Measurement of Tax Progressivity," *American Economic Review* 67 (September 1977): 747–52, esp. p. 750; Okner, "Individual Taxes and the Distribution of Income," pp. 53–57; Joseph A. Pechman and Benjamin A. Okner, *Who Bears the Tax Burden?* (Washington, D. C.: The Brookings Institution, 1974), pp. 3–10, 55; Benjamin A. Okner and Joseph A. Pechman, "Who Paid the Taxes in 1966?" *American Economic Review* 64 (May 1974):173; Joseph A. Pechman, "Distribution of Federal and State Income Taxes by Income Classes," *Journal of Finance* 27 (May 1972):190; Tom Oberhofer, "The Redistributive Effect of the Federal Income Tax," *National Tax Journal* 28 (March 1975):127–33; Benjamin A. Okner, "Taxes and Income: A Microunit Analysis," *Review of Income and Wealth* 21 (September 1975):279–99, esp. 298.

12. In 1976 personal income taxes as a proportion of total tax revenues

amounted to 33 percent, social security taxes comprised 25 percent, and corporate income taxes were 10 percent. See *Revenue Statistics of OECD Member Countries, 1965–1976* (Paris: OECD, 1978), pp. 85–86.

13. See Suits, "Measurement of Tax Progressivity," p. 750; Okner, "Individual Taxes and the Distribution of Income," pp. 58–59; John Snee, "Analysis of Issues in Payroll Tax Relief," *Reducing Social Security Contributions for Low-Income Workers: Issues and Analysis,* Staff Paper No. 16 (Washington, D. C.: U. S. Department of Health, Education, and Welfare, Social Security Administration, 1974), pp. 5–65; "Social Security Returns to Solvency," *Dollars and Sense,* no. 33 (January 1978), p. 7. Suits found that in 1970 the social security payroll tax was about as regressive as sales and excise taxes.

14. See Richard A. Musgrave and Peggy B. Musgrave, *Public Finance in Theory and Practice,* 2nd ed. (New York: McGraw-Hill, 1976), pp. 283, 331, 354, 366, 391; Reynolds and Smolensky, *Public Expenditures, Taxes and the Distribution of Income,* pp. 87, 118, 121; Diane Fuchs, "A Look at the Sales Tax," *People and Taxes* 6 (January 1978):7; Diane Fuchs, "State and Local Systems: Taxes Down Home," *People and Taxes* 5 (December 1977):5; Diane Fuchs and Anne G. Witte, "Where Now, States?" *People and Taxes* 6 (September 1978):2–3; Robert C. Brown and C. Lowell Harriss, "The Impact of Inflation on Property Taxation," *Governmental Finance* 6 (November 1977):16–23; Thomas Mayer, "The Distribution of the Tax Burden and Permanent Income," *National Tax Journal* 27 (March 1974):144; Richard A. Musgrave, Karl Case, and Herman Leonard, "The Distribution of Fiscal Burdens and Benefits," *Public Finance Quarterly* 2 (July 1974):263; Pechman and Okner, *Who Bears the Tax Burden?* pp. 62–65; Joseph A. Pechman, "The Rich, the Poor, and the Taxes They Pay," in Charles F. Andrain, ed., *Political Life and Social Change: Readings for Introductory Political Science* (Belmont, Calif.: Wadsworth, 1971), pp. 213–15; Robin Barlow, "The Incidence of Selected Taxes by Income Classes," in James M. Morgan, ed., *Five Thousand American Families—Patterns of Economic Progress* (Ann Arbor, Mich.: Survey Research Center, Institute for Social Research, University of Michigan, 1974), vol. 2, pp. 230–36. Suits, "Measurement of Tax Progressivity," pp. 749–50, found that in 1970 taxes on personal property and motor vehicles were slightly regressive, whereas property taxes were about as progressive as the individual income tax. Henry Aaron argues that the local property tax is not regressive; however, according to his data, in 1966 people earning between $20,000 and $25,000 paid about the same percentage of their income in property taxes as did people with less than $5,000 a year. Groups making $10,000 to $15,000 annually paid the lowest property taxes as a percentage of their income. See Henry Aaron, "A New View of Property Tax Incidence," *American Economic Review* 64 (May 1974):212–21. In *Who Pays the Property Tax? A New View* (Washington, D. C.: The Brookings Institution, 1975), p. 90, Henry Aaron admits that the property tax is not based on the ability to pay, although he still argues that it is progressive or at best proportional.

15. See Reynolds and Smolensky, *Public Expenditures, Taxes and the Distribution of Income,* pp. 84–85; Musgrave et al., "The Distribution of Fiscal Burdens and Benefits," pp. 267–69; Okner, "Individual Taxes and the Distribution of Income," pp. 60–61; Suits, "Measurement of Tax Progressivity," pp. 747, 750.

16. W. Irwin Gillespie, "On the Redistribution of Income in Canada," *Canadian Tax Journal* 24 (July-August 1976):419–450, esp. p. 445; C. P. Khetan and

S. N. Poddar, "Measurement of Income Tax Progression in a Growing Economy: The Canadian Experience," *Canadian Journal of Economics* 9 (November 1976):624; Kakwani, "Measurement of Tax Progressivity," p. 79; David A. Dodge, "Impact of Tax, Transfer, and Expenditure Policies of Government on the Distribution of Personal Income in Canada," *The Review of Income and Wealth* 21 (March 1975):1–52; Allan M. Maslove, *The Pattern of Taxation in Canada* (Ottawa: Information Canada, 1973); G. C. Ruggeri, "On the Regressivity of Provincial Sales Taxation in Canada," *Canadian Public Policy* 4 (Summer 1978):364–72.

17. J. L. Nicholson, "The Distribution and Redistribution of Income in the United Kingdom," in Dorothy Wedderburn, ed., *Poverty, Inequality, and Class Structure* (London: Cambridge University Press, 1974), pp. 77–80; J. C. Kincaid, *Poverty and Equality in Britain: A Study of Social Security and Taxation* (Harmondsworth, Middlesex: Penguin Books, 1973), pp. 106–08.

18. Thomas Franzén, Kerstin Lövgren, and Irma Rosenberg, "Redistributional Effects of Taxes and Public Expenditures in Sweden," *Swedish Journal of Economics* 77, no. 1 (1975):31–55; Steven D. Gold, "Scandinavian Local Income Taxation: Lessons for the United States," *Public Finance Quarterly* 5 (October 1977):471–88; Assar Lindbeck, "Inequality and Redistribution Policy Issues," p. 307. According to *Revenue Statistics of OECD Member Countries, 1965–1976*, in 1976 taxes on goods and services amounted to 23 percent, taxes on income and profits constituted 47 percent, and social security contributions were 23 percent of total tax revenues. See pp. 84, 86, 89.

19. Alain Foulon, Georges Hatchuel, and Pierre Kende, "Un premier bilan de la redistribution des revenus en France: Les impôts et cotisations sociales à la charge des ménages en 1965," *Consommation* 20 (Octobre-Décembre 1973):111, 137; Gilbert Mathieu, "Taxes and the Frenchman," *The Manchester Guardian Weekly* 115 (November 28, 1976), p. 13; Gilbert Mathieu, "An Unequal Tax Burden," *The Manchester Guardian Weekly* 117 (September 11, 1977), p. 13; *Revenue Statistics of OECD Member Countries, 1965–1976*, p. 84.

20. See, for example, the following studies carried out in the United States, Canada, Britain, and Sweden: Reynolds and Smolensky, *Public Expenditures, Taxes, and the Distribution of Income*, pp. 51–52; Robin Shannon, "Inequality in the Distribution of Personal Income," in *Education, Inequality and Life Chances*, vol. 1, pp. 135–36; Benjamin A. Okner and Alice M. Rivlin, "Income Distribution Policy in the United States," in *Education, Inequality and Life Chances*, vol. 2, pp. 204–05; Gillespie, "On the Redistribution of Income in Canada," p. 435; Miller and Rein, "The Possibilities of Income Transformation," pp. 133–35; Dodge, "Impact of Tax, Transfer, and Expenditure Policies of Government on the Distribution of Personal Income in Canada," p. 35; Maslove, *The Pattern of Taxation in Canada*, p. 64; Kakwani, "Measurement of Tax Progressivity," p. 79; Nicholson, "The Distribution and Redistribution of Income in the United Kingdom," pp. 77–80; A. J. Culyer, *The Economics of Social Policy* (London: Martin Robertson, 1973), pp. 52–55; Julian Le Grand, "Who Benefits from Public Expenditure?" *New Society* 45 (September 21, 1978):614–16; Franzén, "Redistributional Effects of Taxes and Public Expenditures in Sweden," pp. 46–53; Lindbeck, "Inequality and Redistribution Policy Issues," p. 332.

21. Okner, "Individual Taxes and the Distribution of Income," pp. 62–66; Musgrave et al., "The Distribution of Fiscal Burdens and Benefits," pp. 285–

96; Musgrave and Musgrave, *Public Finance in Theory and Practice*, pp. 682–86; Culyer, *The Economics of Social Policy*, p. 51.

22. Sheldon Danziger and Robert Plotnick, "Demographic Change, Government Transfers, and Income Distribution," *Monthly Labor Review* 100 (April 1977):7–11; Sylvia Lane, "Effectiveness of Public Income Redistributive Programs on Lower Income Groups," *American Journal of Agricultural Economics* 57 (December 1975):963; Natalie Jaffe, *Public Welfare: Facts, Myths, and Prospects*, Public Affairs Pamphlet no. 554 (New York: Public Affairs Committee, 1977), pp. 5–11; Richard Coe, Greg Duncan, and James N. Morgan, "Dependency and Poverty in the Short and Long Run," *Economic Outlook USA* 4 (Summer 1977):43–45.

23. Martha N. Ozawa, "Income Redistribution and Social Security," *Social Service Review* 50 (June 1976):209–23; Sheldon Danziger, "Income Redistribution and Social Security: Further Evidence," *Social Service Review* 51 (March 1977):179–84; Gordon Tullock, "The Charity of the Uncharitable," *Western Economic Journal* 9 (December 1971):385.

24. Musgrave, "The Distribution of Fiscal Burdens and Benefits," p. 285; Tullock, "The Charity of the Uncharitable"; William C. Mitchell, "The American Polity and the Redistribution of Income," *American Behavioral Scientist* 13 (November/December 1969):206–08; Theodore J. Lowi, *The End of Liberalism: Ideology, Policy, and the Crisis of Public Authority* (New York: W. W. Norton, 1969), pp. 250–66.

25. See Charles Brown and James Medoff, "Revenue Sharing: The Share of the Poor," *Public Policy* 22 (Spring 1974):169–88; Dennis A. Rondinelli, "Revenue Sharing and American Cities: Analysis of the Federal Experiment in Local Assistance," *Journal of the American Institute of Planning* 41 (September 1975): 319–33; David A. Caputo and Richard L. Cole, "The Initial Impact of Revenue Sharing on the Spending Patterns of American Cities," in Kenneth M. Dolbeare, ed., *Public Policy Evaluation* (Beverly Hills, Calif.: Sage Publications, 1975), pp. 119–52, esp. p. 125; David A. Caputo and Richard L. Cole, "General Revenue Sharing: Its Impact on American Cities," *Governmental Finance* 6 (November 1977):24–33.

26. Sawyer, "Income Distribution in OECD Countries," p. 21; Wilfred Beckerman, "Are the Poor Always With Us?" *New Statesman* 92 (September 10, 1976):334–36. In both France and Germany wealthier students benefit more from expenditures for public higher education than do poorer students. See Martin Pfaff and Gerhard Fuchs, "Education, Inequality and Life Income: A Report on the Federal Republic of Germany," in *Education, Inequality and Life Chances*, vol. 2, pp. 76, 96–99; Jean Claude Eicher and Alain Mingat, "Education et Egalité en France," in *Education, Inequality and Life Chances*, vol. 1, pp. 258, 290.

27. See Gillespie, "On the Redistribution of Income in Canada," pp. 426–27; Franzén, "Redistributional Effects of Taxes and Public Expenditures in Sweden," p. 41; Hugh Heclo, *Modern Social Politics in Britain and Sweden: From Relief to Income Maintenance* (New Haven, Conn.: Yale University Press, 1974), pp. 62–63, 301–04; Roger Friedland, Francis Fox Piven, and Robert R. Alford, "Political Conflict, Urban Structure, and the Fiscal Crisis," in Douglas E. Ashford, ed., *Comparing Public Policies: New Concepts and Methods*, (Beverly Hills, Calif.: Sage Publications, 1978), pp. 210–13.

28. I have used a modified version of the formula suggested by Christopher Hewitt, "The Effect of Political Democracy and Social Democracy in Industrial Societies: A Cross-National Comparison," *American Sociological Review* 42 (June 1977):453–54.

29. Because of measurement problems, economists carrying out longitudinal analyses within the United States have reached varied conclusions about the decline of economic inequality since World War II. Most assume that the degree of income inequality has remained roughly constant. For data substantiating this position, see Reynolds and Smolensky, *Public Expenditures, Taxes, and the Distribution of Income,* pp. 65–90; Morgan Reynolds and Eugene Smolensky, "The Fading Effect of Government on Inequality," *Challenge* 21 (July-August 1978):32–37; Danziger and Plotnick, "Demographic Change, Government Transfers, and Income Distribution," p. 9; Okner and Rivlin, "Income Distribution Policy in the United States," pp. 183–89; Alice M. Rivlin, "Income Distribution—Can Economists Help?" *American Economic Review* 65 (May 1975):4–10; Herman P. Miller, "Inequality, Poverty, and Taxes," *Dissent* 22 (Winter 1975):40–49. Those who argue that income inequality has decreased since World War II include Andrew F. Brimmer, "Inflation and Income Distribution in the United States," *The Review of Economics and Statistics* 53 (February 1971):41; Paglin, "The Measurement and Trend of Inequality," 588–609; Hagerbaumer, "The Gini Concentration Ratio and the Minor Concentration Ratio," p. 379. Peter Henle, "Exploring the Distribution of Earned Income," *Monthly Labor Review* 95 (December 1972):16–17, believes that inequality has increased.

Some reasons for the different conclusions about longitudinal trends in income inequality stem from the diverse methods of measuring "income" and income units. For instance, Henle analyzed pretax earned income, not income after taxes and government transfers; hence, he discovered increasing inequality over time. Studies, like those conducted by Paglin, which view equality as the degree to which the same age groups possess the same income, have found decreased inequality since 1947. The Gini coefficients remained about the same between 1947 and 1961 (they were .303 in 1947 and .286 in 1961), declined to .233 in 1969, and showed practically no change from 1969 through 1972. Thus the growth in economic equality occurred primarily in the 1960s during the administrations of Presidents Kennedy and Johnson; during this time unemployment levels declined from 6.7 percent in 1961 to 3.5 percent in 1969. Between 1961 and 1965, prices never rose more than 2 percent a year. The purchasing power of the workers therefore increased.

Certain changes in the labor force also contributed to growing income equality during the 1960s. More members of a family took jobs. The number of farm workers, who earn low salaries, declined, while the number of more highly paid white-collar workers rose. Certain government programs benefiting the poor began during the Kennedy-Johnson administrations. Throughout the sixties federal government expenditures for social insurance, education, public assistance, medicare, medicaid, rent supplements, day care centers, and veterans' programs increased as a proportion of the gross national product.

30. See Sawyer, "Income Distribution in OECD Countries," pp. 26–29; Gillespie, "On the Redistribution of Income in Canada," p. 420; Shannon, "Inequality in the Distribution of Personal Income," pp. 147, 156; Pfaff and Fuchs, "Education, Inequality and Life Income," p. 40; Schnitzer, *Income Distribution,*

pp. 79, 110, 182; A. R. Ilersic, "Personal Incomes: Home and Abroad," *Canadian Tax Journal* 26 (March-April 1978):240–44; Woldemar Koch, "Income Stratification and the Tax Scale," *The German Economic Review* 14, no. 3–4 (1976):181–203.

Even in Sweden one public policy, state pensions for the elderly, has not reduced income inequalities among the aged, especially retired manual workers. During the 1950s and the early 1960s, inequalities between the aged and the rest of the population actually increased. See Hugh Heclo, "Social Politics and Policy Impacts," in Matthew Holden, Jr. and Dennis L. Dresang, eds., *What Government Does, Sage Yearbook in Politics and Public Policy* (Beverly Hills, Calif.: Sage Publications, 1975), vol. I, pp. 161–65.

31. See Jorg Munstermann, "Wages and Prices: The West German View," *New Society* 31 (January 2, 1975):13–15; Fave, "On the Structure of Egalitarianism"; Joe R. Feagin, *Subordinating the Poor: Welfare and American Beliefs* (Englewood Cliffs, N. J.: Prentice-Hall, 1975), pp. 91–141; Miller and Rein, "The Possibilities of Income Transformation," pp. 128–42; Miller and Rein, "Can Income Redistribution Work?" pp. 3–18; Charles W. Anderson, "The Logic of Public Problems: Evaluation in Comparative Policy Research," in Douglas E. Ashford, ed., *Comparing Public Policies: New Concepts and Methods* (Beverly Hills, Calif.: Sage Publications, 1978), pp. 27–30.

32. See Sidney Verba and Norman H. Nie, *Participation in America; Political Democracy and Social Equality* (New York: Harper & Row, 1972), p. 340; Norman H. Nie and Sidney Verba, "Political Participation," in Fred I. Greenstein and Nelson W. Polsby, eds., *Handbook of Political Science* (Reading, Mass.: Addison-Wesley, 1975), vol. 4, pp. 38–48; James D. Wright, *The Dissent of the Governed: Alienation and Democracy in America* (New York: Academic Press, 1976), pp. 135–37; Lester W. Milbrath and M. L. Goel, *Political Participation: How and Why Do People Get Involved in Politics?* 2nd ed. (Chicago, Illinois: Rand McNally, 1977), pp. 57–61, 92–106.

33. David H. Freedman, "Inflation in the United States, 1959–74: Its Impact on Employment, Incomes and Industrial Relations," *International Labour Review* 112 (August-September 1975):142; Williamson, " 'Strategic' Wage Goods, Prices, and Inequality," pp. 29–41; Nat Goldfinger, "The Economic Squeeze on the Worker, 1974," *AFL-CIO American Federationist* 81 (August 1974):7–11; Arnold Cantor, "The Widening Gap in Incomes," *AFL-CIO American Federationist* 82 (March 1975):11–15; Lindbeck, "Inequality and Redistribution Policy Issues," pp. 325–26.

34. Joachim Vogel, "Taxation and Public Opinion in Sweden: An Interpretation of Recent Survey Data," *National Tax Journal* 27 (December 1974):502–03. For an analysis of the relationship between occupation and attitudes toward taxes in Britain, West Germany, and France, see Richard M. Coughlin, *Ideology and Social Policy: A Comparative Study of the Structure of Public Opinion in Eight Rich Nations,* unpublished Ph.D. dissertation, Department of Sociology, University of California at Berkeley, 1977, pp. 381–89. According to Coughlin, in 1975 high-status white-collar workers (for example, company directors, executives, and managers) showed the greatest support for improving social security and health programs, even at the cost of higher taxes. They also revealed the least enthusiasm for reducing taxes, especially if the government had to curtail

these programs. In Germany, however, executives, managers, and directors were the occupational group most in favor of reducing taxes and cutting these two programs.

For data on the United States, see V. O. Key, Jr., *Public Opinion and American Democracy* (New York: Alfred A. Knopf, 1961), pp. 166–68. Key, p. 168, captures the policy dilemma quite well when he observes: "Taxation to finance welfare programs meets opposition among those who favor welfare programs even more frequently than among those who oppose them. Progressive taxation is offered as the solution, but it meets opposition from persons who oppose both welfare programs and higher taxation of themselves. . . . The balance of forces drives policymakers back toward concealed and indirect taxation, which may be regressive in its incidence."

For an analysis of popular attitudes toward government taxes and spending in nine American cities, see Peter A. Lupsha, "Social Position and Public Regardingness: A New Test of an Old Hypothesis," *The Western Political Quarterly* 28 (December 1975):618–34. According to this 1970 survey, the higher the social status, the stronger was the preference for raising taxes rather than cutting city services as the better way to prevent the rise of costs. Whereas 76 percent of the upper class would accept a raise in taxes, only 45 percent of the lower class desired increased taxes; 55 percent of low-income persons preferred a cut in services. The lower the social status, the stronger was the perception that city taxes were too high. Low-income people sought increased city spending for health services and low-cost housing. In contrast, higher-income individuals wanted to see greater spending for education, public transportation, and curbs on air pollution. Finally, low-status citizens expressed a stronger preference for the users themselves paying for public transportation and library services. However, the upper-status individuals were more willing to pay for these city services through tax money.

35. See Arnold J. Heidenheimer, Hugh Heclo, and Carolyn Teich Adams, *Comparative Public Policy: The Politics of Social Choice in Europe and America* (New York: St. Martin's Press, 1975), pp. 13–43, 69–96, 187–226; Winifred Bell, Robert Lekachman, and Alvin L. Schorr, *Public Policy and Income Distribution* (New York: New York University School of Social Work, Center for Studies in Income Maintenance Policy, 1974), pp. 29–43.

36. Between 1965 and 1976 personal income taxes as a proportion of total tax revenues increased, while taxes on goods and services fell. Since these more progressive changes counterbalanced the regressive effects of declining corporate income taxes and rising social security contributions, the extent of income inequality after taxes remained about the same over this period. See *Revenue Statistics of OECD Member Countries, 1965–1976*, pp. 85–89.

37. Schnitzer, *Income Distribution,* pp. 47–54, 66, 115–20, 184–90; Joseph A. Pechman, "International Trends in the Distribution of Tax Burdens: Implications for Tax Policy," *Bulletin for International Fiscal Documentation* 27 (December 1973):487–95; Culyer, *The Economics of Social Policy,* pp. 57–59; Kincaid, *Poverty and Equality in Britain,* pp. 110–12; Heidenheimer, *Comparative Public Policy,* pp. 227–51.

38. Sawyer, "Income Distribution in OECD Countries," pp. 13, 21; Foulon, "Un premier bilan de la redistribution des revenus en France," p. 109.

39. Vogel, "Taxation and Public Opinion in Sweden," pp. 508–11.

PART
III *Conclusion*

Political analysts who study public policies have focused on three main aspects of the policy process: goals, structures, and impacts. First, the values and goals of political decisionmakers help to shape ideas about the relative desirability of particular economic policies. Second, public officials rely on structures like government institutions, business firms, and labor unions to help them attain their goals. Third, the interaction between values and structural conditions influences economic outcomes. In short, the distinction among goals, structures, and outcomes clarifies three dimensions of the policy process. Chapter 8 examines these features and offers a general overview of the public policy process in seven Western democracies.

The Policy Process

During the mid 1970s Western democracies entered a period of economic crisis. Unemployment rates in some countries exceeded 8 percent. Annual price increases soared to the highest levels since World War II. After 1973 the rate of economic growth began to decline. Faced with growing joblessness, severe inflation, and declining production, Western political leaders became more sensitized to the problems of economic inequalities than at any time since the Depression.

This book has investigated the ways in which North American and European leaders have tried to cope with these economic problems through public policies. The public policy process revolves around three related aspects: the *goals* of the policy officials, the *structures* through which they try to implement these goals, and the economic *outcomes,* that is, the extent to which the policy objectives have been realized. Let us look at each variable to ascertain the strategies for dealing with the growing economic crisis and the successes of the policies.

Policy Goals

The general concepts of freedom and equality influence both the specific policy objectives sought by political leaders and the priority accorded to dealing with certain issues through governmental means. After analyzing four key political ideologies—democratic socialism, the Leninist interpretation of communism, fascism as espoused by Adolf Hitler, and capitalism—Milton Rokeach concluded that freedom and equality are the two most distinctively political values; although ascribing diverse

Chapter Eight

meanings to these values, political leaders made more references to them than to any other beliefs.[1]

Why do freedom and equality rank so high in political leaders' belief systems? More than any other values, these two focus on actual and preferred conditions in the social stratification system. If political activity revolves around the struggle for scarce resources, issues of freedom and equality become especially important in this struggle. Freedom relates to the expansion of choices in the use of scarce resources. Equality means a general similarity in the distribution of resources, including political authority, wealth, knowledge, rectitude, and human respect. From this perspective, groups and individuals who possess the crucial resources and have the freedom to use these resources in the policy process exert the greatest political power to change or maintain the social stratification system. The ways they interpret freedom and equality influence their priorities for political action and the specific policy goals that they seek to attain.

Among the four ideologies dominant in the Western world—conservatism, liberalism, democratic socialism, and communism—liberalism has been most influential in the United States. American liberals accord greater priority to freedom than to equality of economic conditions. For them, freedom has meant the right to accumulate private property and to retain independence from government control over economic production; government should regulate private business firms only if they restrain free competition and deny equal opportunities to others. According to liberal principles, equality of individual opportunity takes precedence over equality of economic rewards. Unequal incomes and wages provide an incentive for individuals to work hard and to produce more. In the ideal liberal society, individuals' economic rewards should be based on their abilities and achievements, not on cash transfers granted by the government.

In accordance with liberal interpretations of freedom and equality, the U.S. national government has played a relatively passive role in dealing with the problems of unemployment, inflation, and economic inequalities. Compared with Canadian and European business leaders, U.S. private business executives retain greater freedom to influence public policies. Measures to curb inflation occupy a higher place on the political agenda than do programs to curtail unemployment. Private banks heavily influence monetary policies enacted by the Federal Reserve Board. Private businesses receive government subsidies to train unemployed workers. Interest groups representing private corporations successfully discourage national legislators from passing laws that would make the tax structure more egalitarian. Social services and cash grants are allocated to selected groups, mainly the aged and the poor, rather than to the working poor of all ages.

On the European continent, however, not only liberalism but a variety of belief systems compete for influence. Democratic socialist parties exercise considerable power in Britain, West Germany, and Sweden. Since World War II conservative and Christian Democratic parties have governed Britain, France, Italy, Germany, and Sweden. At the regional and local government levels in France and Italy, the communist party holds power with the socialists. Although disagreeing with each other on the specific interpretations of freedom and equality, European conservatives, socialists, and communists all assert that the central government should exercise a wide scope of power in the economic sphere. The historical tradition of a strong, positive state has led both the conservatives and the two left-wing parties to establish public enterprises and public health programs that supply low-cost medical care to all citizens. In Germany Chancellor Bismarck, the antagonist of the Social Democrats, implemented government health and social security programs during the late nineteenth century. In Sweden most government enterprises were established before the Socialist party came to power in 1932. At the beginning of the twentieth century in England, the Liberal party, rather than the Labourites, more fervently supported government-funded unemployment insurance and old age pensions. During the early 1970s the greatest extent of nationalized industries and the highest transfer payments as a proportion of the gross domestic product were found in France and Italy, the two European countries where conservative parties have held power in the central governments since the close of the Second World War.

Despite their agreement on the need for government to play an active role in the economic process, conservatives, socialists, and communists take different stands toward government policies for managing the economy and providing social services. Today conservatives, compared with socialists and communists, show greater reluctance to expand social welfare services and to enact government programs that will redistribute wealth according to egalitarian standards. Conservatives also express greater opposition to extending government ownership of industries. Of all Western European major parties, the communists most strongly support nationalization and an active government role in economic planning.[2]

These policy differences among the conservatives, socialists, and communists stem from their diverse interpretations of freedom and equality. Like classical liberalism, conservatism supports the freedom to hold private property and rejects economic leveling, uniformity, and income equality. Yet, in contrast to liberals, conservatives fear that too much freedom will encourage personal indulgence, anarchy, and disorder. They have historically favored a strong state to exert some control over economic policy making. In this regard, mercantilism, the corporate state, and étatisme are all associated with conservative dominance over the central government.

Rather than stressing freedom only for private businesses, democratic socialists have tried to expand economic freedom for workers, consumers, and unorganized groups within society. In the socialist view, government should look after the economic needs of the workers and consumers to ensure that powerful private economic monopolies do not exploit them. Although opposing equality of incomes, most socialists want to narrow sharp differences among members of different classes. A government that provides health services, educational opportunities, and economic security can help to eliminate the special privileges held by the wealthy. Under the ideal socialist arrangements, each individual would gain equal opportunities to realize his or her abilities.

For European communists, economic equality takes precedence over freedom for the private entrepreneur. Communists interpret freedom to mean the emancipation of the poor farmers and the factory working class from economic exploitation. In their view, the government should restrict the freedom of private businesses to manage the economy. Except in Italy, communist parties advocate greater public ownership and more extensive regulation of private industries, especially large-scale corporations. From the communist ideological perspective, full economic equality means more than just the equal opportunity to rise in the capitalist social stratification system. Rather, equality refers to social relations in a society where neither class conflict nor class domination exists. Until the classless society is attained, existing Western governments should implement policies that lessen wage differences, extract more tax revenue from the wealthy, and expand social services for the poor. Communist party leaders in France, Italy, and Sweden believe that even in a capitalist society these economic policies help equalize resources among all people.

Policy Structures

Along with general values and goals, the structures for implementing government decisions have influenced the public policy process in North America and Western Europe. During the last 300 years, Western societies have shown a changing attitude toward the proper scope of political power. As in the past, people today face problems associated with unemployment, price rises, and economic inequalities. In this regard, the most general political issue revolves around the choice of agencies that assume responsibility for trying to resolve these social problems. How do the elites define the scope of political activity? To what extent do political agencies, like governments and parties, take the primary responsibility for posing solutions and then implementing the policies? Throughout the Western world, political leaders have resorted to three alternative strategies: first, the reliance on *private institutions,* such as the family, the church, and business firms; second, the assumption of major responsibilities by the *central government;* third, the emergence of the *corporate state,* under which government bureaucrats, heads of private corporations, and trade union leaders together formulate and carry out basic public policies. Let us look at each strategy in turn.

Originally the family and church, rather than the central government, handled economic issues. Under the feudal system, individuals worked their own land, tilled the soil of the landlord, or raised crops on land owned by the Roman Catholic Church. In this agrarian situation, as long as famine, pestilence, war, and other disasters did not threaten individual survival, unemployment remained a problem for either the Church or the family to handle. Similarly, when most economic transactions occurred through barter, rather than through exchange of monetary currencies, inflation posed fewer problems. Poverty and economic inequalities were accepted as part of the "natural" order. In cases of acute economic distress, the Church, members of the extended family, and perhaps the landlord provided some relief.

Later, local governments joined private organizations in trying to alleviate economic problems. From the sixteenth through the nineteenth centuries, the emerging central governments in Western Europe spent money primarily for military and transportation projects, such as equipping armies, supplying navies, and building roads, railroads, ports, and canals. With the growth of an urban, industrializing economy, unemployment became a more pressing problem than heretofore. Private charities, along with village or city governments, began to offer some economic assistance to the poor and unemployed.

Influenced by the English traditions of decentralized government and economic laissez faire, leaders in the U.S. republic viewed private organizations—economic firms, churches, voluntary associations—and local governments as the primary structures that should handle the problems of poverty and inequality. Beginning in the 1840s, private business owners began to dominate the policy-making process. By the early 1900s, powerful oligopolies, such as United States Steel, General Electric, Standard Oil, and Dupont, had formed. Unlike most European societies, where members of the aristocracy, professional civil service, military corps, and high clergy within the established church all shared political power with private business leaders, in the United States no other institution rivaled the power exercised by private business corporations, especially between 1896 and 1932. Even today American private business firms exert greater influence over public policy formation and implementation than do other private institutions.[3]

What public policy consequences have emerged from the powerful structural role played by private business corporations in the political arena? Compared with European or Canadian governments, the U.S. government shows lower taxes and expenditures as a proportion of the gross national product, lower expenditures on social services and transfer payments as a share of total income, and lower increases in the money supply. Compared with public officials in other nations, U.S. political leaders also place less importance on incomes policies (controls over wages and prices), government economic planning, and publicly owned industries. Even the U.S. Postal Service is operated like a private corporation. Multinational corporations like IBM, Bank of America, Exxon, and Mobil, dominate the programs offered by the "noncommercial" Public Broadcasting System, which is partially funded by the federal government.

On the European continent, however, private business corporations never gained the extensive political power that they have exerted in the United States. Instead, political and economic conditions in Europe facilitated the emergence of a stronger central government, an activist state that achieved a higher centralization of power, a greater coordination of government activities, and a larger number and variety of activities. From the late fifteenth century on, European states were frequently involved in international wars; active involvement in warfare strengthened the state, particularly the professional military and civilian bureaucracies needed to organize resources, both human and material, behind the war effort. Furthermore, most Europeans lived under a rigid feudal system. Although peasants were numerous until the late nineteenth century, they did not play a strong role in the political arena. Coerced, apathetic, and fatalistic, they yielded to the power exerted by state officials and the landed aristocracy. At first kings allied with landlords to restrict peasant rights. Later monarchs built up powerful state bureaucracies that reduced the power of the landed nobility. Particularly before the twentieth century, the feudal structure posed barriers to upward social mobility for both the middle and the working classes. Upwardly mobile members of the middle class wanted a strong state that would break down the feudal barriers to social mobility. European workers did not secure the suffrage until the late 1800s and early 1900s. Since a strong state had arisen before the mass enfranchisement of the working class, the socialist parties that emerged during the late nineteenth century called on state officials to guarantee factory workers both political and economic rights—that is, the right to vote, the right to form trade unions, and the right to receive social services, such as old age pensions, health care, and unemployment insurance.[4]

In short, a strong centralized state emerged at an earlier historical period in Europe than in the United States. Between 1610 and 1914 the North American continent was geographically isolated from overseas warfare. A rigid feudal system never developed. Most white males had gained the right to vote by the 1840s. Thus the two main conditions for a powerful central state—prolonged involvement in war and a rigid sociopolitical structure—did not prevail in the early American republic. For these reasons, whereas professional state bureaucracies were well established in France, Germany, Sweden, and Britain by the end of the nineteenth century, not until the New Deal days of the 1930s did a professional state bureaucracy develop in the United States. Although the U.S. federal government today plays a more positive role in the economy than it did before the 1930s, it still exerts a less dominant role than do European central governments in trying to overcome economic problems.

Contemporary central governments outside the United States have assumed greater responsibility for tackling the economic problems of unemployment, inflation, and inequalities. More and more problems have become politicized, and now fall under the scope of central political authority. National civil servants, rather than family members, the clergy, feudal barons, local officials, or voluntary association leaders, assume the prime responsibility for dealing with major economic issues. How do the national government bureaucrats justify their expanded role? First, they argue that most modern problems linked to unemployment, poverty, and poor health stem from national, not local, causes. Throughout the Western industrial world, private oligarchical industries are organized nationally. Local governments or nonprofit voluntary associations cannot restrain the power of the concentrated industries. As a result, deleterious side effects of economic oligopoly, such as technologically induced unemployment, plague these societies. Second, centralized government can more effectively expand the resources needed for dealing with the personal crises faced by low-income groups. Third, advocates of a strong state assume that a centralized system of policy implementation may afford more equal treatment to all citizens. In this view, centralization brings greater impersonality, impartiality, and uniform standards.[5]

Despite the expanded role for the central government in the economic process, we should not assume that European citizens live under absolutist states. Certainly, the central governments in Western Europe do not exercise the comprehensive powers exerted by the party-state bureaucracies in the Soviet Union, Eastern Europe, China, Vietnam, or Cuba. There, party and government bureaucrats control the production and distribution of economic resources. Government firms produce most goods; citizens buy most goods in state stores. In Western Europe, however, governments must function within a market economy. Local governments and independent physicians implement health care policy. Social services are distributed through local governments. Private business firms receive government subsidies to train the unemployed. Private commercial banks retain some authority over the formulation and implementation of monetary policy.

Rather than private associations or an absolutist central government dominating the policy process, the corporate state has emerged as the most common structural form today, especially in Canada and Western Europe. In the corporate state, government, private business corporations, and labor unions jointly formulate and carry out public policies. The distinction between "public" and "private" activities becomes blurred. The government manages, plans, supervises, and regulates economic activities. Private groups, especially unions and business firms, have some responsibility for implementing public policies. The old system of territorial representation, under which each individual voter makes direct demands on a legislator to enact a preferred public policy, no longer seems so effective. Instead, to exert any influence over the policy process, an individual must be an active member of some organized group that has access to Cabinet ministers and civil servants.

In the corporate state, trade union officials exercise less decisive power than either the national civil service or private business corporations. Among the seven countries, unions are strongest in Sweden, Britain, and Germany. Over 80 percent of the Swedish work force belongs to unions; in Britain and West Germany, between 40 and 50 percent of the labor force is unionized. During the late nineteenth century socialist political parties and unions established close cooperation; both struggled for the expansion of the suffrage and for an improvement in workers' living conditions. Today, when socialist parties hold government power, union leaders can gain easy access to public policymakers. Despite the strength of socialist parties and unions, in these three countries the unions' power to veto policies seems greater than their ability to initiate new policies. Certainly, unions can use the threat of going on strike to veto wage controls devised by the government. However, even in Britain, a country supposedly dominated by the unions, union influence over the civil service and even Labour members of the House of Commons has been limited. The national Trades Union Congress leaders govern a highly fragmented organization. Leaders of individual unions and shop stewards at the local level exert the greatest power. When the demands of party leaders and national trade union officials come into conflict, the Labour MPs sponsored by the unions usually vote according to their party's preferences. In short, the TUC has found it difficult to control the Parliamentary Labour Party, Cabinet members, or the civil servants.[6]

In France, Italy, Canada, and the United States, trade unions have less political strength than they do in Sweden, Germany, or Britain. Not more than one-third of the work force belongs to a union. Democratic socialist parties are weaker. Especially in France and Italy, the union movements are politically fragmented between the communist, socialist, and conservative parties. All these factors reduce their influence over political decision making.

As we have seen, private business firms retain a powerful position in the corporate state. Business executives in all countries help formulate and implement crucial policies dealing with unemployment, inflation, regulation, nationalization, and income distribution. Attempting to curb unemployment, governments grant subsidies to private firms that hire more workers. Heads of the central banks have shown special regard for the recommendations made by private banking officials for decreasing inflation. Particularly in the United States, West Germany, France, and Italy, legislators have offered special tax incentives to businesses. For instance, in 1978 the U.S. Senate and House of Representatives refused to pass tax measures that would have increased taxes on multinational corporations, export firms, airlines, and other private industries. Instead, Congress approved a bill that lowered corporate income tax rates and reduced the capital gains tax.[7]

Within the corporate state, heads of large private corporations enjoy special access to senior civil servants and managers of nationalized industries. For example, representatives of the Confederation of British Industries regularly consult with Cabinet ministers responsible for economic matters. In Germany national industrialists cooperate with the civil servants in preparing new legislation. French administrators seem far less responsive to trade union leaders than to businessmen and industrialists such as highway contractors. Public enterprises operate like private corporations. Even in France and Italy, the states characterized by the highest degree of nationalized industry, the central governments have failed to gain extensive control over either the heads of private corporations or the managers of the publicly owned firms. In France and Italy, directors of both state and private corporations display close cooperation, even to the point of engaging in joint price fixing.[8] In sum, although private businessmen rarely see all their preferences translated into public policies, they, along with the senior civil servants and a few elected government officials, still retain the dominant influence over the policy process.

Among the government officials, Cabinet ministers in parliamentary systems, the president and his staff in France and the United States, and the senior civil servants exercise the greatest power in formulating public policy. Except in the United States, where the House of Representatives and the Senate share considerable power with the president, legislators have virtually no influence over economic policy. In England the rank-and-file Members of Parliament have surrendered their authority to introduce new revenue measures to the Cabinet, which is dominated by the leading ministers and the top civil servants. Elsewhere in Europe legislators lack the power to increase the budget or even to propose new taxes.[9]

As the corporate state grows stronger and engages in more complex, comprehensive activities, not only legislators but also presidents, prime ministers, and Cabinet officials cannot easily establish effective controls over bureaucratic behavior. Civil servants, who always outnumber legislators, have a much longer tenure in office; especially in democratic regimes, parliamentary ministers or presidents experience a rapid turnover in office. Civil servants also possess the crucial resources needed to formulate and carry out public economic policies; these resources include professional expertise, administrative skills, and time. By contrast, legislators, prime ministers, and perhaps even presidents are nonprofessionals, who must divide their time among different groups, including elected representatives, interest group lobbyists, constituents, and officials from other countries. For these reasons, professional bureaucrats dominate policy making.[10]

What roles do political parties play in the public policy process of the corporate state? No Western democratic party has established the elaborate control network organized by the Communist party over the USSR government. In the Soviet Union party agencies parallel government agencies and keep close supervision over them. In all Western societies, however, political party leaders lack either the staff resources or the will to regulate policy implementation. Generally, civil servants function independently of party control.

Even in nations like Britain and Sweden, which have strong social democratic parties, Cabinet members and civil servants, not party leaders, formulate basic policies. For instance, the British Labour Party has historically stressed the crucial role that party members should play in strictly controlling actions taken by Labour Members of Parliament. Despite this injunction, neither the Labour party's annual conference nor even the National Executive Committee has made basic decisions. Instead, the Parliamentary Labour Party members, specifically the top ministers (when the party is in power) and the senior civil servants, formulate policies, sometimes in opposition to the preferences voiced by party activists. Similarly, in Sweden the Social Democrats do not really formulate policy, but rather respond to policy proposals initiated by the civil servants. In short, the political party exercises limited influence over the policy process. Comparing the public policy processes in Britain and Sweden, Hugh Heclo concludes:

> *The major impact of political parties on pensions, unemployment benefits, and superannuation has been in organizing general predispositions to policy choices. . . . Parties have competed in expressing moods toward social policy change; concrete proposals for implementation have come in a distant second. Neither party functionaries nor organizational structures have been prominent in the creation of specific new policy departures.* [11]

The same generalization holds true for other Western countries as well.

Despite the lack of structural control, political parties do influence policy by shaping moods, setting priorities, and recommending tentative solutions to pressing economic problems. As Heclo implies, these attitudinal effects of parties appear stronger than their structural control. In particular, legislators' party affiliation affects their attitudes toward policy issues. At local and national government levels, left-wing parties support positive government actions to realize greater economic equality, such as the extension of social welfare benefits, the institution of more progressive taxes, and greater government management of the economy intended to offset the power exerted by private corporations. Generally, right-wing parties show a weaker commitment to government measures intended to promote more economic equality. Moreover, democratic socialists in Germany and Britain, compared with their conservative party colleagues, have made slightly different policy responses to changes in inflation and jobless levels. When prices have risen, the German Social Democrats have opted for higher interest rates and for a budget surplus. When unemployment has increased, they have resorted to lower interest rates and a budget deficit, the classic Keynesian strategies. Christian Democratic governments, however, have shown less willingness to actively intervene in the market to resolve economic problems. In Britain whereas the Labour party government has used interest rates to curb inflation and budget deficits to reduce unemployment, the Conservative party has relied on monetary policy to cope with both inflation and unemployment.

Regardless of the influence of party affiliation on policy predispositions, legislators do not always translate their parties' positions into public policies, especially at the local level. During the twentieth century, socialist and non-socialist parties have engaged in bitter ideological conflicts; however, when controlling executive power, all parties have followed somewhat similar economic policies. For example, even though German city governments controlled by the Christian Democrats generally spend less for social services like health and education, the policies enacted by the CDU and the Social Democrats are not significantly different. Indeed, blue-collar and white-collar cities dominated by the SPD diverge just as much. In France and Italy, local governments controlled by alliances of communists and socialists try to implement reformist policies, including balanced budgets, honest administration, and the establishment of low-income housing, city planning bureaus, higher unemployment insurance, day-care centers, and better city transportation. Contrary to expectations, the Italian Christian Democrats controlling city governments have enacted more expansionary fiscal policies than have the communists and socialists.

Two general reasons explain the disjunction between stated party positions and legislative policy. First, in the United States and overseas, party activists take programmatic ideology more seriously than do elected officeholders. Everywhere, candidates running for office have broader constituencies; they must gain support from a plurality of voters, who generally regard a coherent, consistent ideology as less important than do party activists. The overriding desire to win office discourages complete ideological consistency and motivates candidates to compromise their party's issue positions. Second, variables other than a party's stands on issues shape the content of public policy. Past historical experiences condition present policies; governments often make minor adjustments to the existing policies. Moreover, in the multiparty systems existing throughout Europe, several parties usually form coalition governments. The need for policy compromises with other parties in the coalition mutes ideological differences. Finally, organizations other than parties participate in the policy process, including trade unions, professional associations, private business corporations, and civil servants. All these groups play crucial roles in shaping the content and the outcomes of public economic policies.[12]

Economic Outcomes

This book has examined the effect of government policies on unemployment, inflation, and income distribution. Table 8–1 summarizes the ranking of the seven Western democracies on these economic outcomes during the first half of the 1970s. Economic conditions in Sweden and Italy show the greatest contrasts. In Sweden unemployment was low, prices increased moderately, the degree of income equality was the highest of the seven nations, and citizens enjoyed the highest gross national product per capita. In contrast, during the early 1970s Italians faced high inflation, moderate unemployment, high income inequality, and the poorest living conditions as measured by the GNP per capita. The British had to cope with similar economic problems; however, they lived under greater income equality. West Germany represented still another pattern. As in Sweden, unemployment was relatively low; yet Germany had less inflation and less economic equality. The French experienced moderate unemployment and inflation rates, but they lived in the most economically unequal society of the seven. Finally, the United States and Canada experienced similar economic conditions during the early 1970s; although unemployment was higher than in the European countries, the degree of income inequality and the severity of inflation placed the North American societies in the intermediate range.

Table 8–1   Economic Outcomes

Country	Unemployment 1971–1975	Price Rise 1971–1975	Gini Index of Inequality[a] 1969–1973	GNP per Capita 1974
United States	6.1%	6.8%	.37	$7099
Canada	6.1	7.4	.35	6935
United Kingdom	3.8	13.2	.33	4089
West Germany	1.6	6.1	.39	6842
Sweden	2.3	8.0	.27	8450
France	3.3	8.8	.42	6386
Italy	3.6	11.5	.40	3074

[a]Low Ginis indicate low income inequality (high equality).
SOURCE: Data from tables 3–2, 4–1, 5–1, and 7–2.

To what extent can public policies explain these outcomes? Comparing inflation and unemployment rates in twelve Western European and North American nations during the 1960s, Douglas A. Hibbs assumes that the parties controlling the government enact policies that produce specified outcomes. According to him, since the close of World War II, countries governed by socialist parties have faced higher inflation and lower unemployment rates than have nations controlled by more conservative political parties.[13]

Our examination of data for seven countries over a fifteen-year time span, however, reveals a more complex pattern. True, Sweden, which was governed by the Social Democrats between 1932 and 1976, has become a relatively wealthy, egalitarian society where unemployment poses fewer problems than does inflation. As expected, Swedish leaders gave priority to expansionary fiscal policies that lowered jobless rates and to redistributive budgetary measures that promoted greater income equality.

The correlations between policy priorities and policy outcomes seem less clear in the other countries, especially Britain and West Germany. Neither the Labour nor the Conservative government in Britain has managed to cope with rising prices and unemployment. Inflation was more severe during the period from 1970 to 1973, when the Conservatives governed, than between 1964 and 1970, when the Labour party held government office. During 1977, unemployment rates soared to nearly 7 percent, the same jobless figure found in the United States— yet a Labour party controlled the government.[14] In West Germany both Christian Democrats and Social Democrats have given the highest priority to curbing prices. During the late 1970s, when the socialists governed in a coalition with the Free Democrats, they achieved greater success in restraining price increases than in lowering unemployment. Although U.S. and Canadian leaders have perceived inflation a more severe problem than unemployment, both North American governments have found it difficult to hold down prices and jobless rates. Here, neither the socialist nor the communist party has exerted great influence over the policy process; yet the degree of income equality has been higher in these two countries than in France or Italy, where the communist and socialist parties occupy over 40 percent of the seats in the parliaments and play a key role in some urban and regional governments. Thus Hibbs' conclusions overstate the impact of political parties and government policies on economic outcomes.

It is more accurate to suggest that economic conditions like income equality, inflation, and unemployment depend on the interaction between the *subjective will* of the policy officials and certain *objective condi-*

tions, like the distribution of political power, level of technology and economic production, class relations, cultural beliefs, and demographic patterns. In a famous passage written over one hundred years ago, Karl Marx observed:

> *Men make their own history, but not of their own free will; not under circumstances they themselves have chosen but under the given and inherited circumstances with which they are directly confronted.* [15]

According to this assumption, the will of the policy leaders to accomplish certain objectives constitutes only one determinant of particular outcomes; subjective priorities must operate within specific historical conditions. For example, however much policy officials desire to restrain inflation, certain conditions largely remain beyond their immediate, direct control. These "objective circumstances" include weather conditions of drought and floods, the actions of concentrated industries to cut production when demand falls, the decision of the OPEC cartel to quadruple oil prices, the expansion of Eurocurrency by multinational corporations and banks, and the pressures of the International Monetary Fund. In contemporary democratic systems, all these conditions remain unresponsive to the traditional fiscal and monetary policies; yet they have profoundly affected the severe inflationary pressures experienced during the 1970s. Similarly, changes in demographic patterns, particularly the growing proportion of the population under twenty-five years old, have raised unemployment rates throughout the Western world. Unless governments adopt expansionary policies to expand total demand and to provide jobs in either the private or the public sector for unemployed youth, jobless rates will continue at a high level. Finally, government policies have played only a limited role in promoting greater income equality. Except in Sweden, the redistributive effect of budgetary policies has not substantially increased economic equality since the close of World War II.

At present the Western world faces the most severe economic crisis since the Depression of the 1930s. What does the future hold? Will the "reserve army of the unemployed" be permanently with us? Will inflation rates once again exceed double-digit figures? Will the gap between rich and poor grow?

The rapidity of social change and the complexities of life pose problems for the policy analyst who attempts to predict the future consequences of current policies. Since the economic environment is not a simple controlled laboratory situation, numerous variables and sources of instability confound our attempts to predict future events.

A complexity of variables, both explicit public policies and factors less subject to direct policy control, affect economic outcomes. The subjective wills of policy officials and citizens change, as do objective conditions. For example, during the early 1960s a negative association between unemployment and inflation prevailed. Countries with high jobless rates faced low price increases. After the first half of the sixties, however, the Phillips curve seemed a less accurate description of the relationship between price rises and joblessness. Especially during the 1970s inflation and unemployment rose concurrently. More than any other condition, the quadrupling of oil prices by OPEC nations late in 1973, combined with restrictions on oil supplies, represented an acute external "supply shock" affecting all Western economies. Escalating oil prices meant higher general inflation. Increased costs for oil also lowered the disposable incomes of households, businesses, and governments. As production and consumption declined, demand fell and unemployment rates rose. Under these changing international conditions, traditional monetary and fiscal policies no longer appeared able to produce desired outcomes.

Both policy analysts and political leaders find it difficult to predict accurately the future outcomes of policies. The German philosopher Hegel (1770–1831) referred to the "cunning of reason"—that is, the contradiction between the subjective intentions of leaders and the objective consequences of their actions.[16] Often leaders' public policies have unintended, unanticipated effects. For example, although political leaders intended that higher interest rates should produce lower inflation rates, the opposite effect ensued. Rather than pulling down aggregate demand, increased interest rates pushed up the costs of supplies, thereby aggravating the general inflation. In this way, the "cunning of reason" hindered the efforts of political leaders, as well as policy analysts, to predict the impact of public policies.

Because of such problems, this book has sought to understand the past outcomes of public economic policies, rather than to predict future events. As the economist Lester Thurow advises:

> Most physical sciences understand rather than predict. To understand a phenomenon is to be able to predict the outcome of a laboratory or controlled environmental experiment where "other" variables are held constant and stochastic [random, uncontrolled] processes are limited. With the single exception of heavenly motion, physical scientists predict outcomes in controlled environments. They are no better, for example, at predicting the real world's meteorological phenomena than economists are at predicting the real world's economic events.[17]

By taking a comparative view of the content and impact of economic policies in seven Western democracies, this book has tried to explain the cultural and structural bases of the policy process. Consistent with Thurow's perspective, it has concentrated on understanding past economic conditions. As both Hegel and Marx well understood, historical events do affect the present situation. Whatever the difficulties, understanding the past places us in a better position to explain, if not accurately predict, future economic changes.

Notes

1. See Milton Rokeach, *The Nature of Human Values* (New York: The Free Press, 1973), pp. 168–86.

2. John Clayton Thomas, *The Decline of Ideology in Western Political Parties: A Study of Changing Policy Orientations,* Sage Professional Paper in Contemporary Political Sociology, vol. 1, series no. 06–012 (Beverly Hills, Calif.: Sage Publications, 1975), esp. pp. 8–9, 56–64. For analyses of the ideological viewpoints of political party leaders within specific countries, see the following studies: (1) United States: Allen H. Barton, "Consensus and Conflict among American Leaders," *Public Opinion Quarterly* 38 (Winter 1974/1975):507–30; Aage R. Clausen, *How Congressmen Decide: A Policy Focus* (New York: St. Martin's Press, 1973); (2) France: Denis Lacorne, "On the Fringe of the French Political System: The Beliefs of Communist Municipal Elites," *Comparative Politics* 9 (July 1977):421–41; "The French Left," *Monthly Review* 29 (February 1978):14–16; (3) Italy: Alan J. Stern, "Rudimentary Political Belief Systems in Four Italian Communities," *The Journal of Politics* 37 (February 1975):241–43; (4) Britain: Richard Rose, *Politics in England,* 2nd ed. (Boston: Little, Brown, 1974), pp. 306–14; (5) Sweden: Michael Lindén, "Political Dimensions and Relative Party Positions: A Factor Analytical Study of Swedish Attitude Data," *Scandinavian Journal of Psychology* 16, no. 2 (1975):97–107. According to Linden, Conservative, Socialist, and Communist candidates for local government office in Sweden answered questions dealing with these issues: (1) nationalization of domestic natural resources, private insurance companies, and commercial banks; (2) greater government control of the economy; (3) increase of the inheritance tax; (4) lessening of income and pay differences. On all these policy measures, the Communist party candidates expressed the greatest support, the Conservatives voiced the strongest opposition, and the Social Democrats took an intermediate position, closer to the Communists than to Conservative party leaders.

3. David Vogel, "Why Businessmen Distrust Their State: The Political Consciousness of American Corporate Executives," *British Journal of Political Science* 8 (January 1978):64.

4. For a historical analysis of the emergence of the nation-state in Western Europe, see Charles Tilly, "Reflections on the History of European State-Making," in Charles Tilly, ed., *The Formation of National States in Western Europe* (Prince-

ton, N. J.: Princeton University Press, 1975), pp. 3–83; Immanuel Wallerstein, *The Modern World-System* (New York: Academic Press, 1974), pp. 107–62.

5. See Norman Furniss and Timothy Tilton, *The Case for the Welfare State* (Bloomington: Indiana University Press, 1977), esp. chapters 2, 3, and 4. For Furniss and Tilton, Sweden most closely approximates the ideal welfare state, since its leaders show a commitment to the values of equality and freedom and it has demonstrated "superior techniques of social organization."

6. See Richard J. Willey, "Trade Unions and Political Parties in the Federal Republic of Germany," *Industrial and Labor Relations Review* 28 (October 1974):38–59; Nils Elvander, "In Search of New Relationships: Parties, Unions, and Salaried Employees' Associations in Sweden," *Industrial and Labor Relations Review* 28 (October 1974): 60–74; Lewis Minkin, "The British Labour Party and the Trade Unions: Crisis and Compact," *Industrial and Labor Relations Review* 28 (October 1974):7–37; William D. Muller, "Union–M. P. Conflict: An Overview," *Parliamentary Affairs* 26 (Summer 1973):336–55; Timothy May and Michael Moran, "Trade Unions as Pressure Groups," *New Society* 25 (September 6, 1973):570–73; "Collective Bargaining and Government Policies," *OECD Observer* no. 94 (September 1978):3–6.

7. Charles E. Lindblom, *Politics and Markets: The World's Political-Economic Systems* (New York: Basic Books, 1977), pp. 173–200, 229–30, 347; Ralph Miliband, *The State in Capitalist Society: An Analysis of the Western System of Power* (New York: Basic Books, 1969); *People and Taxes* 6 (October 1978):4–6.

8. Lindblom, *Politics and Markets,* pp. 112–13, 181–87; Ezra N. Suleiman, *Politics, Power, and Bureaucracy in France: The Administrative Elite* (Princeton, N. J.: Princeton University Press, 1974), pp. 297–99, 323–31.

9. Robert W. Gilmer, "Fiscal Policy and Public Finance," *Challenge* 19 (September-October 1976):50–51.

10. See Michael R. Gordon, "Civil Servants, Politicians, and Parties: Shortcomings in the British Policy Process," *Comparative Politics* 4 (October 1971):29–58. The same generalizations about the role of the civil servants in the British policy process also apply to other Western democratic societies.

11. Hugh Heclo, *Modern Social Politics in Britain and Sweden: From Relief to Income Maintenance* (New Haven, Conn.: Yale University Press, 1974), p. 295.

12. See Andrew T. Cowart, "The Economic Policies of European Governments, Part I: Monetary Policy; Part II: Fiscal Policy," *British Journal of Political Science* 8 (July, October 1978): 285–311, 425–39; Robert C. Fried, "Party and Policy in West German Cities," *The American Political Science Review* 69 (March 1976):11–24; Robert Fried, "Comparative Urban Policy and Performance," in Fred I. Greenstein and Nelson W. Polsby, eds., *Handbook of Political Science* (Reading, Mass.: Addison-Wesley, 1975), vol. 6, pp. 323–46; Sidney Tarrow, "Communism in Italy and France; Adaptation and Change," in Donald L. M. Blackmer and Sidney Tarrow, eds., *Communism in Italy and France* (Princeton, N. J.: Princeton University Press, 1975), p. 624; Georges Lavau, "The PCF, the State, and the Revolution," in *Communism in Italy and France,* pp. 127–28; Alan J. Stern, "The Italian CP at the Grass Roots," *Problems of Communism* 23 (March-April 1974):50; Joseph A. Schlesinger, "The Primary Goals of Political Parties: A Clarification of Positive Theory," *The American Political Science Review* 69 (September 1975):840–49.

13. Douglas A. Hibbs, Jr., "Political Parties and Macroeconomic Policy," *The American Political Science Review* 71 (December 1977):1473. Hibbs admits that variables other than policy choices and factors external to national decision making, like the quadrupling of oil prices in late 1973, shape both inflation and unemployment. Yet he concludes, p. 1487, "Macroeconomic outcomes . . . obviously are influenced to a significant extent by long- and short-term political choices."

14. See *OECD Economic Outlook,* no. 23 (July 1978):14. In 1977 the unemployment rate in the United Kingdom was 6.9 percent of the total labor force, 6.9 percent in the United States and 8.1 percent in Canada. In retrospect, Hibbs's assertion, p. 1474, that "rates of unemployment even approaching those typical of Canada and the United States are simply not politically feasible or acceptable in countries with large Socialist-Labor parties that are frequently governed by the Left" seems a bit outdated.

15. Karl Marx, "The Eighteenth Brumaire of Louis Bonaparte," in Karl Marx, *Surveys from Exile: Political Writings Volume II,* David Fernbach, ed. (New York: Vintage Books, 1974), p. 146.

16. Shlomo Avineri, *Hegel's Theory of the Modern State* (London: Cambridge University Press, 1974), p. 232.

17. Lester Thurow, "Economics 1977," *Daedalus* 106 (Fall 1977):87. The quotation is reprinted with permission of the author and of the managing editor of *Daedalus.* Robert L. Heilbroner, "The Missing Link(s)," *Challenge* 21 (March/April 1978):16–17, and John Kenneth Galbraith take a similar position. According to Galbraith, *Almost Everyone's Guide to Economics,* with Nicole Salinger (Boston: Houghton Mifflin, 1978), p. 8: "There are very great limits to what economists can predict. We must be judged by what we explain and what results from the policies we urge, not by what we foretell as to the stock market or the price of oil. You must always remember that prediction itself derives from the fact that no one knows. If something can be known, for example that the sun will rise tomorrow morning and at exactly 6:24.24, then no one predicts it, not even on television."

Index

inflation, 94–99, 100–101, 114. *See also* Monetary policies, effect on inflation
Interstate Commerce Commission: 25, 115
Italy, economic problems and policies: central banking system, 21; economic development and non-defense expenditures, 44, 45; economic outcomes, 224–225; elitism and populism, 35, 37–38; government institutions, 38–39; government ownership policies, 24, 26, 27; income distribution and economic inequality, 199, 200, 202; income distribution and fiscal policies, 194–197; income distribution and government expenditures, 190–191, 193; income distribution and taxes, 184–185; income inequality, 178, 179–183; inflation and capital investment, 100, 102; inflation and concentrated industries, 107, 110–113; inflation and fiscal policies, 91–93; inflation and government, 92–93, 95–96, 114–115, 118–119; inflation and labor unions, 119–125; inflation and manufacturing workers, 127; inflation and monetary policies, 92–99; inflation and personal saving, 90; inflation rate, 86–87; interest rate, 18, 19; labor unions and political power, 46–47, 50; monetary supply, 18, 19, 20; policy goals, 214, 215; policy structures, 217, 220, 221, 223; political parties, 40, 42–43; private business and political power, 52; taxes and expenditures, 11, 12, 14, 15, 16; trade and foreign investment, 150–151; trade deficit and currency devaluation, 149; tradeoff between unemployment and inflation, 142–144; unemployment rates, 65–70, 77–81

Job security: 79
Jobless rate. *See* headings under Unemployment
Johnson, Lyndon: 157

Keynes, John and Keynesian theory: 31, 70, 75, 91, 97, 141; Swedish tradeoff, 164; United States tradeoff, 156, 157. *See also* Aggregate demand, insufficient as explanation for unemployment; Phillips curve, tradeoff theory and

Labor, effect on public policies: 43–44
Labor mobility: 71
Labor supply, efforts to decrease: 79
Labor unions, explanation for tradeoff: 167; Sweden, 164–165; United Kingdom, 154–156; United States, 158, 162–163; West Germany, 153
Labor unions, impact on inflation: 119; unit labor costs, 120–122; wage increases, 119–121, 122, 123–124
Labor unions, political power and economic policies: 49–51; attitude of firms towards, 49; membership differences, 46–47; political unity, 47–48; reformist policies, 45–46
Land, effect on public policies: 43–44
Lane, Robert: 173
Left-wing parties: 40–43
Lindblom, Charles: 51, 54
Locke, John: 34, 36
Loose oligopoly: 104

Manufacturing workers: effect of inflation on, 128–129; income equality of, 178, 180–183
"Markup," effect on inflation: 108
Marx, Karl: 226, 228
Military expenditures: 13
Monetarist explanations of inflation. *See* Monetary policies, effect on inflation